Richard Pryor

Richard Pryor

THE LIFE AND LEGACY

OF A

"CRAZY" BLACK MAN

EDITED BY

Audrey Thomas McCluskey

Indiana University Press

BLOOMINGTON AND INDIANAPOLIS

This book is a publication of

Indiana University Press
601 North Morton Street
Bloomington, IN 47404-3797 USA

http://iupress.indiana.edu

Telephone orders 800-842-6796
Fax orders   812-855-7931
Orders by e-mail iuporder@indiana.edu

Library of Congress Cataloging-in-Publication Data

Richard Pryor : the life and legacy of a "crazy" Black man / edited by Audrey
Thomas McCluskey.
    p. cm.
Includes bibliographical references and index.
ISBN 978-0-253-35202-6 (cloth : alk. paper) — ISBN 978-0-253-22011-0 (pbk.
: alk. paper) 1. Pryor, Richard—Criticism and interpretation. I. McCluskey,
Audrey T.
PN2287.P77R53 2008
792.702′8092—dc22
[B]
2008004229

1 2 3 4 5 13 12 11 10 09 08

CONTENTS

III. Reviews

IV. Social and Cultural Criticism

ACKNOWLEDGMENTS

The list of people to thank for their contributions to this project is long. In fact, some who contributed may not realize that they did. For example, the couple from Ellettsville, Indiana (a small 99.9 percent white town near Bloomington), who told me that they had never felt the need to visit Indiana University before, but when they read in the local paper that the Black Film Center/Archive was "doing a special program" on Richard Pryor, they jumped on their Harley and came. That program of events in 2001, titled, "Is He Crazy? A Retrospective of the Career of Richard Pryor," attracted a wide and diverse audience. I want to express my appreciation to all who attended, including those who came to the standing-room-only keynote lecture by writer James Alan McPherson. McPherson, generous with his time and wisdom, contributed to and encouraged this project. He, along with the audience, inspired me to extend the retrospective to book-length form. I also benefited from discussions with filmmaker Avon Kirkland, who is working on a Pryor film project. The staff of the BFC/A deserves to be singled out for magnificent service, without which neither the retrospective nor this book would ever have been as well executed. That list of worthy warriors begins with Paul Heyde, former archivist and head of technical services, whose efficiency and dedication were like money in the bank. It also includes a bevy of graduate assistants who worked at the BFC/A between 2001 and 2006—Crystal Keels, Tyrone Simpson, Ketwana Wilson-McCormack, Damien Strecker, and Jennifer Heusel. The list of "thank yous" also extends to the many friends of the BFC/A whose financial and moral support make the work of the BFC/A possible. The same goes for those who, like Nelson George, Bob Avakian, and Jim McPherson, gave their gracious consent to republish essays without charge. I want to acknowledge the new contributors for their wonderful essays, and for enduring my pestering for months. Bless them. I thank Michael Schultz, a busy Hollywood director, who took time out of his schedule to share with me his memories of Richard. My work was made easier by the supportive accommodations I found during my sabbatical stay as a fellow-in-residence at the Institute for Advanced Study at Indiana University. I thank the former director, Alfred Aman, staff assistant Victor Kinzer, and most of all, assistant director/academic specialist Ivona Hedin, who has been a nurturing presence for all lucky enough be invited to the IAS. My sincere appreciation goes also to my colleague and friend Alyce Miller for her thoughtful and helpful comments on a part of this manuscript. Then, there are friends and Pryor aficionados such as Gladys and Gene Devane, Vicki Roberts, Richard Reed, Yvonne Reed, Paul and Louise McQuirter, Margaret McDay and the late Bill McDay, Bob and Holly Stephens, and others who used to get together at house parties "back in the day" to listen to Richard Pryor records and literally roll on the floor and cry with laughter.

I thank Indiana University Press and Bob Sloan for believing in the project and holding fast despite missed deadlines. Finally, my extended family—the McCluskeys, Alexises, and Garners—is my "A" team, and I appreciate their support, as always.

Richard Pryor

Introduction

RICHARD PRYOR: COMIC GENIUS, TORTURED SOUL

Audrey Thomas McCluskey

It would be easy to call the late Richard Pryor a genius and leave it at that. But there was more complexity to his genius than his ability to make us laugh. Even as we felt the prickly sting of truth about ourselves and society amidst his extravagantly elegant "lies" and self-revelations, we knew that his genius came with lots of scars attached. It is telling that in her recent memoir about growing up as the daughter of the famous comedian, and as one of his seven offspring by different women, Rain Pryor calls her father selfish, "anti-romantic, and downright mean."[1] He was obsessed with sex, she charges. It was "pussy, pussy, pussy," all the time. When he failed to show up to pick up Rain, the newborn, and her mother from the hospital, her mother had to take a cab home, only to find him in bed with the housekeeper.[2] While he enjoyed the unprecedented accolades and crossover fame of a certified comic genius, being declared a "crazy" nigger bestowed a reckless freedom upon him, and an abandon which he embraced. Historically, the designation of "crazy nigger" generally identified someone who defied the dictates of convention.[3] It could apply to a range of behaviors, including rebelling against injustice, being a social misfit, or acting "buck wild" and just not giving a damn. Richard Pryor may have embodied a little of each type. Some might suggest that the perplexity of his early life—its unconventionality and instability—fueled his brilliance, and his edgy self-destructive rebellion. Growing up in a brothel run by his grandmother, with a mother who was one of the sex workers and a father who beat women, left its imprint. This, combined with his craving for attention and mastery of the blues aesthetics of his environment, created in him a bluesy persona that turned pain into art. Like the bluesman, Richard Pryor kept looking for sunshine in a cloudy and ominous sky.[4]

Writers of several different stripes, from Ralph Ellison to Richard Powell to Kalamu ya Salaam and Amiri Baraka, among others, have wrestled with the notion of a transcendent suffering in the black psyche which has come to be known as the "blues aesthetic"—an ethos that manifests itself in everything that blues people do, not just the music. It is a philosophical orientation that resolves (or displaces) grief through motion.[5] It allows one—in Ellisonian vernacular—to "finger the jagged edge" of tragedy in order to transcend it. To art historian Powell, this aesthetic is an organizing principle in African American artistic expression.[6] In Baraka's cosmology, it is a conduit for rage, and a highly politicized response to oppression.[7]

There *was* a simmering rage in Richard Pryor that found expression in his performance. His life illustrated the essence of the blues aesthetic. The genius that lurked in him sprang from his ability to channel tragedy and rage into art. Moreover, it has been argued that just as black music reaches its level of genius through egalitarian complexity (it is available to everyone who can hear),[8] Pryor's humor was both multifaceted and egalitarian in its targets and scope. It traversed racial and class boundaries, yet remained "territorialized" within a black milieu.[9] Also like black music, his comic imagination was a "gift" of slavery and racism.[10] In "Bicentennial Nigger," which he considered his most politically charged recording, his genius is on display. Pryor first explains that the ironic nature of black humor derives from its origins on the slave ship, when slaves contemplated their fate of being royalty one day and slaves the next. He then assumes the persona of a two-hundred-year-old slave who returns to "celebrate" the U.S. bicentennial made up in blackface and painted in red, white, and blue stripes. With the slowly rising volume of a drum and bugle corps playing "The Battle Hymn of the Republic" in the background, the Bicentennial Nigger—in blackface and with a chuckling laugh—begins his story:

> I'm just so thrilled to be here, over here in America. So glad y'all took me out of Dahomey. I used to could live to be a hundred and fifty, now I die of high blood pressure by the time I'm fifty-two, and that thrills me to death. I'm just so pleased that America is gonna last. They brought me over here in a boat. It was four hundred of us come over here. Three hundred and sixty of us died on the way over here. I love

that. That just thrills me so. I don't know, you white folks are so good to us. Got over here, another twenty of us died from disease. But you didn't have no doctors to take care of us. I am so sorry you didn't. Upset you all some, too, didn't it? Then they split us all up. Yessirree. Took my mama over that-a-way, my wife that way, took my kids over yonder. I am just so happy. I don't know what to do, I don't know what to do if I don't get two hundred more years of this. Lawd a mercy. Yesirree. I don't know where my old mama is now. She up yonder in that big white folks in the sky. Y'all probably done forgot about it, but I ain't gonna never forget.

In this highly satirical piece, the blues self does not surrender the painful memory, but rather forges it into his consciousness and identity. This character is drawn from the African American folkloric tradition of the "revolutionary trickster"[11] who manages to survive overwhelming circumstances through his wit and guile.

Clearly, Richard Pryor's gutsy public posture did not seek to ease white fears or conform to white expectations. As the first "crossover" black comic, he brought everyone into his world. His topical observations and critiques of racism and police brutality were meshed into his routines along with candid revelations about his sex life and drug use. On his hit album . . . *Is It Something I Said?* the personal is political when he injects the broader racial context while discussing his own time in jail: "They give niggers time like it's lunch, down there. You go looking for justice, and that is what you find, just us."

The simultaneity of rage and vulnerability that was at the core of Pryor's physical, on-the-edge comedy is suggested by the images on many of his album covers. The cover of . . . *Is It Something I Said?* for example shows a staged scene with Richard in a monk's robe, tied to the stakes, with stacked firewood at his feet, and surrounded by figures dressed in black capes, head to toe, holding torches aimed at him. His expression is quizzical and pleading, as if asking: "IS it something I said?" The image on the self-titled *Richard Pryor* album cover is of Richard sitting on the ground near a cave, naked except for beads and a ring in his nose. He is holding a bow and arrows. The image evokes several levels of meaning—the primordial state of mankind, an African past, and an obscurant notion of "the primitive." His nakedness also denotes the truthfulness of his confessional style, as well as the danger and vulnerability that threaten to overtake his primitive defenses.

Viewing his own life as a "cosmic joke," Pryor made it his primary source material. His use of personal stories freed him from external constraints, doubts, and fears about overstepping the arbitrary line of political correctness. He spoke with the power of an authenticity derived from his own flaws and open wounds. Yet comedy, being a mirror image of tragedy, served his survival instincts well by turning negative personal situations into lessons about enduring. Making people laugh got him out of lots of sticky situations in his youth—at home, at school, in his 'hood, and in jail. "You said whatever you had to say to stay out of trouble."[12] His vulnerable, non-heroic self-presentation allowed people across different social and cultural barriers to understand, if not identify with, his foibles.

The years from the mid-1970s through the late 1980s saw Pryor's popularity explode on the American popular culture scene. Praised for his comedy writing and performance, he set a new standard and leaped over racial barriers in the entertainment industry. His irreverent style, mostly free of joke-telling and steeped in the language and liveliness of black underclass life, was unapologetic and daring. With his character-driven comedy, he understood, like few before him, that black humor derived not from exotica, or burlesque minstrelsy created for white audiences, but from black people's ways of knowing and being in the world.

Pryor's success as a comic easily transferred to his popularity as a movie star. His ascent in becoming the "most powerful black man in Hollywood" carried a heavy burden. Not only was he charged with helping other blacks by giving them opportunities in the film industry, but he became the "go to" black actor whom everyone wanted in their films. He became the standard-bearer for comics, especially black ones, by whom everyone else was judged. The observation that he prepared the way for comedians such as Eddie Murphy, the Wayans brothers, and others is an easy one. You can see Pryor's influence in their work. Chris Rock said that if there were no Richard Pryor, he would still be a comedian—"the only difference is I'd really suck."[13] It may be less obvious how Pryor bestowed a kind of permission upon those who followed him in comedy by clearing a path for them. As a pioneer, he gave them permission to break the mold, to do different kinds of black comedy. Filmmaker Reginald Hudlin admits that his hit film *House Party* (1990) was inspired and shaped by a Pryor sketch—"Have Your Ass Home by Eleven," on the *That Nigger's Crazy* recording.

Pryor is viewed as a predecessor by black and white comedians. "I just dreamed about being like Richard Pryor," said Keenen Ivory Wayans. "Pryor started it all. He's Yoda. If Pryor had not come along, there would

See No Evil, Hear No Evil. Copyright 1989 TriStar Pictures, Inc. All Rights Reserved. Courtesy of Columbia Pictures.

not be an Eddie Murphy or a Keenen Ivory Wayans or a Damon Wayans or
an Arsenio Hall—or even a [white comedian like] Sam Kinison," he
continued.[14] Comedy audiences have always been segmented by race and
certain racial tropes. That is why *Good Times,* the seventies television
sitcom, was believed to depict a "real" black family, while the eighties
sitcom *The Cosby Show* was said to show a "fake" black family. Pryor was
able to subvert such thinking by moving beyond predictable tropes and

See No Evil, Hear No Evil. Copyright 1989 TriStar Pictures, Inc. All Rights Reserved. Courtesy of Columbia Pictures.

themes without sacrificing his ethnicity. "I am everyone I create,"[15] he said, amassing a global repertoire of humanity that included different races, ages, and sexes, and all living things. Admittedly, the ethos behind "black" and "white" comedy is quite different, and few since Pryor have been able to bridge the divide. Bill Cosby, who preceded Pryor, is a notable exception. Perhaps Sinbad, but he has not achieved similar stature. Arguably, no white comedians have attracted a crossover audience. When Pryor first did it, the revelatory aspects of his observations were quite funny to both races. White people, he surmised, are uptight, and in extreme control of their emotions; black people are inflammatory and demonstrative. That Pryor bridged a racial chasm with these essentialist observations surprised many observers. White people who came to his shows and bought his records knew that they would be made fun of and stereotyped as square, dumb, or countrified—and more often than not, racist. He perfected, through artful mimicry and lithe physicality, a

See No Evil, Hear No Evil. Copyright 1989 TriStar Pictures, Inc. All Rights Reserved. Courtesy of Columbia Pictures.

white-black binary that spared no one. Contrasting behavior by race has become an overworked cliché in the hands of some recent comics, but Pryor was able to strike a core of truth within a hyperbolic frame. Through performance, he actually eased racial tensions rather than exacerbated them by allowing people to laugh at themselves. A memorable routine that would probably not be funny except in Pryor's rendition of it showed how black and white people react differently to the police. Whites, he suggested, tend to see the police as friends; blacks are fearful of them. He illustrated the difference by imagining through voice and movement how a white man and a black man react, as each one is getting out of his car, upon being stopped by a traffic cop. White man: "Hey officer, glad to be of help." Black man: "I am reach-ing . . . in-to my pocket . . . for my li-cense. I don't want to be no motherfucking accident!" This shows Pryor's identification with the sense of rage and discontent among many black men and is another example of what Herman Beavers has called Pryor's "protoradicalism,"[16] in which his subjectivity suggests a revision of notions about the black male subject.

Everyone who was a fan had a favorite Pryor sketch. In my informal survey, Mudbone's philosophical witticisms were mentioned several times, as were two routines about Chinese people. The "Chinese man

Stir Crazy. Copyright 1980 Columbia Pictures Industries, Inc. All Rights Reserved.
Courtesy of Columbia Pictures.

who stutters" was an exercise in mimicry that had Pryor affecting a
stutter with a staccato, syncopated "Chinese" accent. "Chinese Food" was
a routine in which Pryor expressed amazement at how Chinese people
eat so efficiently with "two sticks," while black people "lose three pounds
of food with a knife and fork!" Another favorite is "Our Text for Today,"
in which he imitates the performance style of a black preacher, preaching
from the "Book of [Stevie] Wonder." In "The Wino and the Junkie,"
Pryor becomes the affecting persona of these two social outcasts as they
match wits with each other. The well-remembered "I Went to Africa,"
and the "The Motherland" were particularly prescient observations
about black America's quest for identification with Africa. The breadth
of his themes made people view him as more than a comic. According to
novelist Walter Mosley, "calling Richard Pryor a comic, is like calling
Martin Luther King, Jr. a minister from the South."[17]

Richard Franklin Lennox Pryor III, who was born in Peoria, Illinois, in
1941, was not the first black comedian of national stature to break free of
the coon-show minstrelsy that intended to amuse whites and confirm the
most debilitating stereotypes of black inferiority. By the time he arrived
on the national scene in the early 1960s, a trickle of articulate, self-aware

Stir Crazy. Copyright 1980 Columbia Pictures Industries, Inc. All Rights Reserved. Courtesy of Columbia Pictures.

black comedians had begun abandoning the neo-vaudeville routines of the "chitlin' circuit." Beginning in the 1950s, several emerged from this strong tradition of black comedic performance to gain widespread notoriety, including Rudy Ray Moore, Dick Gregory, Godfrey Cambridge, Slappy White, Jackie "Moms" Mabley, Redd Foxx, La Wanda Page, Flip Wilson, and Bill Cosby, among others. Moore, for example, recorded his live performances and ushered in the era of the black "party" record, with its raw and unfiltered language and heavy use of black folkloric characters such as Stagolee and Petey Wheatstraw. Others, including Cambridge and Gregory, inspired by the Civil Rights Movement, embraced a more socially aware comedy that "kicked sand" in the face of American racism. Each, in his or her own way, pushed the boundaries of the black comedic tradition. But it was Pryor who, after finding his footing in the hopes, hurts, and voice of black folk culture, sandblasted his irreverent, socially aware, self-referential style of comedy all over the national mindscape. Drawing upon extraordinary skills of observation, mimicry, and hyperbole, his "lies" held the sting of truth. With these weapons he was able to expand the scope of comedic performance—not only for black comics as noted by Carlin, but for everybody.

Richard Pryor, of the unusual childhood and self-destructive tendencies, seemed an unlikely vessel for cross-cultural stardom. Yet be-

Wholly Moses. Copyright 1980 Columbia Pictures Industries, Inc. All Rights Reserved. Courtesy of Columbia Pictures.

cause comedy, in the classic sense, destroys pretensions and promotes social reintegration, the racial and political disruptions of the day provided an ideal backdrop for his iconoclasm. He embodied the ambiguities and contradictions of the American dream, racial and otherwise, while his flawed and vulnerable persona became the perfect voice for the advent of a hybridized "post"–civil rights society. By the late 1970s, black America had lost most of its heroes. Medgar was dead. So were Malcolm and King. The civil rights agenda had stalled, the Black Panthers and other "threats" to the homeland had evaporated, and Nixonian America was soon followed by the era of Reaganomics.

Brimming with ambition and energy, Richard Pryor stepped into this void and became the man who brought state pomposity and arrogance down to size by smashing white male authority and common racial myths to shards. He did it with levity and in-your-face defiance. After Watergate and the presidential pardon, Pryor observed: "Nixon would not have lasted two days in jail. Niggers was waiting for him." Similarly, a cultural myth that instilled white supremacy was dispensed with in a few lines: "Tarzan wouldn't last a week in Africa. [In Africa they call him] the crazy white man, [who is] back up in the trees with the baboons, [and] Jane is in Nairobi, whoring."

With best-selling albums and hit movies, including an Academy Award nomination for best supporting actor, live concerts, a television show, and an Emmy for television writing, Pryor was touted as the most influential black man in America. Film and culture critic Pauline Kael upped the ante, calling him, "the only great poet and satirist among our comics." To suggest that the history of comedic performance has a chronological dividing line of before and after Richard Pryor, writer Mel Watkins titles the concluding chapter in his history of black comedy "Pryor and Thereafter."[18]

That he was born and raised in a city that is the *sine qua non* of Midwestern white bread dullness, and the exemplar of mainstream virtues and hypocrisy, situates him outside the Deep South's neurotically racist culture. Yet blacks who migrated to the city in search of jobs in the meat-packing industry brought with them the southern mannerisms and sensibilities that Pryor absorbed and that permeated his most memorable characterizations, including the sagacious Mudbone. He depicted the nuances of lives on the outside of the American dream—and mixed them with his own jarring ensnarement in life on the edge.

It was a life that made artistic use of his contradictions, ambition, and insecurities, and revealed his vulnerabilities. This torturous trajectory also subjected him to a cycle of bad circumstances, including poor health—having a heart attack and being burned up in a drug-related incident, which some insist was a suicide attempt.[19] Pryor could, at different times, be magnanimous and cruel,[20] caring and aloof, protective and self-destructive, volatile and vulnerable, crass and profound, misogynistic and an admirer of women. "I love strong, smart women,"[21] he professed, but there were also stories about how he hated it when Pam Grier, his girlfriend at one time, beat him at tennis, and about his physical confrontations with his wives and lovers. He loved his strong, enterprising grandmother dearly and was devastated by the death of this woman who had raised him. It was his deep depression after her death that his daughter blames for his suicide attempt. He also felt very close to a teacher, Juliette Whittaker, who recognized his giftedness. Yet, his insecurities caused him to break up with several wives, girlfriends, best friends, and business partners, and to shoot up his wife's car and to bring a gun into a script meeting.[22] Jim Brown, whom he publicly proclaimed as a hero and friend, stated that Pryor hurt him deeply when he summarily dismissed him as president of Indigo Films, the company that Pryor had founded with forty million dollars from Columbia Pictures, telling him, "I want my company back."[23] Brown believed that his dismissal came because Pryor felt that he was "too black" and had a different vision for the company. Such unpredictability, which may have indicated psychological stress, was ignored by family and friends and even added to his iconic stature.[24] The demons that bedeviled him were like wicked muses that jolted his creative genius, but gave him no peace. The edginess of his humor was matched by, or more accurately, perhaps, provoked by living life on the edge. Some of his angst was pure rebellion. He once told an audience of mostly white people that if they didn't like his show, they could "kiss my happy, rich black ass."[25] To many black people his combination of temerity and side-splitting truth made him into a folk hero.[26] With such insults veiled by humor and self-derision, he got away with it.

He brought the same caustic approach to other controversies. In Zimbabwe [where the black leadership wrested power from the racist white minority] he observed that white folks are "always smiling, and friendly-like." Refusing to sentimentalize his near-death from the self-inflicted burns, he said in his comeback album, *Live on the Sunset Strip,* "Catching on fire is inspiring. They should use it for the Olympics. I did the 100 yard dash in about 4.6 . . . and when you run down the street on fire, people will move out of your way." With this performance he won the public over with details about his "accident" and recovery, again deriving lessons and blues-like transcendence from the painful experience.

Pryor's uncensored, X-rated observations—especially about sex and race—were filled with coarse language, dominated by a recurrence of the words that made up his unholy trinity: "bitch," "nigger," and "mother-fucker." He used these words not for shock effect, but as intertwined and inseparable parts of his comedic phrasing. This language brought consternation and condemnation in many quarters and charges of racism, sexism, and a vulgarity that violated common decency. It can be argued that his use of unsavory references to women in his performances showed his socialization in a sexist culture, and his yearning to fit into a masculine paradigm. The unathletic Pryor idolized athletes, especially Muhammad Ali and Jim Brown, both of whom had plenty of women and a complicated relationship with them. But much of Pryor's sexist material and his exaggerated male swagger had the effect of subverting male privilege because, more often than not, it showed his inability to impose male authority. In one routine drawn from his real life, he recalled how he resorted to "shooting his wife's car" in a desperate effort to gain control of a domestic situation. In another routine he assumes the persona of "Macho Man" in the bedroom, but he is divested of all pretensions when the woman assumes sexual control.[27] Nevertheless, the word "bitch" remained his synonym for woman throughout his life. There would be no epiphany about the negative and degrading effects of its use as there would be with his use of the N-word.

Richard Pryor brought into the mainstream a word that to many is the most devastating word in the English language—"nigger." His constant use of the word, until a trip to Africa raised his consciousness to its debilitating effects, was grating at the time, but not because black people did not use it with each other; in fact the word is a mainstay in non-elite black linguistic expression. Pryor grew up with the word being part of his family's daily conversation. But until his crossover appeal drew a white audience, the unstated rule was to never use it in racially mixed company. Pryor was suspicious of white people who pretended to be shocked by its use. When Barbara Walters interviewed Pryor, after his accident, she asked him about his use of the N-word, which she said she could not bear to repeat. Pryor helped her sound it out, and then declared in a sly voice, "Well, good. You said it pretty good. . . . That's not the first time you said it."[28] He removed the pretension of shock about language, implicitly asserting that it is the bad deeds that we should worry about, not the words. Pryor, no doubt, bears some of the blame for the ubiquity of the word in popular culture, especially hip hop. His first trip to Africa in 1979 was reportedly the turning point that filled him with pride about his heritage and made him feel ashamed of his use of the word. He saw "no niggers" in Africa, and declared that he would no longer say that word. He bemoaned his lack of education about Africa, and declared himself changed by the experience:

> I also left regretting ever having uttered the word "nigger" on a stage or off it. It was a wretched word. Its connotations weren't funny, even when people laughed. To this day I wish I'd never said the word. I felt its lameness. It was misunderstood by people. They didn't get what I was talking about.
> Neither did I.[29]

If any one word dominated his performances to the end, it was "motherfucker." He used it as a prop, as a bridge, for sonorous effect, and as an all-purpose utilitarian word whose meaning was determined by the context of usage, not the literal definition. His rhythmic intonations and cursing had film critic Pauline Kael describing Pryor as a "master of lyrical obscenity." His poetic cursing becomes a way to reverse injury, and to interrupt the historicity of hurtful language, argues scholar Kate Brown in her essay in this collection.

The rough language of his public persona belied a more gentle side that showed up in interviews. In a soft, sometimes barely audible voice, Pryor could be quite reflective about his life and his career. He admitted to sometimes phoning in his performances, and to putting his name on inferior projects just to get paid. He also acknowledged an inner drive and quest to express himself at the highest level, but admitted to sometimes falling short of his own standards. "I wasn't courageous and honest. It was hard enough to get this laugh, [so I'd] leave it at that. I try to do new and different stuff, and sometimes I don't get there."[30]

He also showed apprehension about losing himself in the creation of the Richard Pryor persona. "I live in his house, I spend his money, [but] it ain't me."[31] His inner conflict and his quest for greatness were the yin and yang of his existence. In his 1995 autobiography, in which he interspersed some of his old routines with reflections about his life in the wake of his multiple sclerosis diagnosis, the conflicts seemed to have been resolved. He contemplated death with the same sense of humor and irony that defined his best stand-up:

> When my body shuffles off to Buffalo, I want to be cremated. I don't want nobody fucking with me again. Because there are people who like to fuck with dead people. Twist their toes around and shit. I don't want nobody fucking with my toes. Or my nuts![32]

When he died in 2005 he had been, for more than a decade, hampered by the debilitating effects of that dreaded disease.

At his peak, Richard Pryor was without equal as a storyteller, comic performer, and insightful commentator on the foibles of race in America. In Hollywood his name alone could green-light a project, regardless of its artistic merits. He became the most prolific and the highest-earning black American in entertainment history. But what makes Richard Pryor, even in death, such an enthralling and enigmatic figure is the mystifying alchemy that produced him. His genius did not come free. It was fraught with excruciating insecurities and pain that even the salve of drugs and sex did not ease. His daughter Rain says that it was easier to love Richard Pryor if you did not know him, but, lucky for us, we thought we knew him very well. We understand how hard and tiring it must have been to keep pushing back the clouds and to try to keep some sunshine on his face.[33]

The idea for this collection grew out of a film retrospective on Pryor sponsored by the Black Film Center/Archive at Indiana University. "Is He Crazy? A Retrospective of the Career of Richard Pryor" took place in the fall of 2001 and included screenings of several of his films plus a keynote lecture by Pulitzer Prize–winning author James Alan McPherson. In his lecture, titled "Crazy like a Fox: The Vernacular Style of Richard Pryor," McPherson compared Pryor to the ancient Greek poet Homer. McPherson believes that like Homer, Pryor drew upon the expressive language of everyday people and found profundity in their wit and wisdom. He conducted one of the earliest in-depth interviews with Pryor, which was the basis of the 1975 *New York Times Magazine* article that is included in this volume. These events attracted large audiences of baby boomers who wanted to recapture some hilarious Pryor moments, and younger college students who had only heard about him and wanted to know what the fuss was about. In my introductory remarks at the opening event, I said the following: "Richard Pryor has had a lasting effect on people, even those who initially disliked his often provocative material. It has been said that he could be simultaneously profane and profound in his social critiques, and that is a quality that has been distorted in today's emphasis on being shocking and shallow. In his movie roles, Pryor's characterizations could lift the most pedestrian films. This retrospective is an opportunity to reintroduce Pryor to some, and introduce him to a younger generation who missed out."

The same can be said for this anthology, which includes some of the best previously published writing about Pryor, dating back over thirty years and extending up to five years before his death in 2005. The new essays offer a range of interesting perspectives on Pryor by scholars in several disciplines, including cultural studies, English, philosophy, communication, film and media studies, and African American studies. By combining older writings about Pryor with new perspectives, along with a personal recollection, this collection seeks to capture Richard Pryor in real time, from his meteoric ascent through the entire trajectory of a brilliant and tragic career. It also seeks to apply the wider lens of history in looking back, and also forward, to examine his legacy and to understand why he cast such a giant shadow.

Earlier writings by journalists and scholars date from 1975 to 2001. In the excerpted chapters from John A. Williams and Dennis A. Williams's book, *If I Stop I'll Die: The Comedy and Tragedy of Richard Pryor,* this father-son writing team views the genius of Pryor's comedy, in part, as a response to racial injustice and his own raging demons. Using more of a psychological and biographical approach, Joseph Nazel seeks clues to Pryor's artistry in his youth in Peoria, Illinois, and the culture of black lower-class street life. James Allen McPherson, who conducted one of the earliest in-depth interviews with the often guarded Pryor, stresses the moral dimensions of his themes. David Felton's essay, "Jive Times: Richard Pryor, Lily Tomlin, and the Theater of the Routine" focuses on the astounding dynamics and creative genius of a 1974 television performance by Pryor and Lily Tomlin that he argues created "a new path for other entertainers to follow." In "Richard and Me," culture critic and filmmaker Nelson George bemoans Pryor's erratic behavior even as he praises his brilliance, singling out his overlooked performance in *Which Way Is Up*, a film directed by Michael Schultz. The short essay by socialist author Bob Avakian is an example of the political ideas that attached themselves to Pryor's commentaries. Pryor's distrust of the police resonates strongly with Avakian. Scholar Siva Vaidhyanathan argues in "Now's the Time: The Richard Pryor Phenomenon and the Triumph of Black Culture" that his arrival on the popular culture scene with his irreverent, unapologetic humor was just in time to benefit from the opening up of society and its embrace of black cultural and artistic forms. Similarly, in his essay, "A Pryor Love," Hilton Als credits Pryor with "reinventing standup" and seizing it from the borscht-belt comedians in a style that compares favorably to that of novelists. Kate Brown offers a scholarly meditation on "eruptive voices" in Pryor's comedic style. The author finds in the poetics of Pryor's cursing a "citational strategy" that is purposeful as well as political.

Two reviews by the famed film critic Pauline Kael—of *Superman III* (1985) and *Live on the Sunset Strip* (1982), his concert film—are included. Kael, who considered Pryor an even better comic actor than Charlie Chaplin, also faulted him for sometimes phoning in his performance, rather than pushing it to the extent of his talent. Closing out the review section is "Richard Pryor: The Real Slim Shady," by Rob Sheffield. He finds in Pryor's work the template for much of what is now in vogue in popular culture.

Beginning with my interview with director Michael Schultz, the new writings look back, after his death, at the man and his unparalleled career. Schultz, who directed him in four films, provides an inside view of his work habits and unique artistry. Margo Natalie Crawford's essay, "The Crisis of Masculinity in *Jo Jo Dancer: Your Life is Calling*," identifies in the semi-autobiographical film a symbolic reenactment of Pryor's ongoing struggle to locate black power within the anti-black world. Similarly, Keith M. Harris (" 'That Nigger's Crazy': Richard Pryor, Racial Performativity, Cultural Critique") sees in Pryor's continual use of auto-biography across his films and comedy albums "the trajectory of truth and self" that is very much in the black cultural tradition. Malik D. McCluskey's essay, " '. . . And It's Deep Too': The Philosophical Comedy of Richard Pryor," provides a seldom-used metric in popular culture—philosophy—to show that Pryor's insights have a philosophical resonance that prompts self-examination among his audience. Tyrone Simpson's essay, "When Keeping It Real Goes Wrong: Pryor, Chappelle, and the Comedic Politics of the Post Soul," situates the comedy of Pryor and Dave Chappelle in their socio-political contexts and argues that Chappelle, as an inheritor of Pryor's pro-black, conscious comedy, has found it difficult to adjudicate a meaningful black presence in this post-race, post-soul environment. My essay, "Was It Something He Said? Censorship and the Richard Pryor Television Show, 1977," examines the politics of censorship that marred his debut as host of a network variety show. In "Br'er Richard: Fascinatin' Storyteller," storyteller and professor Maxine LeGall connects Pryor to a long tradition of the best storytellers both within and outside of the black folkloric vernacular. "We Owe a Debt to Richard Pryor," my final short tribute to Pryor, was published as an op-ed essay when he died in December 2005.

A filmography, a discography, a chronology of events in Pryor's life, and an extensive bibliography provide additional information and interesting details about the life and legacy of this uniquely gifted American artist.

NOTES

1. Rain Pryor (with Cathy Crimmins), *Jokes My Father Never Taught Me: Life, Love, and Loss with Richard Pryor* (New York: Regan Books, 2006), 29.

2. Rain Pryor, 35.

3. Although this is a well-documented and frequently used term, there are variations in the way it is used and defined. For the purposes of this essay, I like the definition given by Renford Reese: "These individuals, are not necessarily social activists or race conscious; they are not bound by the conventions or customs of the day; they are nonconformists and play by their own rules and are willing to live with the consequences of their actions." Reese, "The Socio-Political Context of the Integration of Sport in America," *Journal of African American Men* 4, no. 3 (Spring 1999), appendix.

4. Richard Pryor with Todd Gold, *Pryor Convictions, and Other Life Sentences* (New York: Pantheon Books, 1995), 8.

5. Cat Moses, "The Blues Aesthetic in Toni Morrison's *The Bluest Eye*," *African American Review,* Winter 1999, 1.

6. See Richard J. Powell, *Black Art and Culture in the Twentieth Century* (New York: W. W. Norton, 1997); Ralph Ellison, "Richard Wright's Blues," *Shadow and Act* (New York: Vintage Books, 1964).

7. Mary Ellison, "Kalamu Ya Salaam and the Black Blues Subversive Self," *Race and Class* 45, no. 1: 79–95. Also see LeRoi Jones (Amiri Baraka), *Blues People* (New York: William Morrow, 1963 [1999]).

8. Mary Ellison, in "Kalamu Ya Salaam," makes this point as a comparison to an elitist aesthetic that it requires a specialized knowledge and access to decipher.

9. Herman Beavers, "The Cool Pose: Intersectionality, Masculinity, and Quiescence in the Comedy of Richard Pryor and Eddie Murphy," in *Race and the Subject of Masculinities,* ed. Harry Stecopoulas and Michael Vebel (Durham, N.C.: Duke University Press, 1997), 256. Beavers contrasts Pryor with Eddie Murphy, who, he argues, plays characters who are usually "transferred into a predominately white world."

10. John A. Williams and Dennis A. Williams, *If I Stop I'll Die: The Comedy and Tragedy of Richard Pryor* (New York: Thunder Mouth Press, 1991), 1.

11. Larry G. Coleman, "Black Comic Performance in the African Diaspora: A Comparison of the Comedy of Richard Pryor and Paul Keens-Douglas," *Journal of Black Studies* 15, no. 1 (September 1984): 67–78.

12. Pryor with Gold, 34.

13. Richard Pryor, Reggie Collins, and Steve Pokorny, ". . . *And It's Deep Too!*": *The Complete Warner Brothers Recordings (1968–1992),* 9 CDs, Warner Bros./Rhino, 2000, booklet, 52.

14. Black History: Biographies: Richard Pryor, http://www.galegroup.com/free _resources/bhm/bio/pryor_r.htm (accessed 7 May 2002).

15. "Richard on Richard" [Barbara Walters interview], from ". . . *And It's Deep Too!*" booklet.

16. Beavers, 262.

17. Walter Mosley, "The Stage of Life," in ". . . *And It's Deep Too!*" booklet, 15.

18. Mel Watkins, *On the Real Side: A History of African American Comedy* (New York: Simon and Schuster, 1994).

19. Rain Pryor, 102.

20. Instances of generosity to friends and strangers alike are detailed in several Pryor biographies. Stories about domestic violence also appear.

21. Fred Robbins and Dave Ragan, *Richard Pryor: This Cat's Got Nine Lives!* (New York: Delilah Books, 1982), 26.

22. Andy Breckman, a screenwriter, recounts a script meeting for one of Pryor's later low-quality comedy roles. He says that when Pryor objected to a scene in which an old, senile woman is supposed to defecate in broad daylight, and the screenwriter didn't want to take it out, Pryor pulled out a Derringer and laid it on the table. Breckman uses this episode to call Pryor a "pathetic, self-hating junkie." "Nobody Move! It's Richard Pryor," www.wfmu.org/lcd/20/pryor.html (accessed [3 May 2005]). Author's note: His adamancy could also reflect Pryor's humanity and respect for human dignity in not wanting to have an old woman treated like a dog. The gun—well, Pryor loved guns, but tended to used them on inanimate things like cars.

23. Quote from Jim Brown in *Jim Brown: All American* (40 Acres and a Mule Film Co., 2002), a documentary by Spike Lee. In Pryor's version of this story, he admits that he simply did not want the burden of owning a company. Pryor with Gold, 210.

24. Pryor talked about how his family overlooked his drug problem in *Live on the Sunset Strip.*

25. Pryor was invited by his friend Lily Tomlin in 1978 to appear at a human rights campaign benefit that was in fact a gay rights benefit. Pryor did not like how it was going down and this comment preceded his exit. Tomlin recalls the incident in a tribute to Pryor, upon his death, on National Public Radio, *Talk of the Nation,* 12 December 2005.

26. Williams and Williams, *If I Stop I'll Die,* vi.

27. This agrees with Beavers's notion of "protoradicalism" (cited earlier). While Pryor's constant search for an authentic self did not make him anti-sexist, or even lead him to question male prerogatives, he was always aware of the self's limitations.

28. "Richard on Richard" [Barbara Walters interview], from "*. . . And It's Deep Too!*" booklet, 59.

29. Pryor with Gold, 175.

30. Interview track no. 15 [unpublished], recorded at the Comedy Store, 1983. Bonus track from "*. . . And It's Deep Too!*" 2002.

31. Interview track no. 15.

32. Pryor with Gold, 244.

33. Pryor with Gold, 8.

New Essays

1 "That Nigger's Crazy"

RICHARD PRYOR, RACIAL PERFORMATIVITY, CULTURAL CRITIQUE

KEITH M. HARRIS

[As the character Mudbone]: You start telling the truth to people, and people gonna look at you like you was askin' to fuck their mama or somethin'. The truth is gonna be funny, but it's gonna scare the shit outta folks.[1]

What I am saying might be profane, but it also profound.[2]

The two opening quotes from Richard Pryor address, in his language, two sets of objects elaborated in this essay: truth and profanity, comedy and profundity. In my language, these two sets of objects are explored as performativity and critique in the stand-up comedy of Richard Pryor from the period of his seventies reinvention of himself to his eighties work, specifically the concert films *Richard Pryor Live and Smokin'* (Jeff Blum, 1971), *Richard Pryor: Live! In Concert* (Jeff Margolis, 1979), *Richard Pryor Live on the Sunset Strip* (Joe Layton, 1982), and *Richard Pryor: Here and Now* (Richard Pryor, 1983). The emphasis is on the mining of his life and childhood and the use of autobiography as it informs his performance; and racial performativity and the critique of the American contemporary that his comedy performs.

Richard Pryor's biography is a matter of public record, and was a prominent aspect of his public persona. His life was variously one of abandonment, abuse, a fair manner of indifference, self-indulgence, and personal perseverance, tempered with great success as a writer, performer, and actor. That his mother was a prostitute, working out of one of his grandmother's in-town brothels; that he was married eight times; that he had coke and alcohol problems, which culminated in the now-infamous freebasing incident; that he had two heart attacks, and a quadruple bypass; that he was debilitated by multiple sclerosis before his death: the intricacies of his life, private and public, are very central to his humor from the earliest points in his career.[3] How these biographical moments enter his humor as autobiography and the extension of these moments to the critique of race, nation, and masculinity that his humor achieves is where we begin with performativity.

The notion of racial performativity that I use is developed through Judith Butler's work on gender performativity and Henry Louis Gates's work on signifyin(g).[4] From Butler, I draw on her elaborations of J. L. Austin's notion of the performative as an utterance, as a speech act, and "the issuing of an utterance [as] the performing of the action."[5] With the performative, Butler expands upon gender performativity as a citational subjectification in which the first person, singular "I" is not a presupposed subject, but instead a citational chain, a re-signification of power and authority, a reiteration of the discursive formation embedded in the performative. Butler's gender performativity is disciplinary and regulatory as a practice of subjective formation.

I expand upon this notion of gender performativity by positing Gates's theory of signifyin(g) as part of the black vernacular tradition, as social discursivity that is best described as performativity as well. For Gates, signifyin(g) is a tropological endeavor in which the given sign (in this case the sign of blackness) is emptied of meaning in the process of signifyin(g) and, therefore, shifts from a semantic significatory practice to a rhetorical one.[6] The shift to the rhetorical demonstrates the sign as mutable and conceptual; denotation is disrupted in that it is doubled, given double meaning, becoming double-voiced, in Gates's words. Signifyin(g), as a process of doubling, mediates mutability and meaning through interpretation and revision.

In augmenting Butler with Gates, we arrive at signifyin(g) as a gender- and racial-performative construct that allows us to examine both gender and race. Gender performativity and signifyin(g) as re-theorized here are racial performativity. Such racial performativity, for my purposes, offers a better hermeneutic for understanding the performance of race and the performativity of race that are found in instances such as the cool poser, the down low brother, the snap queens, the black divas, and the performance that Pryor foregrounds. Racial performativity, then, describes a racial parody, in which the difference of race and the static meanings of color are given privilege as critical agency, and, I argue in the case of Richard Pryor, in which that racial performativity is returned to its rhetorical foundations. By this I mean that ideas of the performative and performativity are already rhetorical, and with Pryor's stand-up, racial performativity is revealed as a rhetoric of race.

Explicit to any discussion of racial performativity is the figuration of race as a trope. Race as trope specifically counters notions of race which envision it as natural, instinctive, and to some extent universal. This idea of racial performativity, of race as a trope, is something more akin to the performances and propositions of identity formation found in the work of Anna Deavere Smith. In Smith's work, as Debby Thompson notes, racial performativity is a post-structuralist critique of liberal humanist models of identity.[7] For Thompson, Smith's notion of identity is one of racial performativity, and identity, then, "is not something *there*, but something constantly made and remade," something that can shift and change.[8] Smith's notion of identity is "radically performative," emphasizing the individual's battle against the scripted or discursively pre-constituted. This identity battle, the alienation of it in performance as performativity, does not, contrary to essentialist theories of race and identity, suggest that because race is performative it has no contemporary significance or meaning; instead, the battle of the performative acknowledges race, through its legacies and contradictions, as systematic, as learned, as a discourse, but not as a static, eternal essence. Race as performativity, Thompson notes, emphasizes the "fact" and the "act" of race.[9] Thompson considers this critique through a discussion of the model of acting that Smith puts forth in her writing and performance. I want to look at the comedic performance, the stand-up of Pryor in a similar fashion, attending to the performative foregrounding of the instability of race and gender.

The Richard Pryor stand-up performances with which we are most familiar, arguably the ones for which he will be remembered, are from the second incarnation of himself. Pryor's first incarnation as a stand-up in the mid-'60s was very much in the mold of Bill Cosby, allowing him to enter the mainstream comedy circuit with an inoffensive style of humor, a "gentrified" style.[10] This was a fairly successful mode for him, but he was not artistically satisfied because of the lack of personal authenticity. After an alleged "breakdown" and a recuperative stay in Berkeley, California, Pryor re-emerged in the 1970s with a new routine and content.[11] The stay in Berkeley allowed him to reposition his humor within the context of the *ethos* with which we have become familiar for the period. This *ethos* of blackness is not colorblind, is aggressively black, is a source of action, a source of doing, calling attention not only to the social condition of African Americans, but also informing aesthetic practices of cultural production.[12] This *ethos* was one inspired by the Black Power Movement, the Black Arts Movement, and the Black Panthers, as well as urban riots and the perceived failure of the Civil Rights Movement, or, as Pryor notes of the environment and his experience in it in *Pryor Convictions*:

> [Living in Berkeley] was the freest time in my life. Berkeley was a circus of exciting, extreme, colorful, militant ideas. Drugs. Hippies. Black Panthers. Antiwar protests. Experimentation. Music, theater, poetry. I was like a lightning rod. I absorbed bits of everything while forging my own uncharted path.[13]

Berkeley becomes the space of coming of age as an artist for Pryor. The comic routine that emerges is formed around character impersonations, replete with exaggerated, expressive body and facial gesture. The content is now raced with the experience of living in the contemporary raced society. His performance relies more on folk traditions of storytelling. His characters are drawn from his life or developed from members of his childhood community in Peoria, Illinois. There is a decidedly more autobiographic tenor to his comedy at this point. The characters of Mudbone and the street junkie appear and are refined in this early period of his career. The humor is vulgar, volatile, and "street," at the same time that it is sincere, sensitive, and vulnerable. There is the greatly expanded and liberal use of the word "nigger" (or the "owning" of the word)[14] in his routine, and significantly, there is the loss of the joke. The humor is located in the narrational style of delivery and the content of the character impersonations.

"I hope I'm funny and shit, 'cause just to be a nigger up here and just be saying nothing, ain't shit."[15] Thus, Richard Pryor begins his routine for the set filmed at The Improvisation Nightclub in New York on April 29, 1971. Within minutes he has transformed himself from a white boy throwing his hair back, to a black schoolboy who is jealous of this, to being Puerto Rican in the Midwest. He continues to explain the rarity of Puerto Ricans in the Midwest, the resulting exoticism, and how "you" can be Puerto Rican with a "process" in the Midwest. Even further, he explains that he can pass for Puerto Rican, which increases the sexual possibilities, until he has an orgasm when his black self is revealed: "Oh! Shit!—that's not Puerto Rican." This first "Puerto Rican" skit leads to the next skit, which begins, "I always wanted to be something but I never wanted to be white. I always wanted to be something other than a nigger because niggers had it so rough."

Pryor is young, obviously nervous, and cautious. Yet, within a few minutes, Pryor has performed race, through his vocal and gestural impersonations, differentiating and hierarchizing racial categories through standards of beauty (the hair) and how these standards can easily be manipulated and appropriated, only to reveal a *pathos* of blackness in which one wishes to escape, to be something else because it is so difficult, as a "nigger," to be. It is in this space of radical juxtaposition between spectacle of self, performance, and specular self, of self-reference and interiority, that we find the performativity. He does this through performance and troping race, giving race shifting embodiment as persona and impersonation.

I want to emphasize the distinction here between performance and performativity. Performance here is an artistic performance, one rendered through script, practice, and a defined set of actions which are assigned. Indeed, it is the performance of race that directs us to the performativity of race, to the constructed, instable, reiterated, and citational discursivity of race. For example, in the above-cited routine, Pryor uses the direct address of "you." Presumably, this "you" is a direct address to African Americans, yet it is simultaneously the sub-standard American English usage of the second person as a generalization, as an address to the third-person "one." The result is a double-voiced address, simultaneously direct and indirect, to the white audience and the implied black audience: the address "You can't be Puerto Rican with a process" implicates the failure of the attempt of a black person to pass as a Puerto Rican, at the same time that it presents the possibility of passing, the fluidity of it, and the failure of it in this instance as a "process." As persona and impersonation, race is externalized, given posture, vocalization, tonal inflection, and difference alongside the revelation of its constructed-ness. What follows in *Live and Smokin'* and in all of his other concert films is how the raced self is learned. However, before we continue with the discussion of racial performativity, I want to examine one more moment in this first concert film, a moment which becomes crucial to Pryor's deconstructive humor.

After the initial opening in which race is projected onto the audience, given external meaning as spectacle, Pryor turns to place and the implications of race. He speaks of growing up in a neighborhood with a lot of whorehouses, the availability of liquor stores in black neighborhoods (and the absence of banks and candy stores), his experience with white men in his neighborhood, and his experience of social and racial differences while visiting a white neighborhood. The American landscape is segregated, geographically and economically, engendering racially different habits, from eating to having sex to the differences between male and female flatulence. Everything is given a stage in this routine, but all in a socially determined field of economic and racial difference.

Next, Pryor turns to his present predicament of being on film, speaking about his desire to be on film and to be like Johnnie Mack Brown, who is jokingly described as "Cool for a faggot." This returns him to the orbit of sexual differences between black men and white men, specifically penis size, which returns him to growing up in a whorehouse and witnessing prostitutes and tricks having sex, further describing his neighborhood as the ghetto, further describing domestic habits as different between black and white. What is significant about this seemingly random monologue is that it posits whiteness as civility and blackness as savagery, while also providing social, economic, geographic, and discursive reasons for this seeming dichotomy: what emerges is whiteness as mechanic, lifeless, routine, and emotionless and blackness as abject.[16] The abjection found in this early routine is that of blackness, as that which is expelled from whiteness and as that which is expelled from within blackness. The abject blackness, the urbanity of it, the sexual economy of it, the class of it, is in contrast to the implied middle-class blackness which counters the characters Pryor creates. In this strategic abjection, within and without blackness, there is a consciousness, a knowing and mastering of environment in abjection. In this sense, Pryor, on the fringes of blackness, indeed expelled from it, is defining it. There is an anti-heroic quality to his routine and the characters created in that the liminality, excessiveness, and vulgarity of the Pryor blackness is that which has to be abjected, that which has to be removed for the civil, middle-class blackness to survive. This use of abjection is never more apparent in his characterizations of black and white than when he turns his routine to the impersonation of "faggots," and I quote at length:

> No, never fuck a faggot, . . . no, I'd like to say this on film, 'cause to all American male persons, never fuck a faggot, 'cause they will lie. They always say, [in a high pitched "faggot" voice] "I won't tell." They lie. They can't wait till you finish fucking 'em: [the high pitched "faggot" voice again, while mimicking the use of a telephone] "Well guess who was here, honey, girl, looka here, well the nigger's got mo' bitch in him than me."
>
> Don't ever give a faggot head, 'cause you really be low down then, right? [looking around to the room] Y'all act like you ain't never sucked a dick or something. Y'all be [in the white voice] "No, sirree, Bob, we've never ever touched a penis in our lives; we're real men."

> I sucked a dick. You can get a habit from sucking dick. You know, become a dick junkie. You can only do it maybe three times. You know, you do it more than that, and you get a habit. You know, you'll be like, [in a hysterical, agitated voice] "I got to have a dick. . . ."
>
> I used to give head to dudes who'd always say don't come in my mouth [a reference to an earlier portion of the sex skit in which he complains about women saying, "Don't come in my mouth"]. [At which point he returns to another skit about being black: "It's Exciting Being Black."]

There is a disturbing homophobia and vulgarity to this "Dick Junkie" segment, yet there is a quiet, subtle, brilliant vulnerability. For, on the one hand, Pryor distances male homosexuality from the orbit of black masculinity by characterizing the homosexual as a faggot, un-masculine, indeed gossipy and feminine, unmanly in the desire to divulge the sexual encounter (as opposed to manly bragging), and as something that "you" (in this case men) should not "do." All male sexual proclivities are allowed, black men having sex with white women, loud orgasms, flatulence after sex, but not homosexuality. Furthermore, in a manner indicative of the black male *ethos* of the time, homosexuality, more specifically being a faggot, is characterized as a white thing, as it were, through distanciation and difference.[17] On the other hand, the entire "Dick Junkie" routine is in a confessional mode, producing oral and anal sex between two men as part of his masculinity and sexuality: having sex with a man who could be identified as a faggot, from where Pryor comes, is indiscreet, but not indiscriminate; oral sex with a man, from where Pryor comes, is a rite of passage, an addiction that is overcome, and at the same time all a part of being black. This skit is not well received, if we note the failure of laughter from the filmic audience, but it is revelatory in the manner in which Pryor puts forth black masculinity as sexual polysemy, with homosexuality as a sexual passage to heterosexuality. This construction of masculinity and blackness in abjection serves to define the limits of both at the same time that it critiques whiteness as a master trope for the configuration of masculinity and race. This frankness with regard to male homosexuality never returns to his routine in this direct commentary, yet the spectre of homosexuality and the liminality of black masculinity remain.[18]

Eight years after *Live and Smokin'*, Pryor releases his first major concert film.[19] By this time Pryor has indeed achieved major popular success in film, television, acting, writing, and producing. He has received a fair amount of press around his health and private life. His humor has garnered him fame and artistic respect. And it is in this moment in his career that we find the Pryor of *Richard Pryor: Live! In Concert*. The routines of *Live! In Concert* are more refined, relying more on his self-characterization as a trickster, fully submerged in folk traditions with the addition of elaborate animal tales. The various experiments found in *Live and Smokin'* are now hallmarks of his concerts: the scatology, the racial performance, the frank discussion of sex, the autobiographical moments, and the emphasis on location (here Southern California and Long Beach, which inspire racial commentary about blacks, whites, Mexicans, and Chinese, as opposed to St. Louis, Peoria, and the Midwest, and the commentary on whites, blacks, and Puerto Ricans), and in keeping with the autobiographical import, there is a greater emphasis on class, as is reflected in his humorous bits about his own upward mobility and class ascent.

What remains from the confessional masculinity and sexuality of *Live and Smokin'* is, in comparison to the transparency of the confession, an opaque, yet salient, critique of masculinity as that which is fallible, as that which is frail, mortal, even penetrable (the masturbating monkey that sticks its penis in men's ears), and ultimately unreliable. This figuration of masculinity is most apparent in his skit re-enacting his heart attack. In this skit, Pryor figuratively separates in two, and literally falls down on stage. The skit is a pronounced example of the loss of control of one's body, complete with a heart, his heart, given voice, agency, and control *over* masculine agency and subjectivity.

What is noteworthy about this rendering of masculinity is that it is done within the nationalist *ethos* of blackness. Pryor's critique, indeed, could be said to be sanctioned by nationalism. On the one hand, this sanctioning adds to the political currency of his public persona and his routine, aligning him with the likes of Jim Brown, Huey Newton (who, though not seen on camera, is acknowledged by Pryor during the performance), Muhammad Ali, and Leon Spinks. On the other hand, given the context of performing before a broad multiracial audience, this rendering of masculinity promotes a radical, all-encompassing celebration of blackness, as when Pryor, in praise of Spinks, says,

I don't like to hear when white people would be saying, [Spinks] is dumb, ain't he? And niggers be agreeing with them, though, that's what tickles me. Be happy for any nigger doing any thing.[20]

For white people to talk about Spinks, pass judgment on his character, is distasteful, but in the direct address to the black members of the audience and in the rhetoric of nationalism, Pryor encourages pride in black accomplishment, no matter how that accomplishment manifests itself.

In his next concert film, *Live on the Sunset Strip,* Pryor offers even more self-revision and progressive nationalism at the same time that the liminality of black masculinity perfected in concerts like *Live and Smokin'* and *Live! In Concert* is more deeply personalized. *Sunset Strip* builds and leads to his routine about the events of and recuperation from the "free-basing incident," but before that there are two significant moments that warrant explication. First, there is his intimate rendering of love, sex, emotions, and masculinity in the "Feelings" segment. Here Pryor, again through his own life experiences, provides a contradictory figuration of masculinity and the differences between men and women with regard to love and relationships. The performance of men in love and of angry men presents masculinity as irrational, emotionally hysterical, more emotional than women, yet less expressive than women. This performance of masculinity is counter to the social discourse of men as being reasonable, emotionally contained, and in control of themselves and their feelings. In fact, this performance deconstructs that received image by exposing masculinity as hysterical and reconstituting the popular image of masculinity as in control: the trajectory of the skit goes from hysteria to neurotic containment of emotion, thereby revealing masculinity and masculine emotional expression, or the lack of it, as a mask, indeed as masking.

The second significant moment in *Sunset Strip* is the renunciation of the word "nigger." The renunciation is part of a narrative of return and reunion in blackness. It begins with Pryor's critique of racism, in which he directly addresses white people as purveyors of racism and black people as the victims, ending with humanist description of the impact of racism:

> It's hard enough just to walk through life decent, as a person. But here is another element added to it when you're black. Them mothers got that little edge on us. It's enough to make you crazy. 'Cause if you're in an argument with another man, he may be white, but it's man on man for a minute—and the shit get rough, he end up calling you "nigger." You go, "Oh, shit. Fuck." Now I ain't no man no more. I'm nigger now.[21]

This prelude to the "The Motherland" skit is the first time that Pryor has used the word nigger in this performance, and for the first time, it does not identify blackness. Here it is an affront to blackness, a dehumanizing, emasculating insult.

Continuing, Pryor tells the story of visiting Africa, the motherland. His conception of the motherland is romantic and quite revisionist. On the one hand, Africa is constructed as the nationalist-envisioned place of all black people, without any understanding of the history of the continent or the differences among the countries on the continent; on the other hand, Africa is historicized as the birthplace of humanity. His praise of the motherland then has to be qualified: "I went home to the motherland, and everybody should go home, to Africa. Everybody, especially black people."[22] Africa is home to us all and everyone should go there. Again there is the double-voiced direct and indirect address which is inclusive, but clarifying.

"The Motherland" leads into the "N-Word" part of the routine and Pryor begins to tell of his epiphany that there were no niggers in Africa. The significance is that at this point in his career the use of "nigger" has come full circle, from the militant, uncompromising use of it in the reinvention of himself in the early '70s—from the owning of it—to the rejection of it as a descriptor of blackness. Within the figuration of blackness in Pryor's body of work, this moment is more than a staging of black pride. The "N-Word" routine disrupts the significatory possibilities of the trope of "nigger." By this I mean that in his earlier routines "nigger" is not only a descriptor and a direct address to an implied audience, but it is also an utterance of blackness, speaking, as it were, a peripheral subject position within blackness, and at this point in Pryor's ongoing self-invention, the word is disarticulated, unable to give utterance to his subject position.

Of the four concert films under discussion, perhaps the most compelling is *Richard Pryor: Here and Now.* In this last film we find the staples of Pryor's comedy, finely honed and tuned, and elements of introspection and confession that have not been present in his films since *Live and Smokin'.* Of the four, *Here and Now* is the only one written and directed by Pryor, and in form, it is at times closer to documentary than concert film. The film begins with a prologue: an establishing shot of the crowd outside the theater, followed by a series of shots which contain sound bites from a multiracial and multiethnic crowd of concert-goers, intercut with backstage shots of Pryor. The use of Pryor's voice-over explaining his relationship to his audience as one of exchange, familiarity, and necessity creates an intimacy in this opening. In the voice-over, Pryor acknowledges that, "After all that's why I am here. It's not something that was made up in some agent's office."[23] As this quiet prologue continues, there is a sequence of shots of Pryor on stage (at what looks like a supper club, not the Saenger Theatre in New Orleans, where most of the film is shot) directly addressing an audience member in the persona of Mudbone. This sequence is guided by a voice-over sound bridge in which Pryor confesses, "And I'm sober. I'm not doing drugs. That's a damn good accomplishment."[24] This confession begins the credit sequence in which we see Pryor, escorted by Jim Brown, upon his arrival at the theater. The credit sequence itself is a series of shots of the crowd outside entering the theater, Pryor onstage before an empty auditorium, Pryor backstage in makeup, followed by shots of the crowded auditorium, concluding with a long take of Pryor, dressed and ready, walking from his dressing room onto the stage. The music of the credit sequence, The SOS Band's "Just Be Good to Me," fades to the sound of the crowd chanting, "We want Richard! We want Richard!" as the announcer says, "Ladies and gentlemen, the two most beautiful words in the world of comedy, Richard Pryor."[25]

I have gone through this detailed account of the beginning of *Here and Now* in order to emphasize the visual rhetoric of authenticity and artistry initiated in the prologue and credit sequence. We are given images of Pryor onstage, backstage, in rehearsal, and in exchange with his fans, all accompanied by his own confession of self. There is a manner in which the prologue and credit sequence visualize Pryor in film and concert as a culmination of a career and, with the confessional voice-over, as a culmination of the self. Pryor is individuated in his artistic virtuosity and transcendent in his popularity.

The humor of the concert is as irreverent as ever, yet tame, more than usual about his experiences of fame. Pryor immediately racializes the crowd, identifies the front row as the "garden row," the row on which he urinates if his show is not funny, makes fun of the set design and his own wardrobe. When an audience member shouts out, "Hey, Rich, how's your mama?" Pryor responds, "How's my mama. I beg your pardon. I'll slap you in the mouth with my dick."[26] Direct commentary on American politics, which has had a slight presence in his stand-up until this point, is prominent with his critique of then President Ronald Reagan. There is the additional Japanese impersonation in the "Dropping the Bomb" skit, a return to Africa as source material; Mudbone and the junkie reappear. However, for the purposes here, it is the final "Public Toilets" skit that is quite telling.

"Public Toilets" is preceded by a skit about the need to inspect your partner's genitals before sex because of the threat of herpes. This cautionary tell leads to the following, and I quote at length:

> No, you gotta be very careful and shit. That's why I go to public toilets man, I be watching them motherfuckers 'cause I know some shit in there waiting for me. I be real careful. Only thing about a public toilet is if somebody recognizes my ass. You know 'cause you can go to the toilet all your life. You can go in the toilet and take a shit and nobody say nothin'. They may make a face when you leave, right? [He grimaces.] But they see me, they start talkin', "Richard Pryor! That was you in there shittin'? Woo hoo whee! Man you don't never need to shit in public. Hey everybody com' in here, Richard Pryor is in here shittin'!"
>
> . . . You ever go into them urinals? . . . And the men go in there and stand right up in the urinal, like they hidin' their shit or somethin' . . . And look each other in the eye. That's the way men look each other in the eye 'cause you don't look down. You look down—what you lookin' at? The only trouble I have in there, people wanna to meet me.[27]

The quotation of this routine does not do it justice. The delivery is replete with facial contortions, expressive movement, vocal riffs, and hand and body gesture. However, close attention to the content is revealing. There is a self-effacement of his star persona, his iconicity, which lends itself to the humor of the skit. Yet, in contrast to the abjection of blackness found so shockingly, and poignantly, in the comedy of *Live and Smokin'*, Pryor in *Here and Now* is no longer the abject: abjection, that which must be removed, is still the quotidian, but now it is his interaction with the quotidian, as the non-quotidian, that mediates the humor and the abjection.

Furthermore, close attention to this portion of the concert reveals Pryor's continued oscillation between the vulgar and the vulnerable. The vulgarity, again, lies in the scatology: this is not new to Pryor's body of work. Yet, it is the metonymic "my ass" that positions Pryor's body as vulnerable. The slippage here is in the space of the routine and the place of homosexuality in Pryor's comedy. The public toilet is a space of homosociality. As such, Pryor, with biting wit, mines the space through the trope of seeing sex. Here the space of the public toilet becomes that of public sex and the threat of homosexuality. Pryor has never shied away from topics of sexuality or, as noted in *Live and Smokin'*, the fluidity of sexuality and masculinity. In this instance, sexuality is mediated by fame.

"I be watching motherfuckers 'cause I know some shit in there waiting for me": what waits for men in public restrooms? Here the spectre of homosexuality, indeed the spectre of the homosexual, is configured and rearticulated in the allegory of recognition: the only trouble he has in the public toilet is that people (men) want to meet him.

As mentioned above, *Here and Now* is a culmination of performance in Pryor's body of work. It is his directorial debut, his last concert film. He is at peak form, and in his autobiographical mode of comedy, he is introspective and retrospective, arguably at peace. To be sure, it is his use of autobiography across his films and albums that allows us to arrive at this conclusion, allows us to see the trajectory of truth and self. Pryor's use of autobiography is not without precedent. There is a long tradition of American and African American autobiography at play in Pryor's comedy. Furthermore, Pryor's use of autobiography is strategic in that in using autobiography he is deploying a familiar and powerful rhetoric, one well established in African American literary and cultural traditions.

The African American autobiography, emerging in the form of the slave narrative, reconciles social, racial, and figurative instantiations of the self through narrative invention and individuation, producing truth and social critique through the exemplar, through the acquisition of personhood.[28] The African American autobiography, as Lewis Gordon argues, stems from an epistemic openness, an insight into blackness, encouraging the possibility of humanity and personhood.[29] William L. Andrews argues that the African American autobiography, in the form of slave narrative, should be distinguished primarily by its rhetorical aims, those of persuading the audience that the slave is "a man and a brother" too and that the black narrator is a truth-teller, a reliable conveyor of the experience and character of black folk.[30] Pryor situates himself squarely in this tradition of African American autobiography, as it is citational of the slave narrative, an autobiography with the rhetoric of equality and truth and experiential authenticity.

That I have concentrated on the "autobiographical moments" in his concert films and in his comedy, and not on his autobiography, allows for an emphasis on racial performativity and the impact of it in the legacy of Richard Pryor. This is not to deny that the written autobiography is performative. For, to look at the films and attend to the performance allows one to see the autobiographical moments as they foreground performativity. In other words, it is important to see the strategy, the deliberate deployment of autobiography in order to see the performativity, to see the constructed-ness of race, and the critique of race which is put forward in performativity.

By looking at Pryor's stand-up as racial performativity, we see the "fact and act" of race. Indeed, we see a spectacle of interpellation: we see the Althusserian "hailing," see how Pryor is interpellated into race, class, gender, and sexuality through the exposure of his confessional, auto-biographical self, and we are also given the effects of his interpellation through his constant reinvention of himself, his constant mining of his private life, his trials and tribulations, his accomplishments and failures as a human being.

NOTES

1. Richard Pryor with Todd Gold, *Pryor Convictions, and Other Life Sentences* (New York: Pantheon, 1995), 110.

2. Richard Pryor, qtd. in Fred Robbins and David Ragan, *Richard: Black and Blue* (New York: Bantam Books, 1986), 30.

3. Much of the biographical information comes from a series of interviews and his autobiography. For a sample of these readings see Frederick Murphy, "Richard Pryor: Teetering on Jest, Living by His Wits," *Encore American and Worldwide News,* 24 November 1975, 27–29; Martin Weston, "Richard Pryor: 'Every nigger is a star,'" *Ebony,* September 1976, 55–62; Louie Robinson, "Richard Pryor . . . about love, life, humor, marriage—and what happened to his television show," *Ebony,* January 1978, 116–122; William Brashler, "Berserk Angel," *Playboy,* December 1979, 243–248 and 292–296; "*Ebony* Interview: Richard Pryor talks about Richard Pryor (the old, the new), rejection that led to loneliness and drugs, God, prayer, 'Nigger,' and how he was burned," *Ebony,* October 1980, 33–44; Sid Cassese, "Richard Pryor: No Laughing Matter," *Essence,* March 1986, 79–84; Richard Pryor with Todd Gold, *Pryor Convictions, and Other Life Sentences* (New York: Pantheon, 1995). I would like to thank Matthew Ferrari and Taik Lim for their research assistance in retrieving most of this material.

4. See Judith Butler, *Gender Trouble: Feminism and the Subversion of Identity* (London: Routledge, 1990); and Henry Louis Gates, Jr., *The Signifying Monkey: A Theory of African-American Literary Criticism* (Oxford: Oxford University Press, 1988).

5. J. L. Austin, *How to Do Things with Words: The William James Lectures Delivered at Harvard University in 1955,* ed. J. O. Urmson and Marina Sbisà (Cambridge, Mass.: Harvard University Press, 1962), 6. Also see Butler, *Gender Trouble;* Judith Butler, *Excitable Speech: A Politics of the Performative* (London: Routledge, 1997); Judith Butler, "Performative Acts and Gender Constitution," in *The Performance Studies Reader,* ed. Henry Bial (London: Routledge, 2004), 1554–1556; Eve K. Sedgwick, "Queer Performativity," *GLQ* 1 (1993): 1–16.

6. Gates, 47–48.

7. Debby Thompson, "'Is Race a Trope?' Anna Deavere Smith and the Question of Racial Performativity," *African American Review* 37 (2003): 128.

8. Thompson, 132.

9. Thompson, 137.

10. For a discussion of the gentrified humor of black comedians, see Mel Watkins, *On the Real Side: A History of African American Comedy from Slavery to Chris Rock* (Chicago: Lawrence Hill Books, 1994; rev. 1999), 527–535.

11. Mel Watkins suggests that this transformation began before the breakdown, in 1966–1969, and would appear on his first album, *Richard Pryor* (1969). Indeed, on this first album Pryor introduces his "Supernigger" routine and offers various nuanced characterizations of white folk, black folk, men and women. Though funny, this humor lacks the critique of race and nation that is found in his later work, including *Craps (After Hours)* (1971), *Live and Smokin',* and . . . *Is It Something I Said?* (1975), because there is not the engagement with the *ethos* of blackness which Pryor deploys after Berkeley. See Watkins, 535.

12. Arguably, the *ethos* of blackness that I describe here as located in the '70s is similar to that described by Eric King Watts when he speaks of the African American *ethos* of the Harlem Renaissance: "[The African American *ethos*] was a dynamic forum for deliberations about the appropriate norms, premises, and practices of a distinct black culture; thus, it made available to black intellectuals the symbolic and material resources for the rhetorical invention and the articulation of a black public voice." I want to suggest that in adopting the contemporary *ethos,* this qualification and quality of blackness, Pryor adapts his routines to a then cultural precept and national moment in which blackness is foregrounded as moral and social failure and, in turn, symbolically rearticulated morally and socially as value in the direct response of the aesthetically aggressive negotiations of the various cultural productions and practitioners of the time. See Eric King Watts, "African American *Ethos* and Hermeneutical Rhetoric: An Exploration of Alain Locke's *The New Negro,*" *African American Communications and Identities,* ed. Ronald L. Jackson II (London: Sage, 2004), 73.

13. Pryor with Gold, 115.

14. In speaking about the introduction of the word "nigger" to his routine, Pryor comments that the word "embodied the hatred of racism as well as a legacy of self-hate." And, "Saying it changed me, yes it did. It gave me strength, let me rise above shit." Pryor with Gold, 116–117.

15. *Richard Pryor Live and Smokin',* 1971 (Mpi Home Video, 2001).

16. John Limon notes this mechanization and abjection in reference to *Richard Pryor: Live! In Concert;* however, his critique continues in a slightly different direction, attributing abjection to American humor broadly. I want to emphasize the use of abjection as it is specifically rendered by Pryor as a part of a racial critique. See John Limon, *Stand-up Comedy in Theory, or, Abjection in America* (Durham, N.C.: Duke University Press, 2000), 83–86.

17. Here I am referring to Amiri Baraka's (LeRoi Jones's) famous statement about white masculinity and entitlement: "Most American white men are trained to be faggots." See LeRoi Jones, *Home: Social Essays* (New York: Apollo Editions, 1966), 216.

18. Homosexuality and the liminality of black masculinity does appear in concert on the album . . . *Is It Something I Said?* (1975), with the skit about going to jail and keeping everyone laughing so that no one would think about having sex with him. There is a continued slippery use of "head." Colloquially, head refers to fellatio; however, in Pryor's use and routines, head refers to oral sex, both fellatio and cunnilingus. This frankness found in *Live and Smokin'* about homosexuality as sex, as opposed to identity, appears in interviews with regard to his childhood milieu, and in his autobiography with regard to his experience of dating a transsexual. See his discussion of his childhood community in Murphy, 27. Also, see the discussion of his relationship with Mitrasha and being "gay for two weeks" in Pryor with Gold, 130.

19. I say "first major concert film" because there is no evidence that *Live and Smokin'* was ever released at the time of its production. The film appears later in home video format in 1986. Furthermore, a large portion of the material experimented with in *Live and Smokin'* appears in more refined form on the album *That Nigger's Crazy* (1971).

20. *Richard Pryor: Live! In Concert*, 1979 (Mpi Home Video, 1998).

21. *Richard Pryor Live on the Sunset Strip*, 1982 (Columbia/Tristar Studios, 2003), hereafter cited as *SS*.

22. *SS*.

23. *Richard Pryor: Here and Now*, hereafter cited as *HN*.

24. *HN*.

25. *HN*.

26. *HN*.

27. *HN*.

28. This definition of African American autobiography is informed by a number of writings. See William L. Andrews, *To Tell a Free Story: The First Century of Afro-American Autobiography, 1760–1865* (Bloomington: Indiana University Press, 1986); William L. Andrews, "African-American Autobiography Criticism: Retrospect and Prospect," *American Autobiography*, ed. Paul John Eakin (Madison: University of Wisconsin Press, 1991), 195–215; William L. Andrews, intro. to *African American Autobiography: A Collection of Critical Essays*, ed. William L. Andrews (Englewood, N.J.: Prentice Hall, 1993), 1–8; Lewis Gordon, *Existentia Africana: Understanding African Existential Thought* (London: Routledge, 2000); Crispin Sartwell, *Act Like You Know: African American Autobiography and White Identity* (Chicago: University of Chicago Press, 1998).

29. Gordon, 23.

30. Andrews, *To Tell a Free Story*, 1.

The Crisis of Black Masculinity in *Jo Jo Dancer:*
2 *Your Life Is Calling*

MARGO NATALIE CRAWFORD

Jo Jo Dancer: Your Life Is Calling (1985) begins with a voice-over. Before any visual images of Richard Pryor appear, we hear the words "Jo Jo, what in the fuck is wrong with you? Why can't you enjoy life? [. . .] I just always felt different." Gayatri Spivak's pivotal question, "Can the subaltern speak?" is reshaped in *Jo Jo Dancer: Your Life Is Calling*. "Can the alter ego speak?" is the key question in this film. The alter ego is literally embodied in the film; one of the principal characters is the alter ego. Richard Pryor plays the role of both the alter ego and Jo Jo Dancer. The film is a riveting representation of the ways in which racial trauma is often inseparable from kinship trauma. This film tells the story of Richard Pryor and the story of kinship inflected by post-slavery trauma. The alter ego emerges, in one of the hospital scenes, when Pryor's healed body rises from his horribly burnt body. The alter ego counsels Jo Jo on the pain tied to his memories of his mother, his father, and himself as a young child. The film ultimately becomes an analysis of the duality of Richard Pryor *when* and *as* he recovers from the tragedy. This omnipresent duality underscores that the pre- and post-tragedy subject does not transcend fragmentation. The crisis of black masculinity is visualized, in this film, as the crisis of necessary fragmentation, a fragmentation that is both the cause of the trauma and the only hope for any type of recovery. The film leads to a nexus of questions about the trope of duality that occupies such a central space in African American cultural studies. Has the pain that causes duality been elided in some celebrations of double consciousness? How does Richard Pryor use laughter to express pain as opposed to romanticizing it? How do the images of Pryor cross-dressing compare to the images of his performance of the "angry black man"? A full focus on the racialized sexual politics in this film unveils Pryor's ongoing struggle to locate the black phallus (black power) within the anti-black world. The film expands the individual trauma of Jo Jo into a larger collective trauma tied to the phenomenology of black men in the post-slavery American landscape. In *Male Subjectivity at the Margins,* Kaja Silverman uses the term "historical trauma" as she differentiates between the "dominant fiction" of the equation of the penis and the phallus and the unsettling of this equation (when the penis and the phallus are not commensurable).[1] The "historical trauma" of black masculinity is at the core of *Jo Jo Dancer: Your Life Is Calling.*

Looking through the lens of Frantz Fanon's phenomenology of race and sexuality in *Black Skin, White Masks* (1952), the images of black masculinity in *Jo Jo Dancer* are images of the precariousness of the black phallus in the world of anti-black racism. Fanon paves the way for a study of the meaning of the racialized phallus within Freudian and Lacanian theories of gender and sexuality. In *The Seminar of Jacques Lacan, Book XI* (1973), Lacan uses "anamorphosis" to explain the function of the phallus. Anamorphotic pictures are visual distortions that when viewed in a cylindrical mirror appear undistorted. Lacan uses an image of the tattoo to explain the connection between anamorphosis and the phallus. The text reads, "How is it that nobody has ever thought of connecting this ['a picture that had to be looked at through a hole, so that its distorting value could be appreciated'] with . . . the effect of an erection? Imagine a tattoo traced on the sexual organ *ad hoc* in the state of repose and assuming its, if I may say so, developed form in another state."[2] In the beginning of the film, images abound of the young Jo Jo looking through keyholes in the whorehouse. Young Jo Jo learns about the phallus through the lens of the "distorted hole" of the white and black men who purchase sexual relations with his mother. Lacan's image of the tattooed penis illuminates the meaning of the black phallus in the world of anti-black racism; his image of the tattooed penis clarifies the difference between the black phallus and the black penis. As opposed to the black penis, the black phallus is the visual effect of the full tattoo upon erection. The tattoo can only be seen in its full, glorious form when the penis becomes the sham of transcendence, the phallus. Lacan is interested in the phallus as a distortion that gains a reality effect. The image of the tattooed penis allows us to think about the inscription of the phallus on the penis. *Jo Jo Dancer* raises similar questions about the meaning of the phallus. In the anti-black world, is the phallus white skin? When Jo Jo's face is burnt, does skin become the prime signifier of his castration, the crisis of his black masculinity? The film adds new layers to Fanon's dialogue with Lacan: the move from the phallus is a signifier to the "the Negro is the genital."[3] As Kaja Silverman emphasizes in her focus on the "dominant fiction" of the phallus, the equation of penis and phallus is always a naturalized fiction. In the case of black masculinity, this equation has *always already* been upset. When Fanon proclaims, the "Negro is the genital," he insists on the real difference between the equation of the penis and cultural power, in the dominant fiction of white maleness, and the sexualized racism that often reduces black maleness to the black penis. Jo Jo, throughout the film, has a confused countenance as the camera captures the "Supermasculine Menial" aspect of black maleness—Eldridge Cleaver's apt description, in *Soul on Ice,* of the raw masculinity that coexists with raw subservience.[4]

Lacan's allusion, in "The Signification of the Phallus," to the "famous painting in the Villa di Pompeii" sheds light on Jo Jo's confused countenance, his sheer bewilderment, as the film interrogates the crisis of the black phallus.[5] Lacan counsels: "For the phallus is a signifier, a signifier whose function, in the intrasubjective economy of the analysis, lifts the veil perhaps from the function it performed in the mysteries. For it is the signifier intended to designate as a whole the effects of the signified, in that the signifier conditions them by its presence as a signifier."[6] Lacan refers to the frieze in the Villa of Mysteries, which depicts an initiation ritual into the cult of Dionysus. These mysteries were violently suppressed during the second century BC because they posed a threat to the order and authority of the Roman state. There are six panels in the frieze, and the one Lacan alludes to is at the far end of the hall and confronts viewers as they enter the room. There, to the right of the mask and the bowl, and the sacred marriage of Dionysus and Ariadne, a young woman lifts a veil from the sacred iknon, or winnowing basket, which would have contained, along with the other sacred objects, the phallus that is to be revealed to the initiates. The significance of Lacan's reference to this image is the fact that not only is the phallus not visible to the viewer of the picture, but the initiate herself appears to have averted her eyes from the basket just as she lifts its veil. The frieze locates the phallus as an absence, concealed, buried, and deferred. In *Jo Jo* the black phallus is the puzzling absence and deferral that keep Jo Jo's eyes in such a state of bewilderment. The film renders black maleness a masked hollowness comparable to the basket, in the frieze, that hides the phallus. Lacan appropriated Freudian analyses of the phallus to designate the process of signification itself. Since the phallus is removed from its identification with the penis, and since it receives its potency from its capacity to be a free-floating signifier, the phallus in an anti-black world, as Lewis Gordon argues in *Bad Faith and Antiblack Racism,* really can be represented by white skin.[7] When the film begins with Jo Jo's mirror image and the alter ego that emerges during the hospital scene (after Jo Jo burns himself), self emerges, as Heinz Kohut theorizes, not as a subject, but as an image, a representation. As Kohut explains, contradictory self-representations coexist. The self is formed through empathic mirroring, becoming the internalization of the gaze of the others. The film, like Kohut's theory, extends Lacan's mirror process. As Barbara Johnson writes, "What does Kohut mean by a self? The self, he writes, should not be confused with the ego. The self is not a subject. The self is an image, a representation. Indeed, simultaneous contradictory self-representations may exist in a person."[8] The images of Jo Jo fully demonstrate this simultaneity of contradictory images.

The Black Male Mirror Stage

The film begins with a focus on mirrors that begs to be compared to Lacan's mirror stage. Jo Jo Dancer, performed by Richard Pryor, crawls on the floor to a large mirror as he searches, in sheer desperation, for remnants of the crack cocaine he has depleted. As Jo Jo stares at his mirror image as he crawls on the floor, the images of black male as beast and as infant emerge simultaneously. In this early scene of the film, the story of Jo Jo becomes a meditation on reflections and representations of black masculinity. The black male gaze is highlighted in this scene (the ways in which black men look at the images that have been forced upon their bodies). The film begins with the words "I always felt I was different." When Jo Jo stares at the image of himself crawling on the floor, the *difference* tied to the black male body is the slippage between the construct of the black male as savage, raw sexuality and the image of the black male as a feminized and infantilized non-white masculinity. In the segregation era of the South, the public restroom signs read "Women," "Men," and "Colored." In order to historicize the post-slavery trauma that create the crisis of African American masculinity, we must remember the collapsing of gender difference that occurred in American slavery and the post-slavery legacy of segregation. As Jo Jo confronts the image of himself as an infant and helpless beast, he confronts the collapsing of gender difference in the post-slavery crisis of black masculinity and femininity.

Throughout the second half of the film, Bo Diddley's blues lyrics "I'm a man" echo as the background music. After Jo Jo crawls to the mirror, the scene shifts and his face is burned from the drug use and he is being pushed down the hallway in a hospital. The nonburnt face of Jo Jo emerges from the burnt face as the alter ego of Jo Jo is introduced. The non-burnt face is the imagined wholeness that emerges after the trauma has created the scarred face. The mirror image shifts from the literal mirror to the mirror of the alter ego. As the film progresses, the mirror stage becomes not the typical Lacanian recognition that is a misrecognition (*méconnaissance*), the "truth" of identity that is built upon a fiction (an image)—"It's me, but it's not me"—but rather the recognition that the images were always a misrecognition. As opposed to the Lacanian scheme, the mirror stage in this film is the stage when Jo Jo identifies himself as the contradiction, the recognitions that have always been misrecognitions.

In Lacanian terms, the mirror stage is organized around a fundamental experience of identification in which the child gains a body image. The child's primary identification with this image produces the emergence of the "I" and puts an end to the psychic experience that Lacan refers to as the "fantasy of the fragmented body." Before the mirror stage, the child does not experience her body as a unified totality but as something disjointed. The child's experience in the mirror stage is divided into three periods that mark the progressive move to the unified body image. The first phase indicates an initial confusion between self and the other, based on the fact that the child sees the reflected image as a real being that she tries to approach and touch. In the second phase the child learns that the other in the mirror is not a real being but an image. In the third phase the child recognizes herself in the image; she acquires the conviction that the image is her own. During this mirror stage the child realizes lack and develops the desire to acquire missing objects, a desire which Lacan connects to the unconscious construction of the phallus, the master signifier. The focus on fragmentation and mirror images, in *Jo Jo Dancer* and the larger representation of Pryor in record covers, reveals a mirror stage, overdetermined by race and gender, in which the tension between wholeness and fragmentation and image and reality is the unresolved crisis of black masculinity.

The word and image interplay in the cover of his 1977 album *Who*

Me? I'm Not Him fully captures the connection between Lacan's mirror stage and Pryor's navigation of black maleness. Like *Jo Jo Dancer, Who Me? I'm Not Him* unveils the connections between Pryor's childhood trauma and his comedy. In this album, however, Pryor's comedy sometimes approaches the tone of Bill Cosby as opposed to the more shocking aspects of *Bicentennial Nigger* and *Supernigger*. In this album cover, the words "Who Me? I'm Not Him" might refer to both the visual image of Pryor and the words "Richard Pryor" at the top of the album. The album cover makes the very identity "Richard Pryor" into an amusing mystery. The finger pointing downward rewrites the mirror stage as Pryor refuses Lacan's *méconnaissance* (the "not me" that becomes "me").[9] The feminized angelic infants surround the image of Pryor as the confused anti-angel. The words and images on this cover can be interpreted as Pryor resisting the feminization and softening of black masculinity. This album cover can also be interpreted as Pryor insisting that he is not the "big black male monster" or angry black man, but rather a peaceful and, potentially, angelic man. When we read the interplay between the words and the image through the lens of the classic psychoanalytic understanding of the simultaneity of recognition and disavowal (the disavowal that is always a recognition), the flowing white clothing that Pryor wears in contrast to the naked feminized angelic infants presents the covering of the imagined lack and abundance tied to the black male body. The album cover exposes the animated contradictions between the white gaze's need to feminize black maleness and the need to make black maleness the epitome of virility. The fetishism of black maleness that occurs in the rampant images of the "big black penis" is always an overcompensation for the lack tied to the black male body in our post-slavery landscape. The covered body in this album cover refuses the fetishism of the naked black male body even as the feminized angelic infants remind us that the very assumption of black manhood, within anti-black racism and the dominant fiction of white maleness, requires a move from an infantile state created by the long layers of fabricated Uncle Toms and Sambos (men that were always rendered "boys").

The Birth of a Black Man

Jo Jo's first successful comedy routine is his simulation of the birth of a child. This part of the film takes the viewer back to the very beginning of the film, when Pryor, in a voice-over, states, "I just always felt different . . . When I was born, Ethel [his cousin] threw up on me.

She looked at me and she threw up again." The emphasis placed on these memories of his birth reveals Pryor's interest in the ways that black men are infantilized. The first successful comedy routine appeases the audience's desire to see the nonthreatening infant stage. Jo Jo performs the movement that a fetus makes as it is moving through the birth canal. The twisted movements and the expression of the newborn as he exits the birth canal are the part of the comedy routine that generates great applause and convinces the club managers that Jo Jo will be a lucrative part of the show. One way to fully understand the significance of this simulation of childbirth that gives birth to his career as a comedian is to remember the larger history of representations of the infantile stages of the "black race." This trope abounds not only in the discourse of apologists for American slavery but also in the tradition of African American literature. In the Harlem Renaissance poem "My Race" (1925), written by Helene Johnson, the birth metaphor conveys both the degradation and the uplift of the "race." Johnson writes,

> Ah, my race,
> Hungry race,
> Throbbing and young—
> Ah, my race,
> Wonder race,
> Sobbing with song—
> Ah, my race,
> Laughing race,
> Careless in mirth—
> Ah, my veiled
> Unformed race,
> Fumbling in birth[10]

When Jo Jo makes the birth of a child his odd choice for a comedy act, he places this larger metaphor into the zone of spectacle and entertainment. The birth metaphor loses its force and becomes performance of the infantilization of the black man. As the audience laughs at this comedy routine, their fears of the angry black man are assuaged by the image of the helpless black infant. This simulation of childbirth is peculiar because there is no mother in this act; the child stretches, yawns, and propels himself, limb by limb, out of the womb. As Pryor is assaulted by the lack of response from the white audience, he stumbles upon this act that makes the crowd respond with utter glee. This representation of childbirth as the child's awakening and stepping out the womb (this black male self-generation) begs to be compared to the earlier parts of the film presenting the young Jo Jo in search of his mother, working in the brothel. What makes this performance the key first act that demonstrates to the owners of the club that Jo Jo can make a crowd laugh? As Jo Jo performs this act, he captures the body movements of an infant. As he distorts his face in this scene, he appeases the same desire that makes buffoon and minstrel images of blackness amusing.

This simulated childbirth, the first successful comedy routine, gains more layers when juxtaposed against the cover of the comedy album *Richard Pryor.*[11] The humor that this cover intends to evoke demonstrates the larger significance of the childbirth act. Fanon captures the insidious connection of primitiveness and blackness when he describes his "discovery" of his blackness: "I subjected myself to an objective examination, I discovered my blackness, my ethnic characteristics; and I was battered down by tom-toms, cannibalism, intellectual deficiency, fetishism [*sic*], racial defects, slave-ships, and above all else, above all: 'Sho' good eatin'" (112). Pryor's performance of the "native," in this album cover, must be connected to the larger questions about the performance of race and gender in *Jo Jo Dancer.* The recurrent mirror images in this biographical film underscore Pryor's attempt, as he co-wrote and produced the film, to "discover" the *images* that have claimed his identity. Performing the African native may lead Pryor to a more acute understanding of the crisis of African American masculinity in the post-slavery landscape. Like the tension between the super-masculine black male and the black menial in constructs of African American masculinity, African male "natives" are often rendered as savage masculinity as well as castrated, naked men who have not evolved to civilized manhood. On the album cover of *Richard Pryor* he dramatizes his awareness of the white gaze that often makes African American men a type of primitive that almost loses gender specificity. As Pryor looks directly at the camera and gives the peace sign, he visualizes the white bohemian gaze that fetishizes the black primitive.

A key scene in *Jo Jo Dancer* explodes the racial and sexual politics of white bohemianism. During a feud with his counterculture wife, Jo Jo, who has flowers in his hair for her amusement, is advised by this lover to read Malcolm X. As the feud continues, she accuses Jo Jo of being a chauvinist and Jo Jo responds by telling her, "You ain't Angela Davis." She then slaps Jo Jo. The scene presents a white woman whose maternalism makes her assume that she knows more about the Black Power movement than Jo Jo. The flowers in Jo Jo's hair are a crucial element in the staging of the crisis of black masculinity in this scene. The white wife is the "hippie" who would normally wear these flowers in her hair. When the violence of her white maternalism leads her to assume the role of the missionary teacher and to physically strike Jo Jo, the film stages the "deflowering" of black masculinity. When Jo Jo rages against the white female lover's *need* to educate a black man, there is the visual image of the infuriated black man with flowers in his hair. In spite of the flowers, Jo Jo's response to this woman matches Clay's explosion in Amiri Baraka's *Dutchman* (1964): "You fuck some black man, and right away you're an expert on black people. [. . .] Old bald-headed four-eyed ofays popping their fingers . . . and don't know yet what they're doing. They say, 'I love Bessie Smith.' And don't even understand that Bessie Smith is saying, 'Kiss my ass, kiss my black unruly ass.' "[12] Jo Jo is struck by the white lover just as Clay is killed by Lula at the end of *Dutchman,* but the black male rage echoes in spite of these final containments of the subversion. Like *Dutchman,* this scene in *Jo Jo Dancer* depicts whiteness as the phallus that castrates black men. In this pivotal scene, the Black Power movement emerges as the sign of the fundamental shift from the infantilized black male to the indignant black man who refuses to accept the violence of white maternalism.

The flowers in Jo Jo's hair, in this scene, beg to be compared to the gun in the bikini he wears during the scene when he cross-dresses as he impersonates Satin Doll, the black female nightclub performer who becomes a mother figure for Jo Jo. When he is in drag, imitating Satin Doll, Bo Diddley's song "I'm a Man" (1955) reverberates. The words in the blues song must be remembered in order to understand the larger import of this background music during the cross-dressing. The lyrics are:

Now when I was a little boy,
at the age of five
I had somethin' in my pocket,
keep a lot of folks alive
Now I'm a man,
made twenty-one
You know baby,
we can have a lot of fun
I'm a man,
I spell M-A-N, man
All you pretty women,
stand in line

I can make love to you baby,
in an hour's time
I'm a man,
I spell M-A-N, man
I goin' back down,
to Kansas Stew
Bring back the second cousin,
Little Johnny the cocheroo
I'm a man,
I spell M-A-N, man
The line I shoot,
will never miss
The way I make love to 'em,
they can't resist
I'm a man,
I spell M-A-N, man

As opposed to the earlier images of Jo Jo's timid nature, when he is in drag he becomes most assertive. When he bursts into the office of the white club managers, wearing a female bikini with a gun inside, and demands the money owed to him and Satin Doll, he transforms from the child-like man nurtured by Satin Doll to the protector of Satin Doll. The makeup and female attire do not hinder the performance of the stereotypically masculine behavior, the male hero. As the blues song "I'm a Man" continues, there is tension between the black phallus (black cultural power) and Fanon's recognition that, too often, the "Negro is the genital." This tension emerges from the visual image of the gun in the bikini and the fear *and* amusement of the white club managers as they look at this frail black body and his phallic weapon.

In the final scene of the film, the image of the gun in the bikini is transmuted into the image of "nuts in a vise," the shocking image of white fear of black masculinity. The options for black men are rendered as "nuts in a vise" or the gun in the bikini. The former evokes the social pressure of the imagined hypersexuality of black men, the latter the feminizing of this threatening potency. Both options create the crisis of African American masculinity. Richard Pryor confronts this crisis through a type of humor that, after his self-proclaimed shift in 1967, consciously aims to disturb his listeners and make them think about the unspeakable. Pryor describes this shift in the following manner: "I made a lot of money being Bill

Cosby, [. . .] but I was hiding my personality. I just wanted to be in show business so bad I didn't care how. It started bothering me—I was being a robot comic, repeating the same lines, getting the same laughs for the same jokes. The repetition was killing me."[13] In this closing layer of the film, Jo Jo delivers his own funeral eulogy as he finds humor in his own near-death experience. The pathos of this "extravagance of laughter" (Ralph Ellison's term for this painful humor) fully resonates when Jo Jo states, "I guess that's a smile and I hope that's his face." The film ends, just as it begins, with Jo Jo's creation of distance from his trauma—his insistence, "Who Me? I'm Not Him," like the name of the 1977 comedy album. This attempt to create distance from his own trauma was surely also a painful reliving of the life-threatening burn injury. Like Othello's final speech, in which he stabs himself in the middle of a performance of his heroic deeds, Jo Jo's performance of his drug addiction and death is a performance of that which should not, so it seems, be performative.[14] The recognition of the everyday performance, however, of the crisis of black masculinity reveals that Jo Jo's burn injury and the drug addiction that led to it were the horrible consequences of the hegemonic *script* of the white phallus and the disempowered state that begins, for Jo Jo, at the brothel where his mother's body, like the bodies of the other women, literally became a commodity.

In the early scenes of the film, when the young Jo Jo sneaks into a bedroom with his mother and one of white male clients, his mother asks him, "Will you ever forgive me, Jo?" As Jo Jo moves to the comedy routines that include the riveting representations of Black Power, he continues to fight the images of the infantilized black man that are depicted in *Jo Jo* as the veritable birth of his career. He stumbles across the simulated childbirth as he desperately tries to make his first audience laugh. The production of the laughter testifies that the infantilizing of black men is a common ground for the white audience. The film's representation of Jo Jo must be considered, to a certain extent, as Richard Pryor's self-image. Pryor co-wrote, produced, directed, and starred in this film. The entire film can be viewed as Pryor's dialogue with mirror images, his representation of self-representation. The film is Pryor's representation of self-analysis and his analysis of the crisis of African American masculinity. Jo Jo's masculinity is figured as a shy, nervous energy that can only be assertive when coupled with humor. Black masculinity is figured as a performance that makes black men laugh at themselves. The pain of this laughing at self is coupled with the ability to laugh at the absurdity of the ideologies that produce this crisis of black masculinity. Living this crisis, in the case of Richard Pryor, the celebrity comedian, becomes a revision of Eldridge Cleaver's theory, in *Soul on Ice,* of the black man as the "supermasculine menial." Pryor ultimately emerges as the "super-amusing intellect."

NOTES

1. Kaja Silverman, *Male Subjectivity at the Margins* (New York: Routledge, 1992), 55.

2. Jacques Lacan, *The Seminar of Jacques Lacan, Book XI,* trans. Alan Sheridan, ed. Jacques-Alain Miller (New York: W. W. Norton, 1981), 87.

3. In 1967, Charles Markmann translated the French original (1952), *Peau Noire, Masques Blancs.* (Frantz Fanon, *Black Skin, White Masks,* trans. Charles Markmann [New York: Grove Press, 1967], 180.) All other page references are included in the text.

4. Eldridge Cleaver, *Soul on Ice* (New York: Delta, 1968), 193.

5. Jacques Lacan, *Ecrits: A Selection,* trans. Alan Sheridan (New York: Norton, 1977), 288.

6. Lacan, *Ecrits,* 285.

7. In *Bad Faith and Antiblack Racism,* Lewis Gordon writes, "In an antiblack world, the phallus is white skin" (128). He also argues, "No matter how much the black man chooses to be a man, an antiblack world may still refuse to recognize him as such. But although a white woman may be denied recognition as a male, she faces a different situation when she demands recognition as white—particularly if the situation is against a black male. Black males and white females do not, therefore, stand on equal planes in an antiblack world" (101). Lewis Gordon, *Bad Faith and Antiblack Racism* (Atlantic Highlands, N.J.: Humanities Press, 1995).

8. Barbara Johnson, "The Quicksands of the Self: Nella Larsen and Heinz Kohut," in *Female Subjects in Black and White: Race, Psychoanalysis, Feminism* (Berkeley: University of California Press, 1997), 256.

9. In "The Mirror Stage as Formative of the Function of the I as Revealed in Psychoanalytic Experience," in *Ecrits,* Lacan explains *méconnaissance* in the following manner:

> But the important point is that this form situates the agency of the ego, before its social determination, in a fictional direction, which will always remain irreducible for the individual alone, or rather, which will only rejoin the coming-into-being (*le devenir*) of the subject asymptotically, whatever the success of the dialectical syntheses by which he must resolve as his discordance with his own reality. (2)

10. Helene Johnson, "My Race," in *Shadowed Dreams: Women's Poetry of the Harlem Renaissance,* ed. Maureen Honey (New Brunswick, N.J.: Rutgers University Press, 1989), 102.

11. *Richard Pryor* (Dove/Reprise, 1968).

12. LeRoi Jones, *Dutchman and The Slave* (New York: Perennial, 2001 [1964]), 34.

13. Cited in "Richard Pryor, Iconoclastic Comedian, Dies at 65," *New York Times,* 11 December 2005.

14. Othello insists, "Set you down this, / And say besides that in Aleppo once, / Where a malignant and a turbaned Turk / Beat a Venetian and traduced the state, / I took by th' throat the circumcised dog / And smote him thus."

3 Was It Something He Said?

CENSORSHIP AND THE RICHARD PRYOR TELEVISION SHOW, 1977

AUDREY THOMAS MCCLUSKEY

It was a telling omen that Richard Pryor's original opening remarks launching his much-anticipated television variety show were seen on the evening news, but not on the show. The censors considered his opening unsuitable for television. In it, there is a close-up of a nervously grinning Richard Pryor welcoming the audience. He begins by attempting to dispel rumors that he has had to compromise or give up anything in order to get the show on the air. As the camera trucks out, Pryor, clad in a flesh-colored body stocking that makes him appear to have no sex organ, says: "I'm standing here naked, I have given up absolutely nothing."[1] This unaired segment illustrates the problem with censors that dogged the show throughout its brief run, and led to it being reduced from ten weeks to four—during the contentious period between September 13 and October 20, 1977. One could almost see it coming, given the clash of television's "ideological apparatus"[2]—the goal of appealing to a mass consumer market, and the trajectory of Pryor's insurgent comedy. Yet the roots of the unhappy coupling between network television and Pryor can actually be traced to earlier events.

For the grandson of a bordello owner, growing up in the 1950s in Peoria, Illinois, television, with its black-and-white images and rabbit ears antennas, could not compete with the colorful drama of everyday life. Like most children growing up in the 1950s, Pryor was a fan of television westerns, but the people he met hanging out at the Famous Door, a local bar, and at his grandmother's bordello in the city's rough-and-tumble black neighborhood were more captivating and enthralling to his sensibilities. They were the muse to his artistic genius, which fueled a restlessness in him that was always seeking expression. When he landed on television in the early 1960s as a stand-up comic that restlessness was apparent, but his muse was obscured by funny but predictable comedic routines.

Darnell Hunt reminds us that television functions as a "social space for mediated encounters" that almost never mimic real life.[3] A relevant illustration is the proliferation of current "reality shows," which are heavily scripted constructions designed to fit prevailing formulas. Pryor's sense of the real was different from television's mediated reality. However, in his first appearances on television he attempted to play along and fit into the dominant paradigm. During appearances on *Ed Sullivan, Merv Griffin,* and *The Tonight Show* in the early sixties, he performed the palatable Bill Cosby–like "Rumpelstiltskin" and "First Man on the Sun" routines.[4] His uneasy manner and obvious comedic gift made one think that there was more that he wanted to say, if he could figure out how. Discussing television in an *Ebony* interview in 1976, he voiced this discomfort: "They want you to be something that really doesn't exist at all. . . . I do these shows but I just get bugged."[5]

By the mid-1970s, Pryor had established himself as a writer on such shows as *Sanford and Son, Flip Wilson,* and the Lily Tomlin special in 1973 for which he shared an Emmy. His name recognition swelled due to his ascendancy to Hollywood stardom and several best-selling comedy albums, including the Grammy award–winning *That Nigger's Crazy* (1974) and . . . *Is It Something I Said?* which was voted the best comedy album of 1976.

Pryor's stand-up work began without the constraints he felt on television, and developed into a different type of monologue-based, character-driven comedy that went beyond mere joke-telling. It gave voice to his profanity-spewing muse, whose "blue language" had allowed many earlier black comedians to get their start while traveling the chitlin' circuit. There was an obvious chasm between the mediated discourse of television and the direction his comedy was taking. It made it difficult for him to accept the narrow range of artistic freedom granted by the networks. While guest-hosting *The Mike Douglas Show* he got into an argument with Milton Berle, the man known then as "Mr. Television." But because he was such a "hot" property, Pryor was forgiven and invited to guest-host *Saturday Night Live* in 1975. Much of the material he wrote for that appearance was rejected, despite SNL's reputation as NBC's most progressive and irreverent show. Long-time producer Lorne Michaels, unbeknownst to Pryor, had inserted a five-second delay in Pryor's "live" opening monologue. It angered Pryor when he later found out. Stuart Hall argues that such "systematically distorted communication"[6] is one of the constraints of the television medium, which serves to disconnect the source of the "message" from its audience. Pryor felt constrained in his ability to communicate with the audience, though he blamed it on the arrogance of people like Michaels and the unnamed censors, not the medium itself.

Pryor believed that television could be used to "wake up people" and he agreed to do a show for that reason. His aim was to destroy barriers, traverse the invisible racial wall, and enlarge the terrain of what was permissible on television. Yet he, like other black performers before and after him, was subjected to the ideology that, according to Stuart Hall, operates as a discourse to encode and decode dominant social norms and cultural values.[7] Although Pryor had wooed a racially diverse audience with his live stand-up and albums, he was no match for the ideological and structural constraints imposed by television.

While Pryor made his mark by stoking and ultimately making fun of racial sensitivities, the function of television is to flatten out differences, and he was expected to toe the line. The "ideal viewer" is constructed as white, and it is to that audience and its social norms that producers (and marketers) cater. (The segmentation of television audiences brought about by niche marketing and cable has made this less true today than it was during the networks' heyday.)

Early in the four-week run of his comedy variety series, *The Richard Pryor Show*, he came out before the integrated studio audience—perhaps at the urging of his director—to do a short stand-up routine in order to let the audience get to know him. This was because, as he stated in this opening monologue, "white people get nervous when they see unfamiliar black faces on television." In other words, he needed to comfort, not alienate, the targeted demographic.

Television history bears this out. From its inception, blacks on television were confined to broad, socially accepted stereotypes, and that initial casting has persisted in different forms. According to Herman Gray, stereotypes were necessary for the legitimization of a racial order built on black inferiority and white supremacy: "Black otherness was required for white subjectivity; blacks and whites occupied separate and unequal worlds; black labor was always in the service of white domesticity (*The Jack Benny Show; Life with Father; Beulah*); black humor was necessary for the amusement of whites."[8] In this hegemonic 1950s model, black women were fat and loud, but were nurturing caretakers of white children. In the 1960s, race was "de-contextualized"[9] and made incidental in shows such as *Julia* (whose title character defied the stereotype of black women by being de-raced and assimilated) and *I Spy.* By the early 1970s, proliferating shows such as *Sanford and Son, Good Times, The Jeffersons,* and *That's My Mama,* although black in name, were in fact under the creative control of white executives. Herman Gray has argued that because they catered to the social expectations of white viewers, these shows were *about* black people, not black shows.[10]

There was no real precedent for the type of show that Pryor aspired to have. In the musical variety format, Nat "King" Cole had hosted a show on NBC in the late 1950s that was mainly him singing and playing the piano while joined by a special guest. But Cole's suave sophistication—he often dressed in a tuxedo—invited negative reaction to the show in some Southern television markets and hastened its demise. The show never attracted a national sponsor, and it was demoted to a less desirable time slot. The experience was grueling for Cole. He told *Ebony* magazine that "The men who dictate what Americans see . . . didn't want to play ball."[11] *The Flip Wilson Show* was a popular, Emmy award–winning hit on NBC from 1970 to 1974. Wilson's winning formula was an affable, easygoing personality and his portrayal of a stock of animated but racially benign characters, including his trademark, Miss Geraldine Jones, a sassy black woman who told stories about her unseen boyfriend, Killer. Wilson's comedic philosophy, "if it's serious, leave it out,"[12] partly explains his appeal among a broad audience.

Richard Pryor had a different orientation and ambition. He was not concretely political like his comedic contemporary, Dick Gregory, who used the civil rights struggle as the subject of his incisive commentary. Rather, Pryor's political sensibilities had been seasoned by his close identification with the black underclass and his two-year voluntary exile in Berkeley, California, among black activists and writers in the late 1960s. His comedy was more anti-establishment and irreverent, infused with an incipient black nationalism that emerged from the shared communal experience of everyday black people—like the ones he knew in Peoria. Pryor often used words like "humanity" and "integrity" to describe his subjects.

Just how different his orientation was became evident in his television special in May 1977. Pryor's guests included La Wanda Page, John Belushi, Maya Angelou, and the Pips doing backup vocals—minus Gladys Knight. The opening skit takes place on a slave ship with a whip-cracking captain played by Belushi doling out punishment to the captives. Pryor, a random slave, is given the additional punishment of having his own NBC special. In this short skit Pryor manages to compare his predicament in the white-controlled world of corporate television to slavery. Such barbs against television, particularly against its censorship of his material, characterized his work on network television.

In another politically charged skit on his television special, Pryor portrays a drunk who hustles drinks in a bar, and is immediately recognizable as "the shiftless black man." He penetrates the stereotype, as he does in his other characterizations. With Maya Angelou as his weary but understanding wife, he stumbles home from the bar and promptly passes out on the sofa. Angelou then begins a soliloquy that generates depth and empathy rather than cheap laughs to show how lack of employment and loss of self-esteem contributed to his current situation. Without mounting a soapbox, this skit invoked a history of racism and discrimination that connected it to racial conditions in America. This highly rated special, the high ratings posted for Pryor's hosting of *Saturday Night Live,* and its desperation for a much-needed hit show made NBC gamble and offer a ten-week variety show to this provocative and very talented artist.

The show generated immediate excitement. It was a showcase of high production values, elaborate sets, and a multiracial ensemble of young, talented actors that included several up-and-coming stars. The cast included Robin Williams, Sarah Bernhardt, Paul Mooney, John Belushi, Tim Reid, and Marsha Warfield, plus high-caliber guests such as dancer Paula Kelly and actors Glynn Turman, Thalmus Rasulala, and Juanita Moore. As Louie Robinson of *Ebony* magazine remembers it, *The Richard Pryor Show* was not one that invited you to sit back, relax, and watch—especially if you were black. Instead, you sat on the edge of your chair, he recalls, "ready in case Richard at any moment did something that would make it necessary for every black person in America to suddenly drop whatever he or she was doing and run like hell!"[13] Most black people who owned televisions watched the show. It also attracted a core of white fans. However, being inexplicably scheduled during the so-called 8 PM family hour opposite the hugely popular *Happy Days* and *LaVerne and Shirley* increased the odds against its survival, and invited closer scrutiny by NBC's Bureau of Standards and Practices—better known as the censors.

Feminist theorist Judith Butler argues that while censorship appears to be the simple restriction of speech, it can function more broadly to limit and constrain *conduct* before the speech act.[14] She differentiates between implicit and explicit censorship. Implicit censorship functions as stated or in unstated "rules" that people are expected to observe on television or other public spaces. It relies upon the unstated power of the norm to dictate conduct. Its illegibility—its ability to disguise its coercive effects—makes it formidable.[15] Implicit censorship exists to restrict certain speech and to keep some word acts from happening. Explicit censorship, on the other hand, targets direct and specific word acts or performatives. During its short life *The Richard Pryor Show* was subjected to both types of censorship. His battle with the censors framed his struggle to assert himself—a black male—as subject. He defied both the norm and history in his assertive representation of black males. His stated purpose was to shake the audience out of its slumber. In his view, television had been misused for so long that it has become simply a tool for selling stuff. He imagined that he could be an instrument of change: "One week of truth on TV could just straighten out everything," he said.[16]

Both the network and Pryor underestimated each other. He had no intention of observing the "rules" of television. He thought that his million-selling albums and star power would give him added leeway and license, and he depended on this social capital to defy and make television history. Pryor told *Ebony* magazine that when he signed the contract, he was under the impression that he would be able "to do what he wanted" to do.[17] Yet the historicity of black representation, and the ideological power of television codes and its code enforcers, conspired to rein him in and wear him down. When Pryor realized the bind that he was in, he threatened to quit, saying: "I don't want to be on TV, I'm in a trap."[18] A renegotiation reduced the ten-week schedule to four, but the censors remained vigilant. This caused him to remark that had he stayed for the whole ten shows, "it would have damaged me mentally."[19]

Pryor recognized his problem with censors as a political one, not just a problem of offending the public's sensibilities. "I think it has to do with anybody or anything that communicates a reality and might disturb or wake up people. . . . I think they try to stop that any way they can."[20] The politics included who would control content, and Pryor insisted upon being in the driver's seat, and not going for the same "okeydoke" response to pressure. "I don't just let people write it and I go out and do it. I'm involved from day one to the finished product."[21]

Whereas the network was used to bringing in its stock of writers, Pryor, a seasoned writer who had deepened his social outlook during his Berkeley hiatus among black activists and writers, enlisted an ensemble of politically conscious writers including Mooney and Reid. Black awareness was infused into the skits. Despite the tremendous restraints that the show was subjected to, Pryor was still able to stall, if not disrupt, the network status quo. What he complained about most was the constant interference from people for whom he had no respect, and who had no appreciation for what he was attempting to do. "I think they [the network] hire people, about six thousand of them, to do nothing but mess with people." After working long hours with fellow writers and actors to create something special, only to be told that it was not right, Pryor felt as though they were messing with his manhood. "We're grown men," he continued.[22] Language was frequently changed or deleted, and several skits did not survive the censors because of their themes, while others were changed, or heavily edited. Few were untouched.

Interestingly, the image that Pryor brought to television, although it differed from those of his easygoing predecessors, Nat "King" Cole and Flip Wilson, did not evoke the stereotypic traits of black males supposedly most feared by whites: hypersexuality and violence. Rather, several sketches and skits whose potency survived despite censorship show that by using comedic license to expose white racism and advocate black empowerment, Pryor posed a more real threat to the status quo.

In one skit, Pryor portrays the "40th President of the United States," taking questions at a news conference. The interchange reveals his sensitivity to black issues and cultural norms. When a reporter asks him about unemployment rates, the black president tells the reporter that the rate of black employment is much too high, and he will be introducing solutions to it. To a question about the need for more black quarterbacks in the NFL, he replies: "My jaws are still tight about them firing James Harris" (one of the first black quarterbacks in the league), and then he goes on to say that there is a need for more black coaches and owners in the league. In response to a black reporter's questions about whether Huey P. Newton (the head of the Black Panther Party) is being considered for director of the FBI, the president says yes, he has "all the needed qualifications." A white woman reporter makes the comment that the president has been seen escorting white women, and asks him if he plans to continue doing it. The president looks around nervously and guiltily answers, "As much as I can." The final question is from a thickly accented Southern white male reporter who violates the first black commandment: thou shall not talk about someone's mother. When he asks if the president's mother would clean his house, the president lunges at him and has to be restrained. The room erupts in chaos as the black reporters from *Jet* and *Ebony* join in the mêlée.

What made this skit and the show's engagement with race and power so different from the usual television sketch comedy was its grounding in the authentic experiences and issues of black people. He made little attempt to accommodate white fears or an outsider status. Herman Beavers notes that the use of "a distinctly black idiom"[23] in his comments about race differentiated him from Eddie Murphy, who tried to follow in Pryor's footsteps. But this undiluted blackness no doubt hastened the show's demise.

In a lengthy segment about a G.I. returning from World War II with hopes of marrying his girlfriend, a Harlem nightclub performer called Satin Doll who now has other interests, Pryor manages to show the stylish nightclub scene of wartime Harlem and to present a classy representation of black womanhood. The skit, which disrupts standard portraiture of blacks, does not depend upon punch lines or the usual comedic elements. Rather, it is a tone piece, interested in storytelling and recapturing a rich history.

The Richard Pryor Show not only captured black history, but it also took aim at black people's foibles, such as faith in religious con men. This gullibility among some blacks (and others) was ridiculed in a skit called "Mojo the Healer," in which a fake healer works people into a frenzy with his exaggerated pronouncements. The uncritical search for African roots is taken on in "The Come Back from Man." A sign on the set exclaims, "Find Your Roots Here," as The Come Back from Man—Pryor dressed elaborately in African garb and waving various objects—gives individual consultations to African Americans in search of their roots. To one man who asks where he came from, the answer is: "You come from Cleveland." Another client is shown a picture of his great grandfather. The man protests, saying, "But this is a white man," to which the Come Back from Man answers, "Them's the breaks!" This funny but serious skit served to inject a cautionary note into the overwhelming interest of African Americans in their African ancestry following the monumental *Roots* miniseries that aired on NBC in January, 1977. The performance by an African dance troupe that preceded the skit suggested a more nuanced and real connection among African people.

Particularly iconoclastic and audacious was the show's treatment of institutional white racism. In a bawdy circa-1920s skit titled "Southern Justice," a young black man is on trial in a sweltering *To Kill a Mockingbird*–type Mississippi kangaroo courtroom for raping a white woman. It employs broad stereotypes of both races to make a historical point, including a crying black mama; a humming black choir; potbellied, tobacco-chewing white folks who use the N-word; white women discussing what they will wear to the anticipated hanging; a "carpet-bagging communist pinko" northern Jewish lawyer, played by Robin Williams, who turns out to be in the most peril; and a sluttish "dumb blonde" who reduces the notion of white women's virtue to farcical conceit. The satire suggests that it is the whole Southern justice system that has oppressed blacks for ages, rather than just individuals, who are merely acting out their assigned societal roles.

Another skit aimed at the institutional foundations of white racism that made it past the censors was based upon the "hidden" knowledge that ancient Egyptian civilization was black. In 1909, a team of archeologists that includes Pryor's character and two white men discover a cave that houses a "book of knowledge" documenting black contributions to civilization. Pryor excitedly announces his plans to share this knowledge with the world. This discovery would have provided a formulaic happy ending, except that in this skit, a more sinister truth is injected. The two white archeologists leave Pryor in the cave, seal the door (and his fate), and call for the bulldozer.

One segment satirizes the mindlessness of white youth culture in the pre–hip hop 1970s in which an acid rock band called Black Death, in hooded robes and heavily painted faces, emerge from coffins to titillate the adoring crowd. In a sequence perhaps inspired by the 1969 Manson Family murders, the leader (played by Pryor) dispenses intoxicating drugs and finally mows down the fans with a huge machine gun. The youth succumb willingly to their fate, confirming the self-destructive trajectory of white culture. Not funny stuff. But it was a provocative, perhaps ironic commentary, given his own struggle with drugs.

A skit designed to bait and challenge the censors prefigures television's current fascination with homosexuality. It features a white woman retelling different versions of her lesbian encounter in the park. As she changes details about the encounter, the stamp of the censor fills the screen in time to obliterate what is imagined to be sexually explicit words. Such overt mention of homosexual activity defied the norm of 1970s television. This short segment, sandwiched between unrelated skits, may have seemed out of place and illusory, but it was truly transgressive. In addition to ridiculing the censors, it tested the limits of censorship by subverting white middle-class female conventionality. This introduces the paradoxic element of censorship that is discussed by Judith Butler. She argues that censorship creates the condition for agency as well as expresses its limits.[24]

It is no wonder that playing this type of cat-and-mouse game with the censors kept Pryor on the run psychologically. At the end of each episode, he is shown either being confined or trying to escape. At different times he is guarded by a lion, locked in a cell, or literally huffing and puffing on the run. A representation of the danger inherent in his work as an artist is presented on the cover of his best-selling album . . . *Is It Something I Said?* The cover pictures a frightened Richard Pryor tied up at the stake with kindling wood at his feet, as robe-wearing monks carrying fiery torches encircle him. These dramatizations are illustrations of a state of siege, which was what Pryor himself to be under in pursuing his art and his subjectivity. In one of the final skits, when the cast knew the end was near, they took turns roasting the host and telling what the show had meant to them. No one looked happy, least of all Richard Pryor.

Pryor's battle with the censors meant not only that some words or scenes were excised, but that some skits were kept from airing at all. The "Whitey for a Day" skit is one that was not broadcast, although the script notes do not say why. Its premise was based upon an early 1960s daytime show in which women from different backgrounds compete to be "queen for a day," with the winner being showered with prizes. The script for "Whitey for a Day" describes a competition among three contestants who tell their hard-luck stories, with the most deserving being selected to be "Whitey." One is "a Puerto Rican with no hope, no future." Another contestant is a black man who has lost everything he owns—house, car, wife, kids, dog, and wallet. The contest winner is decided via audience applause. The prize goes to the third contestant, a black woman whose husband lost control of his nervous system when he was shot by the police while walking home from work. He is now in constant pain. She wants to win "something to help her around the house . . . a male nurse . . . virile, strong, twenty-five to thirty, single, six foot four, nice dresser, able to dance. . . ." Among the "Whitey for a Day" prizes are "the re-stringing of their tennis rackets; a mooring for a sailboat; a full set of mink eye lashes from Beverly Hills; 'have a nice day' wallpaper for three rooms in her house; and a ski vacation to Aspen in a brand-new country esquire wagon complete with two white children, a chauffeur, and the live-in male nurse."

Here, language is probably the least of the censors' worries. The skit invokes a sedimented history of oppression fused with an exaggeration of white privilege. It equates whiteness with leisure, while ridiculing its banality and excess.

Other unaired segments that did not make it beyond the scripts include a sketch titled "Pretty Girl," which attempts to demystify society's obsession with beauty. In it, perfectly beautiful women are, one by one, found to be concealing things not considered feminine or beautiful: huge ears, a hairy chest, nose-picking, and breaking wind.

By today's standards, the short-lived *Richard Pryor Show* would probably not raise the alarms that it did in 1977. There are several reasons for this, in particular the fundamental changes that have occurred in how we actually watch television. The rise of cable television, pay-per-view, and other technological advancements make a wide array of choices available to adult subscribers. The segmentation of audiences by race, class, and other demographics has also loosened the stranglehold of the networks and their censors. While this has increased the amount of adult content, Pryor's attempt to introduce authentic characterizations and settings while communicating essential truths about race in America has had few equals in the thirty years since.

Richard Pryor's iconoclastic daring in launching a show that aimed to be high-quality, intelligent, and transgressive all at once was a watershed in American television. His leap into network television history was auspicious, but, due to its short four-week run to a dwindling audience, it was considered a failure by conventional standards. Yet in 1977, it played no small part in disrupting assumptions about the definition of "good" television and paving the way for more ambitious uses of the airwaves. The latitude enjoyed by current television comedians seems light-years from what Pryor experienced, but *Def Comedy Jam* would not have been possible without him. His social and artistic vision can be detected in his writing and characters. Through most of his career, Pryor was interested in maintaining authority over work/art and in valorizing black manhood within the public space that he occupied.[25] In doing so, he had to contend not only with implicit and explicit censorship and the historicity of black representations, but with his own overestimation of his social power and a naïveté about the ideological workings of the television medium. Looking back on these events, Pryor stated the following in his autobiography:

> When I committed to do a ten-week comedy-variety series, I thought I could do something significant. I saw only the possibilities of TV as a way of communicating. . . . [I thought] there's going to be a revolution in the way everybody thinks.
>
> But the reality of what the network censors allowed on prime time undercut all my enthusiasm. . . .

We still managed to deliver an exciting, surprising, and provocative show. . . .

The show was no vanilla milkshake.[26]

Indeed. *The Richard Pryor Show*'s encounter with network censors recalls Rosa Parks's taking a seat in the front section of the bus. According to history and the conventions of segregation she had no previous right to that seat, but in taking it, she assumed personal authority and agency and ignited an "insurrectionary process"[27] that challenged established practices. Likewise, *The Richard Pryor Show*, although its success was overshadowed by failure to attract a large audience and the constant intrusions of network censorship, was an audacious interruption of the network's status quo.

NOTES

1. Unaired footage and text are included in the box set *The Richard Pryor Show* (Los Angeles: Burt Sugarman, 2004).

2. Stuart Hall, "Encoding and Decoding in the Television Discourse" (Centre for Contemporary Cultural Studies, University of Birmingham [England], 1973), reprinted in *Channeling Blackness: Studies on Television and Race in America,* ed. Darnell M. Hunt (New York: Oxford University Press, 2005), 57.

3. Darnell M. Hunt, "Making Sense of Blackness on Television," in *Channeling Blackness,* 1.

4. Christine Acham, *Revolution Televised: Prime Time and the Struggle for Black Power* (Minneapolis: University of Minnesota Press), 144.

5. "Richard Pryor," *Ebony,* September 1976, 55–62.

6. Hall, 57.

7. Hall, 58.

8. Herman Gray, "The Politics of Representation in Network Television," in *Channeling Blackness,* 158.

9. Mark Anthony Neal, *What the Music Said: Black Popular Music and Black Public Culture* (New York: Routledge, 1999) 97.

10. Herman Gray, *Watching Race: Television and the Struggle for Blackness* (Minneapolis: University of Minnesota Press, 2004), 71.

11. Nat "King" Cole [told to Lerone Bennett], "Why I Quit My TV Show," *Ebony,* February 1958.

12. Billy Ingram, "The Odd Disappearance of the Flip Wilson Show," www.tvparty.com/flip.html (accessed 7 May 2002).

13. Louie Robinson, "Richard Pryor Talks," *Ebony,* January 1978, 116.

14. Judith Butler, *Excitable Speech: A Politics of the Performative* (New York: Routledge, 1997), 128.

15. Butler, 134.

16. Robinson, 117.

17. Robinson, 117.

18. Billy Ingram, "The Richard Pryor Show," http://tvparty.com/pryor.html (accessed 7 May 2002).

19. Robinson, 117.

20. Robinson, 117.

21. Robinson, 117.

22. Robinson, 117.

23. Herman Beavers, "The Cool Pose: Intersectionality, Masculinity, and Quiescence in the Comedy and Films of Richard Pryor and Eddie Murphy," in *Race and the Subject of Masculinities,* ed. Harry Stecopoulos and Michael Vebel (Durham, N.C.: Duke University Press, 1997), 263.

24. Butler, 141.

25. Beavers, 260.

26. Richard Pryor with Todd Gold, *Pryor Convictions, and Other Life Sentences* (New York: Pantheon Books), 153, 158.

27. Butler, 147.

Richard Pryor and the
4 Poetics of Cursing

KATE E. BROWN

Miranda: *I pitied thee,*
Took pains to make thee speak, taught thee each hour
One thing or other: when thou didst not, savage,
Know thine own meaning, but wouldst gabble like
A thing most brutish, I endow'd thy purposes
With words that made them known. . . .
Caliban: *You taught me language; and my profit on't*
Is, I know how to curse.
　　—Shakespeare, *The Tempest* (I.ii.355–66), 1611[1]

That shit will fuck up your whole shit.
—Skateboarder, commenting on a fall during a competition, 1990s[2]

　　　The first epigraph to this essay begins to suggest the contestations and paradoxes that structure cursing as a form of speech. In a scene from Shakespeare's *Tempest*, Miranda, a European castaway, protests the ingratitude of her servant Caliban, an indigenous "monster" whom her father has enslaved and whom she has sought to humanize, giving him thought (as she claims) by giving him language (II.ii.29). Caliban's reply at once acknowledges and repudiates the success of her teaching: the "profit" of his linguistic training is an ability to curse his instructor in her own tongue. For Caliban, cursing constitutes a mode of communication that exceeds and thereby also rebukes linguistic standards. For Miranda, in contrast, Caliban's cursing is both a deliberate injury and the sign of his fundamental incapacity for proper, purposive speech. The contradictoriness of her position and its political usefulness emerge more clearly if we read Caliban's original, "brutish" "gabble" as Miranda's uncomprehending description of his native tongue. On such a reading, she has not taught Caliban to speak; she has rather erased his native fluency by requiring him to speak the language of his enslavement. The "purposes" her words give him to "make known" are foreign and degrading, imposing an intelligibility that is another form of silence.[3] If, for Miranda, Caliban's cursing proves his impenetrability to cultivation, for Caliban himself (once "mine own king," I.ii.342), Miranda's pitying and relentless instruction inflicts a linguistic insult comparable to aphasia, which destroys aspects of speech while leaving intact (indeed, liberating) the capacity to curse. Their exchange thus suggests the peculiarity that defines knowing how to curse: cursing is a linguistic acquirement, yet it also a linguistic mode of alienation from language and culture.

Like Caliban, Richard Pryor defines his education as a verbal training whose effects were profoundly damaging. In a routine called "Nigger Babies," recorded in 1968, he says: "I was a kid until I was about eight. Then I became Negro. Cause they made me do it in school. The teachers tell me, 'You are Negro. Now say it. Negro.'" "Saying it" earns him an A, as well as the ability to play (or an inability not to play) the schoolyard game called "last one to the store is a nigger baby." The game of "nigger baby" becomes the stuff of Pryor's comedy, but the joke is on the Negro child and his identification with white culture: "I used to run like hell myself. I didn't want to be it. I didn't know I lost before the race started."[4] African American history, as Pryor describes it, condenses into a linguistic instruction whose purpose is to reconstitute all African peoples, of whatever place and language of origin, into "one tribe: niggers."[5]

Yet the purposes that language can make known are never so reliable as its instructors might wish, as Pryor's comedy in itself demonstrates and as he makes explicit in a routine recorded in 1972 for the *Wattstax* movie:

> When [white folks] found out niggers could talk, other than "doh wah ho," they got scared to death. You know, like one day, some whitey says:
>> "Nigger, talk."
>> "Well, motherfucker, I been wanting to tell you something."
>> "I beg your pardon."[6]

Here, nineteenth-century African slaves still speaking their native tongues emerge into English with the certainty and force of 1960s and '70s black activists. The white response is a shocked refusal to hear, expressed with a propriety of language that is meant to be pedagogical but that fails to silence non-white speech. For if what "I been wanting to tell you" goes unexpressed, there remains the curse, "motherfucker," a word whose force of insult is at once a matter of convention and an eruption of and within convention.

For Pryor, cursing is "all we got left": it is a mode of black fluency that refuses white English as the standard of comprehensible speech and thereby allows for a "saying" that exposes and disrupts, if it cannot fully escape, the game of "nigger baby."[7] This disruptive "saying" is of the essence of Pryor's comedic brilliance. As I hope to show, Pryor's stand-up comedy draws on the special linguistic properties of "nasty" language (as he calls it) to achieve a poetics of cursing that suspends and even reverses the violent misidentifications and disparities imposed by race relations during the period of his career. To elucidate this poetics, I compare Pryor first to Lenny Bruce and then to e. e. cummings. These comparisons do not, I might emphasize, seek to characterize Pryor as "the black Lenny Bruce," a description made with some frequency early in his career and one that Pryor disliked, even as he acknowledged Bruce as an influence. It is easy enough to see why Pryor would resent the assessment of his comedy as an approximation of a white comedian (even one whose cursing sought to declare the non-whiteness of his act).[8] My point, however, is that the comparison is, in any case, invalid: to examine their cursing is also to demonstrate the profound differences in their comedic modes.

In a 1983 performance in New Orleans, Pryor opens by talking about the city itself: "It's just so hot down here. It get *hot* down *here*. . . . I don't know how they had no slavery when it be hot down here. Cause slaves would've quit, say, 'Hey, man, fuck you. Shit. Carry that shit your-*self.*'"[9] As this routine suggests, cursing has the capacity to sponsor fantasies of immunity to circumstance even at moments when circumstance presses most closely and affords least dignity. Curse words derive principally from maledictions ("damn you"), from private bodily functions ("fuck," "shit"), and from what we now call hate speech, which compares to the malediction in seeking to effect actual and immediate harm ("nigger," "bitch"). But this semantic content does not constrain the lexical possibilities of cursing, as the second epigraph to this essay makes especially clear. The word "shit," as the skateboarder uses it, could hardly be more expressive, yet it carries meanings that oppose one another and defy explicit definition. Similarly, his use of the word "fuck" is entirely at odds with its original meaning. Shedding semantic content, curse words achieve a lexical and even syntactical mobility that is part of their linguistic impropriety: curse words cannot be contained within—cannot even be assigned—a proper place. And if the semantic meaning of curse words fails to constrain their grammatical usage, still less does it suffice to establish or explain their status as taboo, as we can see by comparing curse words to any of the innumerable synonyms they gener-ate.[10] Such synonyms, however funny or distasteful one might find them, remain at the level of innuendo and euphemism. What characterizes a word as a curse is its singular capacity to offend, which accrues as a cultural endowment over time: curses are words that have absorbed the history of their past speakings *as* curses.[11] Curse words are thus both historically laden and historically dislocated, in that their force always derives from beyond the immediate moment of speech. Instead, they verge toward autonomy, congealing in themselves a quasi-magical capacity to insult so deeply as to cause actual injury. ("I got rid of more white people [by saying 'your mama']," Pryor claims; "I must've killed about twenty.")[12] In vocalizing such words, we lay claim to their own autonomy, thus disavowing the circumstances that have rendered us helpless or ridiculous.

Yet even as they repudiate claims to the immediacy and possessibility of language, curse words confer unusual expressive weight on the speaking body. "I love when white dudes get mad and cuss," Pryor says, in his 1979 concert at Long Beach. " 'Cause y'all are some funny motherfuckers when you cuss."[13] The examples Pryor gives can be transcribed, and they merit attention (for which, see below). But their humor, as, in part, their "whiteness," derives from what cannot be transcribed: the timbre of voice, the pronunciation of words, the ponderous bluster of stance and gesture through which Pryor impersonates the white dude cussing. As Judith Butler remarks in a discussion of hate speech, "there is what is said, and then there is a kind of saying that the bodily 'instrument' of the utterance performs."[14] Precisely because "what is said" by curse words is unleashed from semantics and even grammatical place, cursing lends force to the aspects of language that exceed message, including, for example, volume, timing, tone, rhythm, emphasis, and patterns of sound repetition. For this reason, cursing can enter the realm of play and the nonreferential, which is also the realm of poetry, nonsense, and comedy.

The insistence that the "message" of curse words cannot be determined apart from context—and, in particular, on context defined *as* the speaker—comprises Lenny Bruce's defense of an act that was repeatedly prosecuted for obscenity in the early 1960s:

> I do my act at perhaps 11 o'clock at night. Little do I know that, 11 AM the next morning, before the grand jury somewhere, there's another guy doing my act who's introduced as Lenny Bruce in substance. . . . A peace officer, who is trained . . . to recognize clear and present danger, not make believe, does the act. The grand jury watches him work, and they go, "That stinks." But I get busted! And the irony is that I have to go to court and defend *his* act.[15]

To the extent that Bruce's point here can be taken as advocating free speech, it does so not by denying the potential offensiveness of curse words but by emphasizing the special nature of theater. His central argument is to distinguish between the performative (the "clear and present danger" of words whose utterance constitutes a deed, an obscene act) and performance ("make believe"). "The theater is make believe," he emphasizes: "That's where it's at." But the distinction tends to collapse toward performance, for the crime, as Bruce understands it, consists not in *his* act but in the peace officer's impoverished rendition of it. Representing a complex performance as a toneless list of curse words extracted from their original context, the peace officer restages the act in ways that also vitiate its message: comically charged political satire reduces to an eruption within public space of words whose only "meaning" is their obscenity. Bruce's remedy is to repeat the restaging, incorporating the peace officer's testimony into his act as a single, polysyllabic word: "assballscocksuckercuntfuckmotherfuckerpissshittits." Thus performed, the testimony against him can serve Bruce's own point: as "the bodily 'instrument' of the utterance" (to quote Butler again), Bruce performs a "kind of saying" in which obscenity verges toward nonsense. Curse words lose their impact as curses, emerging instead as a set of alliterative and rhythmically pleasing syllables. The obscenity of utterance, Bruce thereby suggests, cannot be determined apart from the speaking body.

Bruce's emphasis on restaging underscores the several paradoxes of cursing that I have outlined here. Whether performed by Bruce or repeated by a police officer, the words that register as curses are equally recognizable and improper: words become curses only as a matter of convention as it takes shape over time, and every instance of cursing therefore invokes convention, even as it also violates the conventions of linguistic decorum. Such words can only be reiterated: they have no original moment of speaking, for their force is never a property of the speaker's. In this sense, cursing escapes temporal locatedness. Yet it does so only to privilege the living, immediately speaking voice, whose utterance shapes, if it cannot govern, the impact and meaning of the words. As it happened, however, neither Bruce nor the courts were inclined to acknowledge these paradoxes, although they repeatedly staged them. The transgressive appeal of Bruce's act was, in significant part, a property of the curse words he used (this, presumably, is why he could not simply cut them from the show), although his defense tends not to recognize this. Implicit in his act is, instead, a linguistic claim comparable to Humpty

Dumpty's: "'When *I* use a word,' Humpty Dumpty said, in a rather scornful tone, 'it means just what I choose it to mean—neither more nor less. . . . The question is . . . which is to be master—that's all.'"[16] Conversely, the prosecution treated obscene words as unsensual and eruptive objects, like stones rather than signs, more accurately hurled than spoken. Yet they held the immediate speaker liable for a force that could accrue to words only over time and as a matter of convention. What was lost in this conflict was the comic voice itself, which always lies in performance and so depends not on the ownership of words but on their dislocation. By the time of his 1964 appearance in San Francisco, Bruce's act consists of reading directly from the trial transcripts, followed by impromptu, unfunny, indeed barely coherent commentary. "I'm not a comedian," he insists, with a grandiosity whose pathos he does not grasp: "I'm Lenny Bruce."

Curse words never mean just what the speaking "I" chooses them to mean, though to vocalize them is always to mobilize and even to shape the cultural history that secures their force. It is in exploiting the dislocatedness of the curse word—retaining what Paul de Man describes as "that delicate and ever suspended balance between reference and play that is the condition for aesthetic pleasure"[17]—that cursing can become both comic and poetic. To demonstrate this point, I want to return to Richard Pryor by way of e. e. cummings's poem "my sweet old etcetera." What makes the poem illuminating in this context is that it confers the force of cursing on a particularly vacuous part of language, the phrase "et cetera." In pushing poetry toward curse, cummings also helps to elucidate how cursing can achieve a poetics. I quote the poem in full:

> my sweet old etcetera
> aunt lucy during the recent
> war could and what
> is more did tell you just
> what everybody was fighting
> for,
> my sister
> isabel created hundreds
> (and
> hundreds) of socks not to
> mention shirts fleaproof earwarmers
> etcetera wristers etcetera, my
> mother hoped that

i would die etcetera
bravely of course my father used
to become hoarse talking about how it was
privilege and if only he
could meanwhile my
self etcetera lay quietly
in the deep mud et

cetera
(dreaming,
et
    cetera, of
Your smile
eyes knees and of your Etcetera)[18]

The peculiarity of the phrase "et cetera" is that it claims reference by withholding it. Literally meaning "and other unspecified things of the same class," the phrase purports to contribute to a series through a reference so obvious that it need not be said. In fact, however, the phrase does not *continue* a series so much as *assert* one through its own lack of content. The phrase thus has two notable features. First, under force of "et cetera," the items of a list are translated from particular and necessary things into typical, hence replaceable, examples: list becomes series. Second, "et cetera" itself functions agrammatically. In "my sweet old et-cetera," these two features—the redefinition of the particular into the generic and grammatical mobility—permit "et cetera" to become a strategy of disruption, a sardonic emphasis that undermines and even reverses the flow of meaning. Progressively occupying the place of adjective, noun, adverb, and participle, the phrase "et cetera" mobilizes itself to conscript particular things into a class. In so doing, it diverts prediction: the sweet old aunt mongers war; the mother curses her son with courage; and the sister knits a kind of malediction, her socks, shirts, earwarmers, and wristers (et cetera) anticipating the dismemberment that war will complete. Drafting even familial sentiment into the declaration and perpetuation of war, the phrase "et cetera" illustrates a logic of categorical conscription so all-ruthless that it ultimately reverses itself, effecting a dissolution of order itself: the effect of such conscription is, literally, mud. As cummings deploys it, in short, the phrase "et cetera" comes both to demonstrate and to condemn the logic of military mobilization.

Like a curse, cummings's "et cetera" must be characterized in terms of its disruptive effects rather than its semantic content. As with all curses, however, these disruptive effects are not easily owned or arrested, for the phrase introduces temporal indeterminacy and even suspension into the moment of speaking. And if there is any escape from the logic of war within the poem, it is by way of this temporal and spatial dislocation. The suspension of time occurs quite literally in stanza six, where cummings interrupts the father's patriotic blather with the word "meanwhile," which we should take as the translation of "et cetera" into temporal terms. The word "meanwhile" names a temporal divide that also effects—again, quite literally; indeed, graphically—a dislocation within "my / self." Divided between home and trench, as between stanzas, the conscripted, dislocated, yet still-speaking self occupies a space of categorical indeterminacy: my / self, lying quietly in the mud, is neither alive nor dead, neither awake nor asleep, but dreaming what dreams may come in this interruptive space of nonpresence. The phrase "et cetera" thus offers, if it also imposes, a linguistic mode of alienation from the culture of war. In this alienated (and poetic) space, the phrase that has brutally asserted a needlessness to name functions instead to bring into language that which is culturally unspeakable, the part of the body that is definitive of the class "female" yet inevitably also inexpressibly particular. Similarly, this phrase, whose effects were conscriptive and disconnective, comes to permit a direct and desirous address. And the apostrophic address elicits a re-membering ("your smile eyes knees and . . . your Etcetera") that reverses the sister's maledictory knitting. By the end of the poem, the dreaming soldier has himself conscripted the phrase "et cetera," whose semantic emptiness now goes to elicit dreams of love so bodily and so particular that they cannot be spoken but demand to be enacted.

Cummings' poetic strategy forces the generic to recognize and even give utterance to the absolutely particular, with the result that lyric voice can redefine the militarized body as the instrument of speaking love. In so doing, it argues for a reciprocity between cursing and poetry that also characterizes Richard Pryor's comedy.[19] It should be acknowledged, however, that stand-up comedy reverses the poetic situation. If the poetic voice is, by definition, disembodied, the stand-up comic is physically present, his body the irreplaceable instrument of the comic act. This is especially true of Pryor, whose comedy is as much physical as verbal and whose humor often lies in dramatizing the innocence that lies in an unselfconscious immediacy to the moment at hand.[20] But where Lenny Bruce uses performance to insist on his ownership of his act, Pryor offers an act in which there is no identity "prior" to the act itself. His humor relies on the discrepancy between body and voice that always underlies performance and that Pryor puts to lavish use, giving over his physical presence to a catholic array of characters (including Black Power activists, wino philosophers, preachers, pimps and whores, his wives and children, white men and women, dogs, body parts, and cars, as well as the character he calls Richard Pryor). Cummings, occupying the disembodied space of poetry, forces the semantically empty phrase "et cetera" to make reference, to insist on the preciousness of the body, even (especially) in its most unspeakable parts. Pryor, in contrast, uses words characterized by their gravity of insult ("motherfucker," "nigger," "bitch") to interrupt, even shatter, the present moment of speaking. In so doing, he produces a space in which insult can translate into recognition and in which devalued bodies can be granted fantastic immunity to circumstance.

I return, then, to Pryor's version of white men cursing: "I love when white dudes get mad and cuss," he says. "Cause y'all are some funny motherfuckers when you cuss. They'll be saying shit like 'Yeah, come on, peckerhead. Come on, ya fuckin jerkoff. Come on, son of a bitch. Come on. Yeah, you're fuckin A right, buddy.' "[21] As Pryor characterizes it here and in his following commentary, white men curse in a language of approach, friendship, and consensus ("yeah, you're fuckin A right, buddy"). What particularizes "white" cursing is not simply its heavy-handed repetition and its reliance on uninspired name-calling, but also its conversion of affiliative language into insult. This is funny when Pryor dramatizes it, but, as his act also makes clear, white cursing has performative effect. The moment of speaking, as Pryor defines it, is fully structured by white men's capacity to use language as an invitation to violence and a mechanism of racism. He describes, for example, black ticket-holders pulled over by Long Beach police as they try to attend the show, while white people assume their right to the best seats. An act remarkable for its appeal across racial lines thus also serves to bring those lines sharply into view.

Yet within a performance situation structured by racial divide, Pryor offers cursing as a strategy of citation that can interrupt the present so as to envision a different set of possibilities. For Pryor, the profit of knowing how to curse is not to return injury but also to reverse it, translating words of insult and violence into recognition and comedy. "Patti be singing her ass off, don't she?" he says, inviting applause for Patti La-Belle's opening act: "And the band's a bitch, too, man. That band's a motherfucker she got." As Pryor uses them here, words that are normally grave insults serve instead to assert affiliation. In this context, to describe the white dude cussing as a funny motherfucker is to recognize in un-usually generous and even affiliative terms the social privilege that un-derlies not knowing how to curse. A routine from Pryor's 1983 New Orleans performance makes the point more bluntly. After the bit cited earlier, in which cursing is imagined to liberate slaves from their work, Pryor acknowledges the historical reality, that "slaves built all this shit down in here, or carried the shit that built it." The piece builds toward what is not quite a joke, that slave-owners required slaves to walk on water—"I looked at the Mississippi, I said, motherfucker had to walk across that. 'Get your black ass on there and walk. Carry that tree' "—before ending with a genial, even appreciative, address to the white members of the audience: "Y'all are some cold motherfuckers. Your ancestors . . ." Here, as in his routine in which "whitey" demands that Africans speak English and then refuses to hear what they have to say, Pryor conflates ancestors with descendents: "here and now" (as the per-formance is called) remains the extension of a past that continues in the form of violent racial disparities. In this context, the word "mother-fucker" carries its full weight as a curse, insisting with shocking direct-ness on the accountability of white people for the racial injustice they perhaps deplore but always benefit from and more often ignore. Yet this instance of the word follows Pryor's characterization of slaves as them-selves "motherfuckers," and it inevitably recalls his many other uses of it: the word weaves through this performance, as through all of Pryor's concerts, more often as a term of parity and affection than of disgust. Exploiting the semantic mobility that attends obscene words, Pryor's curse both registers and suspends the violence predicated by 1980s racial relations. Perhaps more importantly, it reconceives race as a mobile performance, a matter of linguistic fluency and cultural knowledge, a knowing (or not knowing) how to curse.

In contrast to Lenny Bruce, Richard Pryor does not seek to deny the historicity of curse words and racial insults. Rather, his comic poetics make a history of racial fantasy and injustice the basis for interruption and revision. "Not many black people get bitten by snakes," he maintains. "That's true. Because black people stroll too cool in the woods. Now white people get bit all the time, cause they have a different rhythm."[22] In conferring a physical grace on black men that seems to derive directly, if mysteriously, from their blackness, Pryor exposes and renders into com-edy the fantasy of—and anxieties about—sovereign subjectivity underly-ing racism. In a more explicitly political bit, he depicts a white couple returning from intermission to find that their up-front seats have been taken over by black fans who had been relegated to the back. "Weren't we sitting here, Marge? I think we were sitting here," the white man inquires, in an address to his wife that refuses to recognize both black persons and his own racial fear. "Well, you ain't sitting here now, motherfucker," is the reply. Here, cursing announces the physical presence and cultural history that the white couple both deny and fear, and it makes that denial and fear serve a claim to entitlement that legality would deny. In this bit, Pryor explicitly dramatizes the capacity of cursing to divert predication, transferring the fantasy of sovereign subjectivity from the white to the black speaker. Similarly, he returns throughout his career to the figure of Jim Brown, mocking the miraculous physical prowess of the character Brown plays in his movies but attributing that same prowess to him in real life: "Jim is pretty mean. But he ought to stop that shit in the movies, cause he's going to get a lot of niggers killed. Niggers think that shit is true, right? That's a movie, y'all. . . . Can you imagine that nigger being mad at you, coming after you? . . . I would run from that nigger. Can anybody blame me? . . . Nigger played football nine years, never got hurt. Or tired."[23] To acknowledge the absurdity of Brown's action movies is only to take more satisfaction in the fantasy of his invulnerability—an invulnerability that could not be fantasized apart from his status as a "mean nigger."

Strikingly, however, Pryor excludes himself from this kind of sovereignty, which he can perform but never claims to embody. Indeed, he portrays himself as almost wondrously inept: he mocks Brown behind his back but runs at his approach, he falls into his own pool and can't swim, he shoots his own car to stop his wife from leaving, his pet monkey tries to mate with his ear. Many of his self-portraits dramatize his drug and alcohol use, in which he is never cool but instead inflicts on himself a vast and inventive array of indignities and injuries. In the character he offers of himself, Richard Pryor defines the body more as an event than a location—less the site of subjectivity than a source of unpredictability, something that befalls and befuddles his intentions. Pryor's comedy thus dramatizes the body's capacity to disrupt the fantasy of sovereignty it is supposed to secure. Precisely this disruption, however, liberates the fundamentally unattributable expressivity I have associated with cursing. The body essentialized by racial categories becomes the basis for meaning in its particularity and vitality, the immediate moment of its speaking —a moment that is nonetheless always citational and, in particular, cites the history of degrading racial relations in the speaker's capacity to curse.

If there is a utopian quality to cursing, I would end by suggesting, it has to do with the capacity of such utterance to escape temporal locatedness, to fall out of place or to erupt within and thereby disjoin a preexisting historical or grammatical sequence. Such cursing can be comic even when it is not funny, as I will illustrate by quoting from Pryor's "junkie serenade," a piece from the concert film *Here and Now*, in which Pryor impersonates a heroin junkie as he shoots up and slowly nods off, perhaps to death. As the piece nears its end, the junkie says:

> If I come back, I hope you motherfuckers has this shit right. Cause you done fucked it up this time. Yeah. You wasn't sensitive, you motherfuckers. You wasn't sensitive. You just wasn't . . . you just didn't like . . . motherfuckers . . . sensitive. You run over people. You put them, you put them in a position that they can't do nothing in it. Then, when they can't, y'all say, "See." That wasn't right. That wasn't right. That's the same . . . That ain't right. I *know* it ain't right. And I tell the motherfuckers about it, they tell me I'm crazy. I know this shit is foul. With a capital Foul.

It reflects on Pryor's sense of where wisdom can be found that the junkie has already disqualified himself as an ethical model. His habit, as he openly explains, overrides all other loyalties: "I ain't going to jail for nobody. You dig? Shit. I done told on too many people up there," he tells his dealer. The only job he can imagine wanting is "town junkie," shooting up for the enjoyment of tourists, whose prejudices he would be happy to confirm as long he gets the junk. It need hardly be said that such a job is not on offer at the unemployment center, nor is the junkie otherwise employable. Like the curse, in other words, the junkie represents a violation of the social norms that also produced him, forcing him into a position he "can't do nothing in." Yet as he falls out of social and even temporal place—speaking in curses and non-standard speech, from a position of social alienation and bodily dispossession, at a moment akin to dying—the junkie imagines a future that is comic in its escape from the grip of the past, a future in which people "has this shit right." Such comedy, yearning as it does toward an eruption within or erasure of the present, also bears its load of sorrow. For the junkie, whose wisdom is crazy by social norms, and whose curses fade out with his consciousness, cannot be said to have effected the changes he desires. Indeed, the only possible joke in these closing words lie in his attempt to underscore his certainty about what "ain't right," in which he commits a linguistic error ("With a capital Foul") that in some degree changes the subject from the substance to the form of his commentary. Even as a performance, the character is not heard: his serenade is repeatedly shouted over by audience members who want Pryor to be funnier. If Pryor's junkie matters (and, of course, I think he does), it is in ways that compare to cummings's soldier; that is, in the poetry his cursing achieves. Lying in the mud, speaking from an interruptive space of nonpresence, the junkie succeeds in naming what has been socially negated: the sensitivity, the feelingness, the particularity of persons whose personhood has been conscripted to other uses.

NOTES

This essay expands on material published in Kate E. Brown and Howard I. Kushner, "Eruptive Voices: Coprolalia, Malediction, and the Poetics of Cursing," *New Literary History* 32, no. 3 (Summer 2001): 537–562. The original material on poetry, comedy, and cursing is of my authorship, but my thinking about the nature of cursing is wholly indebted to conversations with my co-author about coprolalia and Tourette Syndrome. For a fuller discussion of Tourette's, see Kushner, *A Cursing Brain? The Histories of Tourette Syndrome* (Cambridge, Mass.: Harvard University Press, 1999).

1. William Shakespeare, *The Tempest,* ed. Northrop Frye, in *The Complete Works,* ed. Alfred Harbage (New York: Viking, 1969, 1977), pp. 1369–1395.

2. I owe this example to Mick Skolnick (by way of Michael Halberstam), who heard it on a live news report.

3. See also Stephen J. Greenblatt, *Learning to Curse: Essays in Early Modern Culture* (New York: Routledge, 1990), 23–26. Greenblatt is interested in language training as a strategy of colonial subjugation but not in the specificity of cursing as mode of speech. For discussions of cursing (and other violations of speech decorum) in the context of race rather than colonialism and of queer rather than hetero sexuality, see Michael L. Cobb, "Insolent Racing, Rough Narrative: The Harlem Renaissance's Impolite Queers," and Marlon Bryan Ross, "Camping the Dirty Dozens: The Queer Resources of Black Nationalist Invective," both in *Callaloo* 23, no. 1 (Winter 2000): 328–351 and 290–312.

4. "Nigger Babies," recorded at PJ's, Hollywood, Calif. (24–26 May 1968); reissued on Richard Pryor, *Evolution/Revolution: The Early Years (1966–1974)* (Warner Brothers, 2005), disc 1. In "New Niggers," from the recording . . . *Is It Something I Said?* (Reprise, 1975), Pryor describes Vietnamese immigrants learning English in American military camps. The first word they are taught is "nigger," a training that will divide them from black people even as it will be applied to them. ("Goddamn!" says one of the Southerners who has adopted a Vietnamese orphan; "What the hell we got here, Margo? . . . Look like one of the neighborhood coons.")

5. "Wattstax Monologue," recorded at the Summit Club, Hollywood, Calif. (8 October 1972) for the movie *Wattstax,* dir. Mel Stuart (Stax Films/Wolper Pictures, 1973) and reissued on *Evolution/Revolution.*

6. "Wattstax Monologue."

7. "Wattstax Monologue."

8. Bruce's stand-up comedy career began immediately after four years' service in

the U.S. Navy during World War II. Although it is not the topic of this essay, I think it is important to acknowledge how significant and shocking it would have been for a Jewish comedian to affiliate himself with non-white minorities in the United States—and to do so from a position of hipness—just as images of the abjection and slaughter of European Jewry in German and Polish concentration camps began to filter into American consciousness. This background may also help to explain the degree of anguish that still surrounds his repeated arrests and early death.

9. Richard Pryor, *Here and Now,* dir. Richard Pryor (Warner Brothers, 1983).

10. For the grand finale of his 1983 concert at Carnegie Hall, George Carlin enunciates a seemingly endless list of synonyms for the seven words you can't say on television. The humor of this lies as much in the vast number of synonyms as in the inventiveness of any particular one.

11. Judith Butler makes the same point about racial epithets in *Excitable Speech: A Politics of the Performative* (New York: Routledge, 1997); see, for example, 36.

12. "Wattstax Monologue."

13. *Richard Pryor: Live! in Concert,* dir. Jeff Margolis (Warner Brothers, 1979).

14. Butler, *Excitable Speech,* 10–11.

15. *The Lenny Bruce Performance Film* (1965), dir. John Magnuson.

16. Lewis Carroll, *Through the Looking Glass and What Alice Found There,* ed. Roger Lancelyn Green (Oxford: Oxford University Press, 1971), 190.

17. Paul de Man, "Hypogram and Inscription," in *The Resistance to Theory* (Minneapolis: University of Minnesota Press, 1986), 27–53; the quotation appears on 36.

18. e. e. cummings, *Is 5,* ed. George James Firmage (New York: Liveright, 1926), n.p. The title of the volume provides cummings's solution to the equation $2 + 2$, and it suggests that poetry, like cursing, seeks to open up a space that is not governed by sequence.

19. As Geoffrey Hughes shows in *Swearing: A Social History of Foul Language, Oaths, and Profanity in English* (Oxford: Basil Blackwell, 1991), the reciprocity between poetry and cursing has a literary history that long precedes cummings; see especially 62–88.

20. Many of Pryor's innocents are, in consequence, also hypocrites, and it is the unselfconsciousness with which they reveal themselves that makes them so funny: the preacher, for example, whose epiphany occurs while eating a tuna sandwich and who defines money as the root of all evil except when it is in his hands. Conversely, as I show more fully at the end of this essay, such self-serving is no bar either to innocence or to wisdom.

21. *Live! in Concert.*

22. Ibid.

23. "Jim Brown" (Alternate Version), recorded at the Comedy Store, Hollywood, Calif. (29 October–1 November 1973) and issued on *Revolution.* Jim Brown also plays a central role in the routine "Freebase," from the filmed concert *Live on the Sunset Strip.*

5 Br'er Richard

FASCINATIN' STORYTELLER

MAXINE A. LEGALL

It was Horace, the Roman poet, who once said, "The story's about you." Richard Pryor, comedian, actor, and writer, exemplified these words in his private and public life. His creative genius for telling the story, and telling it masterfully, flowed from the life he led as a boy growing up in the black ghetto of Peoria, Illinois, and the twists and turns of his adult relationships and life. His passion to "to tell the truth"[1] about his own life and the people of his community unfolded through his many characters, both real and richly imagined. An old African American folk proverb popular in Florida is: "I been in sorrow's kitchen, and I don' licked the pots clean." Pryor was born in sorrow's kitchen; he spent most of his life licking out all of the pots. It was in sorrow's kitchen that he became immersed in African American working-class culture.

Speaking about his most well-known character, Mudbone, Pryor described him as a person who told "fascinatin' stories."[2] Pryor brought those fascinatin' stories to life. Although revered as a stand-up comic and comedic actor, his uniqueness derived from his gift as a storyteller whose work was saturated with the folklore of Africa, the southern plantations, and the black enclaves of Eatonville, Harlem, Detroit, Peoria, and other centers of black life. His use of the black oral tradition can be compared to the work of his predecessors, cultural folklorists/preservationists Langston Hughes and Zora Neale Hurston.

That tradition began with enslaved Africans who "brought with them no material possessions to aid in preserving the arts and customs of their homeland . . . they carried in their minds and hearts a treasure of complex musical forms, dramatic speech, and imaginative stories, which they perpetuated through the vital art of self-expression. Wherever slaves ended up, their African inflected culture flourished in spite of tremendous environmental disadvantages."[3] It thrived as an authentic "underground" culture, shared by word of mouth. This private oral culture existed beyond the reach of their oppressors. It was from such secluded and sheltered cultural space that African American vernacular culture emerged and was passed down to future generations.[4] It has, thus, served "to forge a cultural cohesion and the maintenance of a African American world view in the face of the historic cultural rupture"[5] and dislocation. Pryor's life, a classic case of rupture and dislocation, was steeped in that vernacular and enriched by its humor, ritual, and emphasis on personal interactions. From these interactions among groups of people who share a "common core"[6] of values, folklore is produced. It generates within the individual a sense of group membership and identity.

The black folk culture that evolved from these origins was imbued with "projections of personal experiences, and hopes, and defeats."[7] Humor became a coping device against unrelenting oppression, helping them to blunt their pain with laughter. Humor, and the folk culture it reflected, helped black people sublimate their rage against their oppressors, and prevent their own self-destruction through "cruel and dehumanizing situations. . . . Through it all—-slavery, Jim Crow laws, to the hopeful years of the Civil Rights Movement and beyond—laughter remained a tool of regeneration, transformation, and re-creation."[8]

As noted before, Pryor, like Hughes and Hurston, was a keen observer and collector of folk culture and steeped in its regenerative effects. But he was an "accidental folklorist,"[9] not a studied one, who was well versed in the formal aspects of anthropological preservation. His informality conveyed an authenticity that made his stories convincing. Pryor's repertoire was framed by the universal folkloric themes, as enumerated by noted scholar Stith Thompson.[10] They included animals with human traits; taboo subjects; societal customs; drunkenness; triumph of the weak; social relationships; captivity and escape; and, of course, sex and the tensions of race and social class. These topics were all enlivened by Pryor's injection of personal experience and artful exaggeration. He also revealed his knowledge of the perennial concerns in African American oral narratives: trickster tales, jests, toasts, jokes, the errant preacher tales, sermons, testimonials, and the entire breadth of black music— blues, spirituals, and gospel.[11]

In particular, Pryor's style owes a debt to the trickster tales that have remained popular among the black population in the South and in places affected by the Great Migration of blacks to the North and Midwest. John Burrison notes that these tales "cluster into two main cycles (groups of related stories wherein the same characters recur): the animal tales popularized in literary form by Joel Chandler Harris through his story-telling character, Uncle Remus, . . . and the less publicized but no less significant tales . . . which represent the black perspective on the planta-tion experience."[12] Examples of the second cycle include the Br'er Rabbit tales, the stories about John and Ole Massa, High John de Conqueror, the Signifying Monkey, and Stagolee.

Br'er Rabbit, the quintessential trickster animal in African American folklore, is a popular character with many Americans. One of the recur-ring themes of these tales is how a small, seemingly defenseless, power-less animal (by extension, a person or group of people) manages to overcome obstacles through clever verbal skills,[13] skills like jonin', signi-fyin', crackin' on somebody, playing the dozens, and preachin'. Often seen as amusing, lighthearted entertainment, these tales are illustrative of a clever strategy used by African Americans for the individual and the group's continued existence:[14]

> The American Negro slave, adopting Br'er Rabbit as hero, represented him as the most frightened and helpless of creatures. No hero-animals in Africa or elsewhere were so completely lacking in strength. But the slaves took pains to give Br'er Rabbit other significant qualities. He became in their stories different personas, by turns a practical joker, a braggart, a wit, a glutton, a lady's man, and a trickster, but his essential characteristic was his ability to outwit bigger and stronger animals. To the slave in his condition the theme of weakness overcoming strength through cunning proved endlessly fascinating.[15]

Richard Pryor was Br'er Rabbit reincarnated on the stage; his mod-ern-day, urban briar patch.[16] He was Br'er Rabbit, the trickster, and acting as though he did not want to be thrown into the briar patch, knowing that the briar patch was his home, his place of safety, confidence, and re-juvenation. Pryor used the stage as his own place of security and used his range of rabbit-like personas to "re-present" truths mostly whispered about in consumer society. Add the deleted expletives, a taboo body gesture, a racial slur/reference or two, and a dynamic physical presenta-tion format to a Br'er Rabbit story and you have a story with its message of the truth from the "Pryor Patch" delivered by the master folklorist and storyteller, Br'er Richard.

Part of Pryor's power came from his transgressive wit and ability to take on stronger foes. That Br'er Rabbit quality could be traced to his folkloristic roots and through Hughes, Hurston, and poet Paul Laurence Dunbar. His comedic roots extend from comedians Bert Williams, Butterbeans and Susie, Redd Foxx, Jackie "Moms" Mabley, Dusty Fletcher, Slappy White, Flip Wilson, Dewey "Pigmeat" Markham, Dick Gregory, and Bill Cosby, all of whom drew from aspects of their cultural heritage.[17] Pryor also benefited from his association with the black consciousness movement of the 1960s and writers such as Ishmael Reed.[18] His cultural and personal lineage, plus Pryor's natural ability to unite a diverse audience while delving into socially risky subjects, is what made his storytelling so fascinating.

Storytelling, we are reminded, brings people together to share and create common experiences[19] that allow us to maintain and communicate "ideas, images, motives, and emotions that are universal."[20] Pryor brought people together from different racial, social, and religious groups and molded them into a single new group. Sometimes the teller narrates the story as though there is no audience, though he is aware of the audience. In some instances, the storyteller invites the audience to join in the telling. The storyteller appears to be seeing, or experiencing the story as it unfolds before the audience. In actuality, the teller knows the story from start to finish and may choose to alter it as it is being told. Through creativity, image production,[21] and memory, the storyteller invites the audience to experience the story and to suspend disbelief. Pryor was a master of these skills.

In expounding the qualities of a good storyteller, Marsh Cassady identifies a person who enjoys being with others and who desires to connect emotionally with them. He sees the storyteller as an entertainer —someone who takes pleasure in telling or performing, who sheds light on a subject or individual, and who interprets life for others.[22] The teller must also have a "keen enjoyment of [his] material, a burning desire to share [his] enthusiasm with others."[23] Pryor once said, "Something in me is dying to express itself."[24] His method of expressing that "something" was through the power of storytelling.

Storytelling is above all an act of narration, an oral performance:

> In oral narration, the verbal message . . . is supported by both paraverbal and nonverbal communication. The former includes vocal inflections, silences or pauses (sometimes used to create suspense), rhythm and tempo, and the imitation of sounds and characters' voices. The

latter includes kinesthetics, or body language, such as hand gestures, facial expressions, and body movement and posture, as well as proxemics, or the spatial relationships and interaction between teller and audience (for example, eye contact and touching).[25]

Pryor's narration was direct,[26] specific, and sparse. He knew exactly how much to talk and how much to act out. Every word and motion was chosen to advance the message of the story. Through his sublime use of mimicry he "took" the audience into the world of his characters, which also included talking body parts, cars, and crack pipes.

To accurately portray various forms of "black speech," Pryor delivered his stories in the oral fashion of the African Americans he talked about, as well as other racial groups he mimicked. For blacks he used lines such as "don't nobody kick me" and "I don't wanna be no accident" (double negatives); "you be panicked" and "She be all in that" (use of the verb "to be"); "nuttin'" (substitution for medial "th" of double "t" and deletion of final "g" sound); "truf" (substitution of "f" sound for the voiced "th" sound). He used "man" (male figure), "baby" (woman love interest), "trinklin' down" for trickling down, and "turnt" for the past tense of "turned" and "peoples" and "feets" as plurals of person and foot. He used words, themes, and self-depreciating humor that merged mainstream cultural icons with black cultural references. For example, in his sketch "Supernigger," Pryor says: "Look up in the sky . . . it's a crow . . . a bat . . . faster than a bowl of chittlins."[27] To indicate a white person, or a self-important black person, Pryor frequently used a constrained, high-pitched tone of voice. This was in opposition to his folk characters, who spoke with unconstrained language and liveliness.

His characters were finely crafted even to the use of specific associated hand gestures, as in his portrayal of the junkie's slowly uncurling fist.[28] In that single movement, Pryor demonstrated that he had captured the core identity of the character. In his acclaimed concert film *Richard Pryor: Live! in Concert,* he effected a loping gait to portray himself as a youngster, and the audience instantly knew he was both younger and shorter than his dad when they went hunting together.[29] For the audience to *see* a "cool dude," Pryor changed his posture, stood upright, and carried his body with a certain rhythm, and he *became* that cool dude. The energy that defined his storytelling breathed life into the characters and infused them with physical dimension and presence—mouth, hands, body, stance, walk, fluid movements, animal sounds—that made the characters come alive before the audience. According to

Baker and Greene: "Good stories have something to say . . . they have vision . . . a single theme that's clearly defined . . . a well-developed plot . . . believable characters . . . are faithful to the source material and have dramatic appeal."[30] Pryor's stories and performances illustrated these elements.

By using the shock technique of profanity—blue or salty language, what Gehring refers to as "natural obscenities"[31]—Pryor captured the audience's attention. Take for example the following: "You gon' fuck me, for true?"; "I talked about his ass"; "Fuck it, we're going anyway"; "I love when white dudes get mad and cuss, 'cause you all are some funny motherfuckers when you cuss"; "I told stories when I was in prison all day and night; weren't nobody getting no ass . . ."[32] Cussing, in this context, conferred power, or as Brown and Kushner state, an "unusual expressive weight" from the speaker to the audience, and given the "artistic appeal of Richard Pryor's comedy . . . cursing is integral rather than gratuitous."[33]

Finally, what made him a fascinatin' storyteller was that he took an intimate truth, deconstructed it, and shared it with the world. Folk groups, according to Alan Dundes, are those who "identify themselves by geographical-cultural regions, ethnic, racial, religious and/or occupational domain" with its own way of speaking, its own legends, and in-group jokes and folklore.[34] Typically, what each group experiences is private and intimate, and known mainly to those within the group. Richard Pryor placed in public view the thoughts, language, and behavior once confined to a particular group—black and white, red, brown, or yellow; men and women; different social classes; and every geographical-cultural, national, ethnic, gender, racial, language, religious, or occupational group—when out of range of the other. In the words of Hannah Arendt, he "deprivatized and deindividualized"[35] the thoughts and behavior of the members of those groups through storytelling.

"Pryor 'signified,' 'jived,' and 'testified' using retro-stereotyped characters like 'Mudbone' to expose racism's tragedies, while through stories and one-liners he expressed his outrage over institutionalized discrimination. 'We go down to court looking for justice,' joked Pryor, 'and that's what we find—Just Us!' "[36] Commenting on the plight of blacks, he said, "Whites put us in a situation then express disappointment that we're in that situation." And he wondered out loud, "Whites and blacks get along with each other in the theater, why does the problem occur once they get outside?"[37]

Pryor, like Hurston, collected the stories of everyday black folk, and by performing them, presented the African American way of life to the public. With his comedic talent, he even told the sacred cow of black humor—the self-degrading tales—to mixed audiences. On one hand, one of Pryor's dubious contributions to American culture was his incessant use of words not acceptable to the general public at the time and definitely not spoken before racially mixed audiences, words like "nigger," "bitch," and "motherfucker." Although later in his career he did recant the N-word, he continued to use the other less flattering words and descriptions.

On the other hand, like Hughes, Pryor "returned constantly to the life-affirming folk tradition of the black masses. . . . Hughes' (and Pryor's) genius lay in expressing black consciousness, interpreting to the people the beauty within themselves. . . . 'I don't study the black man,' Hughes said, 'I feel him.' "[38] Pryor also felt his characters deeply, and his genius was in presenting a seldom-viewed black humanity to multiracial, multicultural audiences on his own terms, without embellishment, without apology.

The comedian Chris Rock said that Pryor's "very presence gave black people a chance to laugh and feel good about stuff that usually pissed us off."[39] Alvin Poussaint commented: "It's hard to imagine someone white quite like Richard Pryor or even Eddie Murphy or Bill Cosby. There's that special ethnic black tinge to what they do: taking snatches of life and the caricature and exaggeration, picking up on some of the subtle psychological relationships that go on between people and exposing them."[40] Pryor slapped the audience around with his profanities, his escapades and exposés into the taboos of all the folk groups. Pryor's presentations created a psychological tension that was released through laughter. Williams and Williams note that Pryor combined "humor and folklore, creating original material, and causing laughter to explode over experiences which if not shared are at least known."[41]

As a folk artist, Pryor was deeply concerned with societal ills. He chose to showcase the stories of winos, junkies, prostitutes, and preachers who didn't quite hit the spiritual mark. "Richard Pryor," said Bill Cosby, "is perhaps the only comedian that I know who has captured the total character of the ghetto."[42] The people of the ghetto are often thought of in a derogatory way as peasants or as working-class people. However, Hughes said them, "But then there are the low down folks, the so-called common element, and they are the majority. . . . They do not particularly care whether they are like white folks or anybody else. They furnish a wealth of colorful, distinctive material for any artist because they still hold their own individuality in the face of American standardization."[43] Pryor changed the way people looked at each other. As playwright Q. Terah Jackson noted, "He got people to look at the seemingly hopeless faces of city life, and rather than dehumanizing them, he humanized them."[44]

In their response to his death, White and Mastrangelo observed that by using racial slurs, society, his own frailties, and taboo topics, Pryor "pulled down the curtain that divided private and public discourse. He got people to see the shame and discontent of race relations and forced them to acknowledge shared idiosyncrasies."[45] In doing so, he influenced the iconoclastic styles of Eddie Murphy, Arsenio Hall, Martin Lawrence, the Wayans brothers, Dave Chappelle, Robin Williams, Jamie Foxx, Chris Rock, and an entire generation of comedians, storytelling comedians.

A major part of Pryor's legacy to the history of this country is his contributions as a storyteller and folklorist. By filming and recording his concerts, he preserved a segment of our history not captured in history books. He achieved his goal of telling the truth, even when the truth was hard to look at and difficult to admit. His depictions of the junkies and the winos were not just funny. They were gritty reality for far too many people. At the end of the day he had shattered the myth that his cultural group needed to keep "certain things to itself." He took what had been private and intimate and shared it with the world.

There is an old Liberian proverb and folktale about a hunter named Ogaloussa, recorded in *The Cow-Tale Switch and Other West African Folktales,* that says: "A man is not really dead until he is forgotten."[46] With a trickster's skill and daring, Br'er Richard infused wit and humor into his sly and transgressive stories and truth-tales. They, like the classic African American tradition from which they derive, will continue to enthrall and engage us, and ensure that Richard Pryor, fascinatin' storyteller, will not be forgotten.

NOTES

1. Richard Pryor with Todd Gold, *Pryor Convictions, and Other Life Sentences* (New York: Pantheon Books, 1995), 121.

2. Pryor with Gold, 143. Pryor had his Mudbone; Hughes had his Simple; and Hughes and Hurston had their Mule Bone; the author views Mudbone as one of Pryor's alter egos.

3. J. Mason Brewer, ed., *American Negro Folklore* (Chicago: Quadrangle Books, 1968), ix.

4. Linda Goss and Marian Barnes, eds., *Talk That Talk* (New York: Simon and Schuster, 1989), 17.

5. Anand Prahlad, ed., *The Greenwood Encyclopedia of African American Folklore* (Westport, Conn.: Greenwood Press, 2006), 1:14.

6. Alan Dundes, *Interpreting Folklore* (Bloomington: Indiana University Press, 1980), 2.

7. Langston Hughes and Arna Bontemps, eds., *The Book of Negro Folklore* (New York: Dodd, Mead, 1958), viii.

8. George Houston Bass, introduction to *Mule Bone: A Comedy of Negro Life,* by Langston Hughes and Zora Neale Hurston (New York: Harper Perennial, 1991 [1931]), 3.

9. The term "accidental folklorist" is used by the author to refer to those who are keen observers of a culture but are not bound to or guided by predetermined scientific rules and requirements of the discipline.

10. Stith Thompson, *Motif-Index of Folk-Literature,* vols. 1–6 (Bloomington: Indiana University Press, 1955–1958), volumes 2 and 5, vii–xv. For animals with human traits, see 1:395–422; for taboo subjects, 1:516, 520; for societal customs, 5:111–137; for captivity and escape, 5:197–220; for sex, 5:514; for drunkenness, 5:515; for social relationships, 5:163–166; for triumph of the weak, 5:18–21; for social class, 5:513; for race, 5:514.

11. Hughes and Bontemps, vii–xv.

12. John A. Burrison, *Storytellers: Folktales and Legends from the South* (Athens: University of Georgia Press, 1989), 4.

13. Dwight N. Hopkins, *Shoes That Fit Our Feet: Sources for a Constructive Black Theology* (Maryknoll, N.Y.: Orbis Books, 1993), 127.

14. Burrison, 4; Bass and Gates, 1–3.

15. Hughes and Bontemps, ix.

16. Annie Reed, "Br'er Rabbit and the Briar Patch," in Goss and Barnes, 30–31.

17. Brewer, ix; Larry G. Coleman, "Storytelling and Comic Performance," in Goss and Barnes, 431; Jerry Zolten, "Comedians," in Prahlad, 1:248.

18. Pryor with Gold, 70–71.

19. Augusta Baker and Ellin Greene, *Storytelling: Art and Technique* (New York: R. R. Bowker, 1977), 17.

20. Marsh Cassady, *Storytelling Step by Step* (San Jose, Calif.: Resource Publications, 1990), 5.

21. Gladstone L. Yearwood, *Black Film as Signifying Practice* (Trenton, N.J.: Africa World Press, 2000), 125.

22. Cassady, 8–9.

23. Baker and Greene, 69.

24. *Pryor: Here and Now.*

25. Burrison, 14.

26. Pryor's narratives were direct, especially when compared to those of Aesop's fables.

27. *Richard Pryor: The Anthology (1968–1992).*

28. *Richard Pryor: Here and Now.*

29. *Richard Pryor: Live! in Concert.*

30. Baker and Greene, 27.

31. Wes D. Gehring, *Personality Comedians as Genre* (Westport, Conn.: Greenwood Press, 1997), 12.

32. *Richard Pryor: Here and Now; Richard Pryor: Live! in Concert.*

33. Kate E. Brown and Howard I. Kushner, "Eruptive Voices: Coprolalia, Malediction, and the Poetics of Cursing," *New Literary History* 32 (2001): 550, 554.

34. Alan Dundes, *The Study of Folklore* (Englewood Cliffs, N.J.: Prentice-Hall, 1965), 7.

35. Hannah Arendt, *The Human Condition* (Chicago: Chicago University Press, 1958), 50.

36. Zolten, "Comedians," in Prahlad, 1:249.

37. *Richard Pryor: Here and Now.*

38. Henry Louis Gates, Jr., and Cornel West, *The African American Century: How Black Americans Have Shaped Our Country* (New York: Touchstone, 2000), 100.

39. Marc Peyser and Allison Samuels, "Richard Pryor," *Newsweek,* 19 December 2005, 61.

40. Coleman, 434.

41. John A. Williams and Dennis A. Williams, *If I Stop I'll Die: The Comedy and Tragedy of Richard Pryor* (New York: Thunder's Mouth Press, 1991), 3.

42. Williams and Williams, 97.

43. Langston Hughes, found in Hopkins, 84.

44. Q. Terah Jackson III, personal interview, 3 August 2007.

45. Armond White and Bob Mastrangelo, "Richard Pryor," *Sight and Sound* 16, no. 3 (March 2006): 38–39.

46. Harold Courlander and George Herzog, "The Cow-Tail Switch," in *The Cow-Tail Switch and Other West African Stories* (New York: Henry Holt, 1947), 5–12.

6 "... And It's Deep Too"

THE PHILOSOPHICAL COMEDY OF RICHARD PRYOR

MALIK D. McCLUSKEY

From the earliest days of the academy, its relationship to popular culture has been uneasy and controversial. Historians note that many of the first Western academies—Plato's Academy and Epicurus's Garden, for example—were deliberately isolated from the "real world" and the supposed taint of "pop culture" in order to sustain rigorous engagement with perplexing and abstract questions. Ancient Greeks were treated to the comedy *The Clouds,* in which Aristophanes singled out Socrates (albeit unfairly, as Aristophanes mistakenly linked Socrates to the Sophists, who were itinerant philosophers-for-hire).[1] Perhaps more than other branches of humanistic inquiry, philosophy, a hallmark of the earliest academies, is still widely and mistakenly regarded as disconnected from everyday life. Contemporary popular culture has often ridiculed philosophy's pursuit of wisdom, abstractions, and idealism. This standoff has not fostered a productive working relationship between philosophy and certain elements of popular culture. Although philosophers—particularly those working within the analytic tradition—do not explicitly engage cultural trends per se, postmodern scholars have reminded us that philosophy does not exist in a vacuum and that, at the very least, claims to knowledge must recognize the "situatedness" of the knower. Today, the epistemological conditions and sociopolitical context temper claims to *objective truth,* which had been the goal of the academy for many centuries. However, there are recent indications that philosophers are becoming more self-critical of their epistemic positions. During the last twenty-five years, the Western academy has seen the development of cultural studies wherein philosophical questions about the role of culture are being raised and examined. Philosophers are also displaying a new willingness to examine the immediate sociopolitical and cultural context of late-twentieth/early-twenty-first-century questions. Thus, topics that would have likely offended philosophic sensibilities fifty years ago, such as the social significance of the Beatles, morality issues in *The Sopranos,* and the political philosophy of *Buffy the Vampire Slayer,*[2] are being engaged more frequently. While these philosophical forays into popular culture are uneven, such trends indicate movement away from rigid gatekeeping on behalf of the "purity" in philosophical inquiry. Philosophy's tepid response to popular culture has been particularly notable in its reluctance to embrace the comedic aspects of our lives. In this essay, I argue that philosophy would do well to examine humor and comedy, both in and of itself and specifically as found in the oeuvre of Richard Pryor. While Pryor is widely regarded as a pioneering figure in comedy—the first honoree of the notable Kennedy Center Mark Twain Prize for American Humor—and recognized as a comedic genius, he is known also for his philosophical insights. His comedy was wide in its appeal as well as philosophically rewarding. Colloquially speaking, it was "deep," too. In section one, I also argue that humor and comedy are worthy of philosophical attention. I examine several likely objections to this claim, yet show that, in the best cases, humor and comedy can be much more than simple entertainment. In sections two and three, I assert that Richard Pryor deserves further scrutiny as the subject of philosophical study.

Comedy and Philosophy

In some segments of academia, especially among analytic philosophers, humor and comedy are typically viewed as trivial and unimportant. There are very few philosophical examinations of humor/comedy, the metaphysical riddles of philosophy notwithstanding. This is so in spite of the fact that Wittgenstein's quip that "a serious and good philosophical work could be written consisting entirely of jokes"[3] was made in earnest.

A close philosophical examination of humor may be warranted by its essential status within the human condition. There are also important questions that can be raised about humor—pertinent issues of linguistic representation and mimesis for example—but also questions about the wider dimension of humor in our lives—e.g., its political and social meaning. What we find humorous is deeply contextual, relying upon shared views on metaphysics, morals, politics, and aesthetics. In attempting to gain knowledge about our world, philosophers may well be overlooking an important yet relatively untapped reserve.

The resistance to the general idea of linking comedy and philosophy is likely to stem from the traditional notions that hold popular culture—i.e., "common" and uncritical knowledge—responsible for convicting Socrates. There is also the notion that philosophy is about higher thoughts and contemplations, and that its application to the mundane strips philosophy of its rigor and purity. The inclusion of the ruminations of comedians and other figures from popular culture as "philosophy" might appear to some traditionalists to stretch the term such that it could apply to almost any topic, thus undermining its legitimacy.

Several responses to this criticism can be made. First, there appears to be an elitist tenor to this line of thinking that runs counter to contemporary scholarship that values the inclusion of multiple perspectives. For example, feminist critiques have examined how and why the viewpoints of persons who do not happen to be male (or still further, not white, propertied males) have been summarily suppressed. Such critiques raise serious questions about the inherent biases and the very legitimacy of philosophy itself. Neither, then, can the arguments and theories offered by a comedian be discounted solely because of his or her profession.

In addition, the force of this criticism rests upon certain confusions. For example, broadening the scope of philosophy does not undermine its roots provided care is taken to preserve the philosophical method and to keep the meaning of philosophy "clear and distinct." Thus, the phrase "the philosophy of Richard Pryor" (or of any popular figure or, for that matter, any non-philosopher) is misleading. It is not analogous to "the philosophy of Immanuel Kant" or "Hume's Philosophy," wherein there is a self-conscious effort to present logically consistent arguments and a body of work. Nor is it the case that "philosophy" takes on its common meaning as a collection of personal reflections or rules by which to live. As I will show, positions that may start out merely as personal anecdote may in fact give rise to important philosophical insight.

Another initial negative reaction in linking humor/comedy and philosophy is likely to stem from the aforementioned characterization of philosophy as "deep," serious, abstract, and complex. By contrast, humor and comedy are "light," sometimes crass, and often simplistic. Thus, the comedian's gifts aside, one may object that comedy as such cannot serve the same purposes as philosophy—i.e., the pursuit and love of wisdom.

Rather, comedy, like a great deal of popular culture, is created and is to be evaluated by its ability to entertain, to make us laugh, to allow us to escape our present workaday concerns. Yet, it is precisely in light of this escapist feature that the connection may be closer than first realized. As developed by such examples as Platonic Forms, or the noumenal/phenomenal distinction, philosophy's popular reputation is one of "otherworldly" concerns. Of course, the escapism encountered in philosophy is not for entertainment purposes—even philosophers may scoff at the arguments and theories of their rivals. But this is simply to suggest a point of connection between the two. I will return to this point later to assert that the critique offered by comedians is analogous to the "ideal observer" found in modern moral and political philosophy.

The belief that popular culture (humor/comedy in particular) is beneath philosophical attention suffers from still further flaws that I will briefly highlight. First, as not every novel, film, or television show will admit to philosophical insight, there is no reason to believe that every instance of comedy would elicit philosophical insight. That is to say, one cannot assume that all comedy as such will provide philosophical insight any more than all poetry or novels will do so. Second, to the degree that comedy relies upon a shared worldview—as reflected in the phrase, "did you ever notice that . . . ?"—our understanding of the world can be revealed through comedy. As for all uses of language, in order to be intelligible, comedy must draw upon a particular relationship between concepts and language. Yet, quite beyond mere understanding, comedy is able to elicit smiles and laughs—or, in cases of unsuccessful attempts at comedy, the visceral reaction of groans and "boos."[4] This ability to elicit such responses is worthy of philosophical investigation, as is the ability to reveal important lessons about political and ethical ideas that we hold at the deepest level. In this regard, comedy has a unique place. The material that we find funny may work to confirm our worldview. In order for the comedian to be intelligible, he or she must have a point of commonality with the audience. Comedian and audience must share the same language, the same social and political leanings.[5] Third, while humor can be found in all human cultures, there are wide differences in its content and expression. Fourth, there are important social and political critiques made through humor. In allowing certain social, political, and cultural conventions to be suspended, comedy affords the audience an opportunity to encounter forbidden topics without the hostility that often accompanies divergent thinking. Much like the philosopher's "thought-experiment," wherein the messy norms and rules of humans can be bracketed, the comedian may propose a social or political ideal, and offer it for the democratic endorsement of his or her audience.[6] This is what Richard Pryor did when he became one of the first American comedians to use as a subject of his comedy the cultural differences between African Americans and whites. Although he painted with a large brush in point-ing out the racial differences between black and white women, churches, funerals, and dealings with the police, in Pryor's hands these com-parisons could be artful and illuminating, rather than the uncritical perpetuation of stereotypes.[7] As Socrates' disciples carried on the task of philosophical investigation, many of Pryor's comedic disciples have car-ried on his deconstruction of stereotypes and use of social/ political themes.[8]

In the Socratic dialogues, hubris is shown to impede reflection and true knowledge. Through his relentless interrogation, Socrates exposed the interlocutor's conceit, which then allowed for true reflection and knowledge. A specific way that comedy provides such "philosophical moments" is in its unique ability to confront hubris and arrogance. Similarly, satirists such as Jonathan Swift, Mark Twain, George Orwell, and even the *South Park* and *Doonesbury* cartoons have all used humor to expose and ridicule such hubris. A common target of comedians is the hubris of politicians and celebrities.[9] Pryor's comedy was replete with examples wherein the arrogant receive their comeuppance, and this in-cluded himself. On his *Live on the Sunset Strip* album, Pryor pokes fun at himself and the infamous incident of setting himself on fire.[10] Self-deprecation also illustrates the moral virtue of humility and ethical con-sistency. Although undermining the hubris of others is important, a more immediate effect of comedy is experienced when it causes us to reflect and reconsider our own positions and biases.

I have pointed out some of the virtues of comedy as a valuable source of social and political critique, but it must be noted that comedy is a double-edged sword. While comedy can lead audiences to critically ex-amine themselves and their society, it can "reward" people for not raising these questions. Comedy that trades on widely held or age-old stereotypes reaffirms those beliefs, if only by rehearsing them in a public forum. Given the relatively recent emphasis upon "political correctness" in American society, the expression of these stereotypes is frowned upon if not outright condemned. Individuals that hold these beliefs must hold them in private, solipsistically, or, at best, with a handful of like-minded friends and family members. However, the comedian as a quasi-authority confirms that the individual is not alone in his or her belief. Thus, any epistemic disconnect between private beliefs and public wisdom, a gap which would often motivate an individual to investigate their beliefs, is narrowed. In this way, comedy is able to perpetuate stereotypes and the attack upon a group's self-respect and self-esteem.

The Janus-faced character of comedy/humor—with the potential to enlighten as well as to debase—highlights the ethical dimension of this art form and emotion. As I argue in more detail below, certain moral limits may be placed on comedy/humor in light of its unique character. These limits can fall to both comedian and audience alike. Of course, the exact nature of these moral limitations will remain controversial. Suffice it to say here, however, that at the very least, comedy/humor may engage not only our intellectual powers, but our moral sensibilities as well. Historically, it is precisely this complexity that is "grist" for the philosopher's "mill."

Pryor as Philosopher

Richard Pryor may at first appear to be an unlikely candidate for philosophical investigation. He did not author any treatises and, as we will see, was often inconsistent in his views. As I mentioned above, however, it is in a person's life story that philosophical insights are often discovered. For most people, philosophical commitments are often held and displayed not through an articulated position, but in what they find troubling or amusing. With Pryor as with some other gifted artists, philosophical insight is to be found in the work itself.

I have noted a similarity between Pryor and Socrates. Skeptics of my view that there are connections between Pryor and philosophy may find of interest certain parallels in the lives of the comedic pioneer and the father of Western philosophy. In pointing out these similarities, I am not attempting to legitimize Pryor or, perhaps more unlikely, make Socrates "hip." Needless to say, neither of these figures stands in any need of legitimacy, for the genius of both, as well as their individual failings, stand (or fall) on their own. However, the similarities and continuities that one finds in the lives of these two individuals—separated by over two thousand years and vastly different cultures—point to enduring elements of the human condition that are worthy of philosophical inquiry.

Even the philosophically uninitiated know of Socrates through the commonly used "Socratic method." In this pedagogical method, which has terrified countless aspiring attorneys, a teacher engages a student, repeatedly questioning and requiring that student to provide support for his or her position. In the face of this challenge and critique, the interlocutor must substitute for "common" or received knowledge their own critical thinking.

In similar fashion, Richard Pryor (and some other comedians) challenged us to perceive the world in a new way. Comedians often lay plain the lack of sense or substance behind many aspects of modern life. Once these flawed foundations are made clear, audiences often have no choice but to laugh, thereby acknowledging that they have been caught up in silly constraints or stereotypes. It is at this point that true knowledge—i.e., critical and self-reflective ratiocination—can begin. Pryor challenged audiences in several ways, beginning with his own unusual life. In his autobiography, Pryor acknowledged his mother's ties to prostitution and that he grew up in his grandmother's brothel.[11] From these morally complex surroundings, he rose to become the "King of Comedy" and the toast of Hollywood. His personal journey included time in the U.S. Army, time in prison, heavy drug use, and being married seven times. His unusual life and his keen powers of observation enabled him to strike a chord and a nerve with America, forcing it to look at large social questions of race and the more tragicomic aspects of the human condition. Though sometimes scathing in his wit, like Mark Twain, he projected a generosity of spirit that sought to unite people beyond their differences. Both men were trenchant social critics who often outraged others.[12] The "public philosophizing" of comedians is not always robust or even consistent, given that its purpose is to entertain, not elevate. Yet, gifted comedians like Pryor draw upon "common knowledge" or "folk knowledge" for their material, and this provides the opportunity to critique widely held beliefs and stereotypes, and to lay bare the underpinnings of collective—i.e., popular—wisdom.

While I cannot examine it fully here, there is a complex history in the comic traditions of African Americans.[13] From the earliest days of this nation, African Americans have been valued for their ability to provide entertainment. Slaves were often called upon to provide a song or a dance for their masters' enjoyment and approval. At the same time, forms of entertainment have afforded African Americans some "escape" from extremely difficult social conditions. Spirituals whose lyrics spoke of brighter days and redemption were an important weapon in combating slavery, Jim Crow, and oppressive conditions. Although Pryor's comedy offered social critique, it also occasionally lapsed into well-worn stereotypes about Asians, women, and the economically deprived. Nevertheless, Pryor navigated these complications better than most comedians. In the next section, I will investigate his particular irreverence and willingness to tackle the most personal issues. For example, his drug use and the (infamous) incident when he set himself on fire became part of his comedy routines. These references were presented as unglamorous falls from grace which were predicted by the alter ego, a "wino" that Pryor often used in his comedy: "Told you you wouldn't amount to nothin' boy."[14] This chastisement is meant to keep Pryor humble and grounded in the human condition.

Pryor's Philosophical Themes

Aside from these general points about the philosophical nature of Pryor's work, what are the specific philosophical issues that arise in the life and work of Richard Pryor? Indeed, as philosophy attempts to investigate and establish general arguments and principles, the philosophical questions that arise in Pryor's work ultimately pertain to the human condition, despite his particular grounding in and inspiration from black American culture and its folkways.[15] The recent work of philosopher Anthony Appiah has raised pertinent questions about cultural ownership.[16] What does it means that Pryor appealed to a large crossover audience? Is his comedy "black" comedy? Beyond this basic question of categorization is the actual content of his work. Here I will focus on notions of authenticity, political considerations, and his use of the "N-word."

Authenticity

The philosophical issues that arise in considering the life and work of Richard Pryor may be broadly understood as matters of *authenticity*. He was widely recognized as an "authentic" voice in African American life, an attribute for which he was praised. Pryor gained widespread acclaim after he stopped emulating the highly successful Bill Cosby and instead found his own comedic voice. In making this decision, he displayed the moral virtues of courage and integrity not just because of the financial disincentive to be original, but because of the risk of rejection by audiences—blacks and whites—uneasy with his new assertive brand of comedy. Can we understand this claim of authenticity and its apparent value as a celebration of an innovative (read: iconoclastic) brand of comedy? Or might Pryor's supposed authenticity contain important moral and political virtues as well?

Popularly speaking, where exactly does Pryor's *authenticity* lie? Although both Pryor and Cosby became icons, there are sharp differences between them. While Cosby's comedy was not based upon culturally specific content, Pryor's authenticity was a matter of both content and *substance* that emerged from a black cultural context. Also, in fashioning his own style (not copying Cosby's), he broke from the mainstream trend in American comedy that rewarded non-threatening images of African Americans.

Pryor's authenticity is celebrated then for several reasons. His decision to remain "true" to himself is consistent with Kant's imperative to value one's own dignity and to develop one's talents. The American social context certainly complicates these ethical directives for many African Americans. Pervasive anti-black racism encourages African Americans to internalize a view that they do not have (or deserve) dignity and that their value (as price) comes as a matter of usefulness to those who do possess dignity (whites). Traditionally, this value has been cashed out as physical labor (slavery) and/or entertainment value. Thus, for African American entertainers (including athletes), there is a historical challenge to view oneself as having dignity. By asserting his autonomy and challenging conventions and stereotypes, Pryor took steps to reclaim his dignity.

These Kantian considerations aside, there are what we may call reasons from *integrity* that lead us to celebrate the life and work of Richard Pryor as well. In style as well as substance, Pryor's public life was not markedly different from his private life. This unity is rare, especially for African Americans. In African American philosophy, much has been made of Du Boisian "double consciousness" and, similarly, Fanon's "mask" that individuals from oppressed groups often wear.[17] Richard Pryor's comedic style attempted to ignore the problem of "double consciousness" inherent in African American life. That is, Pryor was less concerned about the white gaze or acceptance of white audiences and focused more on presenting African American experience as it was truly lived, warts and all. Against this backdrop, an African American who dared to speak in decidedly non-genteel or "blue" language could be viewed as asserting autonomy (if not as crazy for doing so.) As he contended with racism—including racist comedy club owners—his approach was to attack these problems honestly, with a realistic view of African American life rather than a mythic, hyper-noble depiction of this community. This decision displayed the virtue of courage, and Pryor's approach touched the "golden mean" between the "vices" of stereotypical portrayals of blacks (deficiency) and heroic valorization (excess); real lives are somewhere in between.

For all of its merits, the celebration of Pryor's authenticity is not without its problems. Earlier, I pointed out the two-edged nature of comedy, and given the provocative nature of many elements in his work, we might ask, at what price is authenticity valued and celebrated? The imperative to develop one's talents is regarded as having certain moral limitations (advocates of various forms of egoism may contest this). Under liberalism, the limit is drawn by "harm to others" such that an individual may do as he or she pleases without interference or moral sanction so long as he or she does not harm the (non-competitive) interests of others.

These questions may provide a particular context in which to examine the ongoing liberalism versus communitarian debate. The African American comic who chafes at or rails against certain restrictions placed upon his or her comedy may, broadly speaking, represent the liberal point of view. On this view, the autonomy of individuals takes center stage, and no restrictions can be placed upon the individual unless it can be demonstrated that there is a substantive harm to others (Millian approach), that the comedy (both its style and substance) does not properly accord dignity to human beings, who, by their rational capacities, are "ends-in-themselves" (Kantian approach). Comedians and musical artists will often deny that they are attacking the character or self-respect of anyone in particular or making a blanket assessment of all individuals of a particular group.

Political Considerations

Given the American social context described above, Pryor's comedy and particularly the assertive, unapologetic exercise of his autonomy can be (and was) taken as symbolic of group self-pride and self-respect. His popularity coincided with similar unapologetic autonomous acts by sports figures—Muhammad Ali refusing the military draft and Tommie Smith and John Carlos giving the Black Power salute at the 1968 Olympics—and by musical artists who dealt with race and injustice, such as Nina Simone and Curtis Mayfield. An evaluation of Pryor and his work must bear in mind the specific political context in which he lived. From above, Aristotle pointed out that the development of virtue is sensitive to context—the "Golden Mean" is not arithmetical, but contextual—and a full assessment of Pryor cannot be made otherwise.

Insofar as Pryor can be viewed as a symbolic figure, the question is: did Pryor (and by extension, other African American artists with wide popularity and acclaim) have a moral obligation to speak to racial issues?

In his famous 1926 "Criteria of Negro Art" article, Du Bois famously remarked that: "all Art is propaganda and ever must be, despite the wailing of the purists. I stand in utter shamelessness and say that whatever art I have for writing has been used always for propaganda for gaining the right of black folk to love and enjoy. I do not care a damn for any art that is not used for propaganda."[18] For Du Bois, art was a means to an end, to uncover and speak Truth. In turn, Du Bois believed (perhaps naively) that Truth would serve the interest of bringing about Justice. Pryor's work presented a challenge to any simplified position on this issue. As I pointed out above, his acclaim as an "authentic" voice can be traced in part to his competent use of the African American vernacular. Yet, this tradition also contains certain problematic elements—compromised group self-respect and morally dubious views of women and gays to take two examples— which, in Pryor's popularity, were further endorsed and perpetuated. Thus, as feminists have pointed out, the assertive reclamation or development of a voice is not the sole consideration in assessing the moral and/or political value of acts of authentic defiance.[19] It remains to be seen how best to account for these intuitions, whether liberalism's "Harm Principle" may temper this drive toward authenticity, or if a communitarian or some other approach best explains these "riders." Still further, if the artist carries this special burden in light of his or her accessibility, Du Bois and other advocates of these "special obligations" face difficult questions. Would less successful artists (read: less commercial) be under any less obligation? How to account for the vicissitudes of art and popular culture? If, to avoid these complications, the special obligation is placed on all artists, why are artists singled out?

It is an empirical question whether Pryor's comedy brought American blacks and whites closer together—thereby lessening racial animosity and improving the general social conditions that African Americans faced. Yet, if in fact Pryor's work had this effect, we must remain mindful that Pryor's "propaganda" may have worked in two directions. The narrowing of the cultural gap between two large groups may have been accomplished through ridicule and, thus, at the expense of the dignity of certain individuals or subgroups.

These constraints on individual artistic expression (particularly of the more popular and accessible artists) present a delicate balancing act between the venerable freedom of expression, artistic integrity, and harm to others. In this way, groundbreaking talents and artists often force us to rethink the age-old individual versus society debate that has taken center stage in Western political philosophy for centuries. Matters are complicated even further by the plasticity of language; words and phrases that are insults in one context are terms of endearment in another context. Perhaps no word has received more attention than the N-word, a word Pryor used quite liberally for much of his career. In fact, a great deal of the use of the N-word in contemporary popular culture—most notably, in music (i.e., hip hop) and comedy—can be traced to Pryor himself. Thus, the current debate about the use of this particular word may benefit from a careful consideration of the issues manifested by Pryor's decision to use (and then, to stop using) the N-word.

The N-Word

Randall Kennedy has noted that the development of the N-word into a racial epithet has been tortuous.[20] From its Latin origin *niger,* meaning "black," the particular development of this word highlights the plasticity of language. Yet, a great deal of the current debate over the N-word fails to consider the critical distinction between *meaning* and *reference* that is central to the philosophy of language. What we mean to convey or communicate by the use of a term—a meaning—relies upon a system of reference, with certain rules governing proper use. It is often claimed that what Pryor (and other African Americans) mean by the N-word is something quite different from what many or most non-blacks mean or could mean.

For example, one may contrast the recent use of the N-word by white comedian Michael Richards (of the popular television show *Seinfeld*) with its use by Richard Pryor and many other African American comedians (Chris Rock and Dave Chappelle are two current examples.) In Richards's case, the word was meant to insult two African American audience members. Richards's intention is manifested by his other comments: "Fifty years ago we'd have you upside down with a fuckin' fork up your ass."[21] Given the history of the word, the default use of the N-word is meant to insult or belittle. Thus Richards, without qualifying his remarks in any way or somehow indicating an unconventional use of the word, drew upon the traditional meaning of the N-word to convey disdain and disrespect for the two audience members. It is this disrespectful attitude that was (or should have been) morally condemned.

By contrast, Pryor's use is not meant to insult, castigate, or injure. That is, Pryor's *intent* is not to harm, but rather to mirror the African American vernacular. One can argue that the use of the N-word by African Americans themselves demonstrates the depths of compromised group self-respect made even worse by the intellectual machinations by those who would defend this usage. Others have suggested that the appropriation of the N-word by African Americans represents linguistic resistance to anti-black ideology. Admittedly, there are fine distinctions to be drawn. Can the context argument be stretched to cover all uses of the N-word by non-blacks? As the intention behind a person's words is not always clear, does the shift to consider intention mark a "cop-out?" The moral condemnation that one faces by use of the word must then await further determination, as one can always claim that it was not one's intent to insult ("I did not mean anything by it. I was only repeating a lyric," etc., etc.) This issue has become more complicated in the forty years since Pryor first shocked his audiences. His defiant exercise of autonomy must be tempered by sober reflection of political, psychological, and linguistic issues central to the African American experience.

Politics

Pryor's work vexed both the African American assimilationist and nationalist alike, even as many in these various camps roared with (sometimes uneasy) laughter at his ruminations on social and political themes. The visceral reaction to his comedy lends credence to his contention that humor can cut through all of that: racism, sexism, and here, political ideologies. As I have argued, his early unrepentant stance on the "N-word" forces people—most particularly, the African American community—to engage in philosophizing. Because his comedy rang true for a large segment of the African American community, dogmatic or doctrinaire critiques of his comedy are not sufficient. Pryor's work expressed the concerns of real people in their vernacular, although use of the vernacular is neither necessary nor sufficient to adequately represent the concerns of the specific group. Pryor denied that he was speaking for others—just "calling it as I see it," he said. Thus, his work raises important questions about social and political authenticity. The *authenticity question* remains a central issue in contemporary African American culture and philosophy: who, if anyone, speaks for this or any other politically and socially disadvantaged group? Under systems of representative democratic states, establishing authenticity is important for determining political legitimacy, to say nothing of the personal dimension of leading an authentic life.

In his influential work, Bernard Boxill has proposed and examined two traditions in African American political thought: the assimilationist/accommodationist and the revolutionary/separatist.[22] Although the separatist tradition appears to have lost adherents, this tradition is kept alive via the revolutionary stance taken by cultural nationalists and some hip hop/rap artists. Such artists often answer the assimilationist, often bourgeoisie, by suggesting that their lyrics are simply "keepin' it real." The lyrics are defended in light of the reflection they offer of real life—or better, the life of a certain subset of African Americans. Chuck D of the rap group Public Enemy famously declared that "rap music is Black America's CNN." By this approach, the popularly discussed authenticity of rap music resides in the ability to accurately reflect the world rather than in the ability to reflect an ideal vision, or even merely in self-expression.

Although this "keepin'-it-real" versus moral uplift debate in African American art has remained a central concern in African American political philosophy, the modern guise of this perennial debate can be traced to Richard Pryor.[23] His use of the "N-word" was an affront to those concerned to demonstrate the moral rectitude of black people. In this regard, his comedy also reflects certain class sensibilities and fissures. An unintended effect of his comedy leads African Americans to rethink certain allegiances: to the poor, the role and status of women, the gay community, etc. In a negative way, he leads us to refine our thinking about the intersection of race, class, and gender.

Pryor cited a visit to Africa as the catalyst behind that which protests by bourgeois African American organizations could not do: namely, his decision to stop using the N-word. By Pryor's own words:

> In Africa, I saw people of all colors and shapes. See any niggers? All the acts I've been doing as an artist. That is a devastating . . . word. It has nothing to do with us. 'Cause we're all family that's it jack 'cause it don't mean anything but some cash.[24]

In this quote, he provided a lesson of self-esteem as well as a proto-Marxian critique on the genesis of racism. Given his enormous popularity, his decision turned out to be a dramatic affirmation of the connections between American blacks and Africa. Although these connections —of history, heritage, folkways, and the like—are now valued and celebrated by African Americans, this has not always been the case for the majority of this population. A great deal has been written about the Euro-American effort to deny Africa and Africans any technological, cultural, or intellectual importance for world civilization. This erasure was an important tool in the justification of white supremacy and has been in place since the inception of American history.

Yet, Pryor's "turn" presents certain philosophical questions. What exactly is the nature of this connection between a people and a legacy? The recent work of Anthony Appiah questions this connection, particularly in light of the cosmopolitanism he celebrates and endorses. Evidently for Pryor, it was the opportunity to witness African achievement firsthand that was sufficient to prompt racial pride. The development of this pride seems to give short shrift to the numerous differences between African Americans and Africans, or even the differences between Africans themselves (North Africa and sub-Saharan Africa, East Africa and West Africa, Ibo and Zulu, etc.). This makes Pryor's "turn" seem simplistic and overly romantic.

Special Moral Obligations

The question of special obligations can be raised with Richard Pryor, not only in light of his art, but in light of his wealth and popular appeal. As with most "stars," Pryor's life was intensely scrutinized, a great deal of his private life made public. There are a number of general philosophical questions that can be raised here: the value of privacy and the acceptable trade-off between fame and privacy to name but two. However, a question that is particularly important for African American philosophy also emerges: namely, what if any are the obligations of those African Americans who are well-off to those who are not? For present purposes, I am construing "well-off" in a wide sense, referring to financial wealth as well as social or cultural capital—i.e., fame. Students of African American history and philosophy will know that this question was famously articulated by W. E. B. DuBois well over a hundred years ago. This debate is perhaps all the more important in contemporary times for several reasons. First, the idea of "African American" is contested. As the idea of "race" itself has become widely contested, this metaphysical paradigm shift will undoubtedly affect our moral and political thinking.

Conclusion

As this essay has shown, the life and work of Richard Pryor present several opportunities for critical philosophical engagement, despite some of the limitations of his "common knowledge" themes and self-contradictions. For those philosophers guided by Marx's famous assertion that "the philosophers have only described the world, in various ways, the point is to change it," the engagement with "common knowledge"[25] can be fruitful. The distinction between the real and what are merely shadows requires critical engagement with popular culture despite the reluctance some philosophers may encounter.

NOTES

1. Aristophanes, *The Clouds*, trans. Jeffrey Henderson (Newburyport, Mass.: Focus Publishing, 1993).

2. See, for example, the Popular Culture and Philosophy Series from Open Court Publishing (Chicago): *The Sopranos and Philosophy: I Kill Therefore I Am,* ed. Richard Greene and Peter Vernezze (2004), and *Buffy the Vampire Slayer and Philosophy: Fear and Trembling in Sunnydale,* ed. James B. South (2003).

3. Norman Malcolm, *Ludwig Wittgenstein: A Memoir* (London: Oxford University Press, 1958).

4. The ability of comedy to elicit emotion may be part of a larger philosophical issue of how to explain the connection between emotion and fiction. See Robert Yanal, *Paradoxes of Emotion and Fiction* (University Park: Pennsylvania State University Press, 1999), and Kendall Walton, "Fearing Fictions," *The Journal of Philosophy* 75, no. 1 (January 1978): 5–27.

5. When I speak of sharing the same social/political leanings or orientations, I mean in a general way. There are certainly degrees, but also limits—a Jon Stewart or Chris Rock might not fare well at a Republican Party dinner, for example. The humor or lack thereof is a matter of their political leanings; to the degree that these do not emerge in the comedy act, audiences may still find the comedian funny. Here it would be interesting to examine what audiences of all types would find humorous—the "war between the sexes" is an obvious choice—and the biases and stereotypes that pervade the culture.

6. For example, the political philosophy of John Rawls and its reliance upon a "veil of ignorance" to determine general principles of justice allows for reflective comparison between current conditions and ideal theory. John Rawls, *A Theory of Justice* (Cambridge, Mass.: Belknap, 2005).

7. It should be noted that Pryor was particularly bold in offering a critique of race, both in the content of his routines as well as his style. In many of his stand-up routines, Pryor would make comments about the white people in the audience. Thus, not only did Pryor invert prevailing social norms in which people were not to talk about race at all, but the very venues in which these discussions were held were places in which racial hierarchies were discarded; no one was above a good-natured ribbing. Of course, not all of Pryor's attempts at transgression were successful. Below, I will discuss respect and political correctness. Here I only want to point out the *opportunities* of transgressive critique afforded to the comedian and to Richard Pryor in particular.

8. For example, Dave Chappelle frequently explores the meaning of race in his comedy. Throughout *Chappelle's Show,* Chappelle examines the ignorance of racist views through a blind African American racist, Clayton Bigsby. In this vignette, white adolescents exult in being called "niggers" by an African American, which only increases their "street credibility." Yet, this "street credibility" comes from a person who cannot see, which only highlights our own blindness in holding such things as important.

9. The recent proliferation of the comedy/newscast—the *Daily Show* is perhaps the most famous example—routinely pokes fun at political figures. While it is a matter of some debate whether the blurring of the line between comedy and news—or of entertainment and news—enriches or impoverishes political debate and engagement in the United States, it is clear that comedians are merciless when hubris is detected.

10. Richard Pryor, "Africa," *Live on the Sunset Strip*, "*. . . And It's Deep Too!" The Complete Warner Bros. Recordings (1968–1992)*, disc 7 (Warner Bros., 2000).

11. Richard Pryor with Todd Gold, *Pryor Convictions, and Other Life Sentences* (New York: Pantheon, 1995).

12. Lawrence J. Wilker, http://www.kennedy-center.org/programs/specialeven ts/marktwain/

13. See Mel Watkins, *On the Real Side: A History of African American Comedy* (Chicago: Lawrence Hill Books, 1999).

14. Pryor, "Wino," *Live on the Sunset Strip*.

15. See Pryor with Gold, *Pryor Convictions*.

16. See *Cosmopolitanism: Ethics in a World of Strangers* (New York: W. W. Norton, 2006); Randall Kennedy, *Nigger: The Strange Career of a Troublesome Word* (New York: Pantheon Books, 2002). For more on the debate of African American identity and cosmopolitanism, see Paul Taylor, "Appiah's Uncompleted Argument: W. E. B. Du Bois and the Reality of Race," *Social Theory and Practice* 26, no. 1 (Spring 2000).

17. Frantz Fanon, "The Fact of Blackness," chap. 5 of *Black Skin, White Masks* (New York: Grove Press, 1967).

18. W. E. B. Du Bois, *Writings* (New York: Library of America, 1987), 1000. Notably, both Frederick Douglass and W. E. B. Du Bois raised this concern for African American art and artists. As an example see Du Bois, "The Sorrow Songs," in *The Souls of Black Folk* in *Writings*, 536–546.

19. The work of African American feminists is particularly important here, as African American women have grappled with both the anti-black racism and the pervasive sexism of American politics and culture. The "authenticity" of blacks and women may leave intact the respective sexism and racism of these groups. See bell hooks, *Ain't I a Woman: Black Women and Feminism* (Boston: South End Press, 1981); Patricia Hill Collins, *Black Feminist Thought: Knowledge, Consciousness, and the Politics of Empowerment* (Boston: Unwin Hyman, 1990); and Michele Wallace, *Black Macho and the Myth of the Superwoman* (New York: Dial, 1979).

20. Randall Kennedy, *Nigger: The Strange Career of a Troublesome Word* (New York: Pantheon Books, 2002).

21. http://www.youtube.com/watch?v=-T7vkvpzVXI (accessed November 2007).

22. Bernard Boxill, "Two Traditions in African-American Political Philosophy," in *African-American Perspectives and Philosophical Traditions*, ed. John Pittman (New York: Routledge, 1996).

23. For more on historical themes in African American comedy see Watkins, *On the Real Side*.

24. Pryor, "Africa."

25. Karl Marx, *Theses on Feuerbach, Collected Works of Karl Marx* (New York: International Publishers, 1975).

7 When Keeping It Real Goes Wrong

PRYOR, CHAPPELLE, AND THE COMEDIC POLITICS OF THE POST-SOUL[1]

TYRONE R. SIMPSON

> So if I wasn't like those people on TV, what did that make me? Where did I fit
> in?   —Richard Pryor[2]

> What would a black man be without his paranoia?
>   —Dave Chappelle[3]

In his attempt to elucidate the angst-ridden, media-saturated epoch we have come to know as postmodernism, Jean-François Lyotard assigns culpability for the day's representational dilemmas to the aggressions of capitalism and the extent to which intense systems of commodification have "derealized" our social condition. Lyotard laments:

> Capitalism in itself has such a capacity to derealize familiar objects,
> social roles, and institutions that so-called realist representations can
> no longer evoke reality except through nostalgia and derision—as an
> occasion for suffering rather than satisfaction.[4]

This idea that exploitation and profit imperatives, if allowed to reign for centuries, would somehow cause us to become alienated from that which makes us most human, would not have taken Western intellectuals by such surprise—indeed would not have occasioned Lyotard's explanatory treatise here—if they had studied with seriousness the derealizing effects that enslavement and colonialism wreaked upon Europe's colored Others. If sometime before the late 1960s these theorists had reckoned with the complaints of the Injun, the coolie, the slave, or the wetback (or if, in a more parochial moment, Europe's own weary white proletariat), they would have encountered how readily the Real evaporates before the compulsions constellated around meeting the economic bottom line.

For one example, race theorists from Phyllis Wheatley to James Baldwin have insisted that the manufacture of the social identity "black," in the American context, was an early, devastating attempt to banish the

Real. In its desperate attempt to prepare African bodies for forced un-compensated labor, the slavery regime cobbled together clans and tribes to make this representational category coherent and logical. From the moment such a moniker was bestowed, "black" people have been clam-oring about this derealizing gesture, screaming in strident tones that important knowledge about themselves, about the world, had been sac-rificed to the discursive emergence of this descriptive term. This loss was only exacerbated by the attributes—primitive, licentious, criminal, frivo-lous—assigned to their character and bodies by means of the overly capacious label. It is no surprise then that Henry Louis Gates has found "signifying" to be a productive staple of black expressive culture. Revis-ing "received sign[s]" was not merely a habit dwelling within the rich reservoir of African cosmology, it was one that was coerced into exercise almost immediately upon African encounters with Europe's imprecise vocabulary and the systems of exploitation that such language enabled.[5]

To assert then that the postmodern condition beset Europe's Others well before Western intellectuals espied the crisis or that these Others have been mourning the passing of the Real far in advance of Lyotard or that the existential injunction organizing much of African American cultural action is that of "representin'" or "keeping it real" at all costs, should hardly cause the casual observer consternation. With the juridical barriers of segregation dissolved, thus enabling blacks to insinuate them-selves into the marketplace and thus more willfully orchestrate their own commodification, the plea to "keep it real" serves as community caution-ary tale and a code of ethics just as poignantly as grandmama's directive not to "go up to them people's place and act the fool." In an attempt to brave the commodifying corridors of postmodernism and collect a small piece of global capital's bounty for themselves, blacks are understandably anxious of being derealized as their predecessors were. Will we force the marketplace to reckon with our humanity while it commands our labor, or allow our spirit, skins, and souls to be reified into a version of black-ness that flatters power and corroborates the global order?

If we accept the spiritual convulsions that marked the careers of Richard Pryor and Dave Chappelle, then the arena of black comedy reveals itself as a site uniquely vexed by this representational conundrum. It is not merely that the comic is asked to submit his/her body and muse to a gaze that is sometimes white; it is that such a gaze—not yet graduated from the seductive pleasure of minstrelsy—is often carnivorous and de-humanizing. That is, the black comedian, when he enfolds himself in the antic disposition that the stage requests, is not readily viewed as clever and shrewd. The black's laughter-provoking material is seen not as a product of wit, but rather, as other forms of black genius have been, as a serendipitous orchestration of the body. The craft must be epidermalized, morphed involuntarily into a Stepin' Fetchit trick (dare I say derealized?) before it can be considered comestible and rapaciously consumed by its whitelike audiences.[6] The treachery of this gaze is certainly palpable to Jack Schiffman, son of the former owner of the Apollo Theatre, who claims that viable black comedy would require the immense concession that "blacks did, in fact, possess intelligence and the ability to think."[7] When to the pressure of confirming black cerebral activity one adds the possibility that the comic may wish to articulate resentment or disdain for the society for which he performs, the hazard of the comedic practice aggrandizes and is made bare.

This essay meditates on the art of both Pryor and Chappelle not merely because audacious social criticism was a commonplace among their comic performances, but because their similarities are too striking to resist juxtaposition. In their formative years, both artists witnessed how oppression profoundly registered its impact on black life. Pryor was raised in a brothel in Peoria, Illinois, while Chappelle witnessed the crack cocaine epidemic of the Reagan-Bush years in Washington, D.C. Both comedians found in mass culture, television in particular, the raw materials from which to cull their humor. As latch-key children of the postwar period, they fed their imaginations on the mythos television pawned off to its watchers as true and mourned the fact that blacks seemed perpetually excluded from the fantasy-life the medium purveyed. The two artists at a certain point in their careers sought to redress these exclusions by hosting their own respective sketch-comedy television series; the elder in 1977, the younger between 2003 and 2005. This forum, as opposed to stand-up or film, ultimately proved itself inhospitable to both artists, moving Pryor and Chappelle to quit production enigmatically and leave behind lucrative contracts that befuddled their fans and proponents. And most profoundly, this duo of comedic dynamos both suffered an artistic identity crisis that compelled their hiatus from professional life for a brief period. The malaise that afflicted them can be fairly diagnosed as the angst of "keeping it real," and protecting what they construed as their pure comic and political voice from forces that sought to discipline or corrupt it.

Not surprisingly, the aforementioned parallels between Pryor and Chappelle have caught the attention of critics and other observers, who have begun to knit the artists into the same comedic cloth. Most recently,

Bambi Haggans, in her fine magisterial work on post-war black comedians, entitled *Laughing Mad*, deems the artists to be phenomena of the same cultural epoch that she describes as "Post-Soul." Leaning on the critical work of Mark Anthony Neal, Haggans understands both Pryor and Chappelle as black folks

> who came to maturity in the age of Reaganomics and experienced the change from urban industrialism to de-industrialism, from segregation to desegregation, from essential notions of blackness to meta-narratives on blackness, without any nostalgic allegiance to the past . . . but firmly in grasp of the existential concerns of his brave new world.[8]

Indisputably both Pryor and Chappelle were/are forward-looking, post-industrial, racial anti-essentialists of the first order whose comedic practice rigorously interrogates what it means to be black amidst the hyper-commercialized milieu of post-apartheid America. Yet I would like to take issue with the slight historical slippage that Haggans's post-Soul conceptualization commits, and point to this misapprehension as crucial to understanding the political output of both artists. Pryor's maturity as an artist is not contemporary to the rise of Reaganism, and his fortuitous temporal escape from the backlash populism of American whiteness that came with the movement differentiates his work in television from that of the younger comic. In fact, it is important to take seriously the decision of Trey Ellis, one of the early theorists of the post-Soul, to identify Richard Pryor as a *progenitor* rather than contemporary practitioner of this comedic genre. In praising Pryor's "molten parodies of black life on his early albums and short lived television show, [which] all helped forge . . . [the] aesthetic," Ellis draws attention to the comic's courage in critiquing performances of resistant blackness and nationalism at a time when the Black Power movement had done everything possible to sacralize blackness, bumptiousness, and racial difference.[9] I argue herein, then, by means of close reading of the comics' public statements and the "unconscious" of their television sketches, that "keeping it real" meant different things for the two comedians, making their respective politics appear anachronistic and timely at the same time. Invested in challenging the racial exclusions of U.S. mediascapes, and of their society more broadly, *The Richard Pryor Special* and *The Richard Pryor Show* embraced an openness to coalitional politics—rather than to a black nationalism with which they were concomitant—that fails to animate Pryor's comedic successor. Having witnessed the depredations of Reaganomic policies on black life and observed a new wave of aggression under a second Bush regime, Chappelle's eponymous television series inclines toward cultural nationalism as a response to the realization that the promise for a more racially just society is being consciously antagonized, if not withdrawn.

"My Eyes Didn't See Any One Color": Pryor's Berkeley-Born Aesthetic

The multiple eulogies paid to Richard Pryor in the past two years are primarily due to the avant-gardism he brought to his trade. It was not merely that Pryor brought courage and candor to his work, but that doing so meant insinuating a sobering eddy of subaltern life into the American mainstream. Early in his career, when success, money, drug addiction, marital disharmony, and legal difficulty all took hold of the comedian with equal speed and vigor, Pryor recognized what would become once and for all his artistic inspiration. In his memoir, the comic admits:

> I saw myself as a victim of the system, an outsider for whom justice was out of reach, a dream, and then I saw how closely my situation mirrored the black man's larger struggle for dignity and equality, and justice in white society. That was me. I was that character. That was the person to whom I had to give voice.[10]

These comments make clear that the zeitgeist of black disenchantment and resistance that consumed the globe in the late 1960s had swept up the comic in its maelstrom. Yet this new political conviction could not survive the powerful, often intolerant, distillation process that sustains the institution of American television. Though Pryor made this political restiveness most explicitly manifest in his stand-up performances and comedy albums, his pro-black sensibility took the form of rewriting the myths that constituted contemporary American culture and challenging their authority over how its consumers saw the world.[11] During his brief tenure as variety-show auteur on television—a one-hour special on May 5, 1977, and four other variety hours taking place on the Tuesdays between September 13th and October 20th of the same year—comedy sketches such as "Star Wars Bar," "Titanic," or "Jekyll and Hyde" would revise major cultural narratives, such as a movie, a technological catastrophe, or a fictional icon, respectively, and insert a black character, normally played by Pryor, as central to and often critical of the experience's mythic standing.[12] Though we may look at such narrative interventions as minor in comparison with the more confrontational content of Pryor's stand-up material, we must keep in mind that staging these correctives on television to an integrating America in 1977 was, as critic Harold Cruse might concur, "truly and effectively radical." By carving out a space for blackness in the American imaginary in this way, Pryor "present[ed] a definitive critique of the entire cultural apparatus" of the nation.[13]

As important as acknowledging this crucial artistic contribution in Pryor's televisual work, however, is the idea that the comic's recognition that he had a share in black existential discomfort and that he should ventriloquize this unrest in his work was indeed a *recognition*—possibly a late one—that he made as an early adult. Previous to this new devotion, Pryor, similar to another icon of the sixties, Malcolm X, was preoccupied with escaping the harsh circumstances that accompanied black life—to the point at which assimilating into American whiteness seemed like the only viable alternative. Pryor suggests this much in reflecting upon his childhood decision to de-racialize himself and adds:

> In my imagination, I gave myself a new identity. I called myself Sun the Secret Prince. As Sun the Secret Prince, I was colorless. I was just light and energy, caroming off the planets. No boundaries. Simply alive. (16)

In the same section of his memoir, Pryor includes one of his quips about "always want[ing] to be something different than a nigger . . ." He also remarks upon once watching and becoming bemused by the sitcom "Father Knows Best," because the characters in the show lived so pleasantly—and thus differently from his family and the other black people he encountered. What I am trying to suggest by highlighting Pryor's self-reflections here is that his childhood started him on an assimilative journey that placed limits on the prospects of his comedic muse becoming a nationalistic one. These limits, which led Pryor to unabashedly ape the vanilla everyman comedy of Bill Cosby in his early professional years, I will argue further, were calcified by another formative moment in his early career: his exile to and ethnography of Berkeley, California.

In 1970 (seven years before his ascension to television host), according to Pryor, he and the man who became his beloved friend and colleague, Paul Mooney,[14] left Las Vegas, the performance mecca in which Pryor's drug-induced behavior had rendered him persona non grata, for northern California in order to "shed the phony image [of himself he]'d created" (96) and "find [his] lost soul" (115). The comic claims that he "[did]n't know why" he wanted to go to Berkeley, but did so because "[he] had it in [his] head" (114). A cursory sense, however, of life and culture in the region at the time may explain why a young/black male adult would flee there to find a more dynamic and political sense of self.

With the help of the mass media and then Governor Ronald Reagan, Berkeley had established itself by 1970 as the home of the American counterculture. It hosted the anti-establishmentarian escapism of Beat writers Gary Snyder and Allen Ginsberg (it was notably the birthplace of the latter's canonized poetic primal scream, "Howl" [1956]), and granted sanctuary to the disaffected bohemians, some of whom had migrated from the north of San Francisco, who came to be known as the "hippies." In the arena of explicit politics, Berkeley was the site of organized youth resistance, starting with the Free Speech Movement in 1964, the emergence of the Black Panther Party in nearby Oakland in 1966, the confrontation with the police and the university over People's Park in 1969, and the strike against the conservative Euro-curriculum of San Francisco State University by the multi-ethnic Third World Liberation Front. In his autobiography, *Pryor Convictions*, Pryor describes what he found when he arrived at Berkeley with rhetorical flourish:

> Among my discoveries in Berkeley was an extremely passionate, highly charged, supersophisticated [sic] renaissance of black intellectual, artistic, and political activity. It was fueled by the minds and fervor of stars like activist Angela Davis and novelist Ishmael Reed, who were smart, proud, committed . . . and uncompromisingly black. (117)

In an atmosphere that brazenly had annihilated convention and in its place exalted personal experimentation, adventure, and dissidence as its organizing ethos, Pryor honed his comedic craft by immersing himself in black radical thought and quotidian life. Not only did Pryor spend his underground hiatus reading recursively a copy of the late Malcolm X's speeches and making Marvin Gaye's countercultural ballad, "What's Going On," his own internal mantra, but, as Mel Watkins tells it, "[Richard also] went to the ghetto and started studying people."[15] This ethnographic practice enabled the comic to conjure up the underworld plots and personages of his old Peoria neighborhood. The mental amalgamation of black experience in both Peoria and Berkeley would be the raw materials from which the comic could invent a more fearless, candid, and utterly more black version of Richard Pryor. This was indeed the result. But the tutorial in radicalism and subalternity did not lead to nationalism. This, I believe, is partially because Northern California boasted a political culture that, though it unquestionably empowered blacks to articulate and act upon their grievances, was firmly built on the idea of coalition. Historian W. J. Rorabaugh explains:

> Here was the paradox: the strength of the liberal coalition and of biracial community ventures in Berkeley made it difficult for blacks to articulate a position of Black Power. Power in Berkeley was destined to be shared through a coalition rather than through any claim to exclusive use of power[, though] the black need to escape the suffocation of white benevolence was just as great in Berkeley as in the rest of Black America.[16]

Simultaneously incendiary and stultifying, Berkeley coalitional politics impressed upon the young comic that talk about a black freedom struggle must be accompanied by talk of other progressive sociopolitical causes. Black Power, then, was a vital, yet modest portion of a larger radical piece. This perspective fit rather nicely with Pryor's ideological propensities preceding his flight to northern California. In his memoir, the comic explains that though he was a contemporary of Malcolm X, he was not adequately familiar with the Muslim leader to have an opinion of him. It took his comedic godfather, Redd Foxx, to explain Malcolm's incandescence, particularly, the idea that the leader's political thought culminated in a commitment to multi-racial justice. Pryor confessed that "after Redd introduced me to him as a person and what he stood for, I missed him terribly" (99).

Motivated by Malcolm X, then, Pryor would not allow black life and the injustices that shaped it to be the sole inspirations for his comedic repertoire. In his memoir, the chapter on his sojourn at Berkeley notably concludes the narrative's first part (hinting at the benchmark significance of the experience). He testifies that after almost a year in the area in 1970, "he just felt full," with a sense of "Richard Pryor the person" (121). He was now prepared to "go back" to his audiences and "tell [them] the truth." He also includes among these culminating remarks the quip, "I could be a revolutionary, but I like white women" (121). The ribald flouting of contemporary racial and sexual taboo aside, the comment signals Pryor's squeamishness when facing the spectre of nationalism and his deeper comfort with a more ecumenical view of political progressivism.[17] This coalitional perspective would ensure that the black cause would not be the only one he championed during his remarkable foray into television comedy in 1977.

Though Pryor articulated his terms of engagement with televisual comedy by having John Belushi pull him out of the hull of a slave ship for the purposes of "going to NBC . . . to do his own special" or by having

Maya Angelou perform an Emmy-calibre soliloquy as a despairing but resigned spouse of the local drunkard (played by Pryor), for our purposes, the most striking sketches of the hour-long special that NBC aired on May 5, 1977, occurred in the special's latter third. The plot unifying the episode was literally pedestrian: Pryor, playing himself, perambulating through the studio corridors toward the stage where he was to begin the live performance that would open the much-anticipated show. But in a meta-textual fashion that has become a hallmark of postmodern cultural production, the host's travel from studio door to stage becomes epic and thus proceeds to constitute the entirety of the show itself. In a clear homage to all of the people and experiences that somehow contributed to him being finally contracted as a network star, Pryor meets several personalities on his way to the proscenium, poised to importune him with "ideas for the show," among them La Wanda Page (as the piously charismatic Aunt Esther of *Sanford and Son*), the affable but no-nonsense Shirley Hemphill (performing as her character by the same first name from the sitcom *What's Happening*), and actor Glynn Thurman (as a hustler who resembles some of the characters featured in the film *Cooley High* [1975], in which he starred). These scenes/personages, however, are not as important as the two black male children who accost Pryor late in his journey. Reminding the host that in television he has "a unique vehicle" at his disposal that he would be wise to employ for "meaningful expression," the two boys join a multicultural coterie of seven other children to perform a musical sketch entitled "This World Was Made for All Men." The masculinism in the message notwithstanding, these singing and dancing children provide a multiethnic spectacle that anticipates the diversity initiatives that elite and academic progressives would embrace in the early 1980s as remedies to past social invisibility and disenfranchisement. In a funky ballet of pre-adolescent cuteness, the young players recant the titular refrain alongside verses that cite historical facts about the United States often lost on the lay viewer. We are reminded that Native Americans have an original claim to the country's land and learn that East Asian labor is responsible for the nation's railways. The sketch couldn't be more explicit: it is Pryor speaking through the mouths of babes, encouraging his "family hour" audience to simultaneously reclaim the innocence and garner the maturity necessary to recognize the very human claims several ethnicities have on the progress of the nation. The preacherly tone is hardly hidden.

This puerile sermon becomes more conspicuous because of the sketch that follows it. In "Writer's Block," a group of Black Power radicals, bedizened in all the militaristic regalia that made the Panthers mesmerizing, corner Pryor and propose a script that "reveals the black man's plight in America" and that "for the first time showcases black unity, dignity, and pride." Noticeably uncomfortable with the situation, Pryor hears out the intimidating band of pitchmen, and expresses his discomfort with their angle by noting that the concept sounds "real heavy" and hardly funny. The comic forecloses the matter by claiming disingenuously that he already has the show planned out. The radicals refuse to take no for an answer, threaten his pets if he fails to perform their script verbatim, and elect to physically march Pryor out to the stage to begin the show just to ensure that he does their bidding. The scene and thus the *Special* itself conclude ironically with Pryor out on the stage, singing the sacred anthem of American performance culture, "There's No Business like Show Business."

From this sequence, Pryor leaves no question about his uneasiness with black nationalism. The entire *Special* is built on curious characters making suggestions to Pryor, posturing as television novice, yet none of these sketches earn the name of "Writer's Block." Black nationalism, however, in the form of an irresistible and violent political polemic, is cast as an impediment to comedic creativity. Far from sharing the youthful yet savvy optimism of the child performers, or Pryor himself, black nationalism appears to be too serious, too dogmatic, and too threatening for prime-time play.

Five months later, energized by the critical acclaim that the *Special* had received, *The Richard Pryor Show* aired four episodes that revealed that Pryor's coalitional worldview would not wane.[18] In the first installment, the show demonstrated a surprising comfort with featuring characters that liberally transgressed gender prescriptions—a freedom of personality toward which nationalism was particularly intolerant. In "Satin Doll," for instance, a soldier played by Pryor braves a wartime black nightclub to rekindle a romance with a woman who has become the establishment's songstress and headliner. Rivaling the intrigue of his inevitable heartbreak is the spectacle of the nightclub's emcee, Big Time Blazes Henry, a dark-skinned black man who opens the show by vocally impersonating both Ella Fitzgerald and Billie Holiday. The perfectly pitched falsetto and the effeminate gestures of Henry discomfit the audience not one wit. Its generous applause not only intimates an openness to gender play, but primes watchers for the trouble racial difference may bring to standard narratives of military heroism. In this story, the guy does not get the girl.

In another sketch, "I Gotta Be Me," viewers encounter a construction worker who, in the safety of his desolate working site after quitting time, progressively undresses to reveal his appreciation for a polka dot bikini, long blond hair, and silver high heels. This transformation occurs while the performer sings and dances to the song that gives the sketch its title. Two factors make this scene remarkable. First, drag and cross-dressing were established and respected practices in American televisual comedy. Yet in the past, particularly in the oeuvres of Milton Berle or Flip Wilson, comics would engage in transvestitism for the purposes of simulating femininity for their audiences.[19] That is, these performances featured males attempting to earnestly assume the persona of women. In these cases, gender lines are crossed only for the purpose of keeping these lines drawn. Pryor's show, in contrast, features a man in woman's clothing acting like a man in woman's clothing. Rather than avoid such gender trouble, the sketch revels in it and asserts it as desirable and normative. Pryor's progressivism, then, appeared to have room for challenging the gender conventions that black nationalism would just as soon leave in place.

Second, and more provocatively, is the deep sense of empathy that this sketch about transvestitism suggests. In articulating a desideratum for the man's gender freedom, the song's lyrics can be detached easily from his desires and applied to other marginalized social identities. For example, one lyric states, "I gotta live, not merely survive, and I won't give up this dream of life that keeps me alive." Beyond its poesy, we find here a blues lyric in drag, one capable of being crooned by the most downtrodden black man or woman we could find. More than any other aspect of Pryor's aesthetic, it is his staging of empathy and cultivation of cross-constituency identification that reveals the comic's coalitional investments and broad conception of social progress.

This empathic, coalitional aesthetic returns in a more sublime form later in the series. In the fourth show, Pryor grants stage time to one of the first Native American stand-up comedians ever to be featured on U.S. television. In the segment bearing his name, Charlie Hill proffers humor which, like Pryor's at times, is unabashedly shaped by ethnic grievances. Hill's personal introduction demonstrates how effectively comedy functions as a Trojan horse for the airing of racialized complaints:

> My name is Charlie Hill Segoli. I'm Oneida, I'm from Wisconsin; that's part of the Iroquois nation. My people are from Wisconsin. We used to be from New York [but] we had a little real estate problem.

Hill turns state-ordered Native relocation policies into a punchline, thereby making the Pryor show a racially non-parochial forum for political wit.

Yet the inclusion of Native stand-up hardly manifests the pinnacle of Pryor's coalitional artistry. This instead, in this analyst's opinion, comes in the third show of the series in a sketch entitled "New Talent." Here we encounter Pryor costumed as the incomparable rock musician Little Richard, performing his classic single "Good Golly, Miss Molly." But shortly after the performance begins the picture fades through snowy static into a shot of a young white woman in a bathrobe seated on a chair. In what appears to be a formal interview between strangers, the woman begins to detail a tryst she has just enjoyed as a byproduct of staying in the rooming house in which she presently resides. Her frank account of a lesbian love that has come and gone is gripping. I have provided her remarks in their entirety below:

(Woman in a mood of romantic celebration): I've fallen in love again. She's a woman here in the rooming house. She has been so kind to me ever since I came here. She brings me things. One day she brought me this enameled coke button with silver filigree. And another time she brought me this pencil. I was in the park last night. I was reading a book and having my dinner and she was there and she sat down with me and told me about her life—a harder one than mine. Everything about her, her voice, her hands, it was more than I could resist. She asked me to walk with her into the woods. We found this small clearing among the trees and the bushes and we CENSORED (frame becomes dark except for this word in white letters) . . . But um today when I saw her, she didn't speak to me. She acted like nothing happened between us. Why? . . .

Actually (woman's mood becomes scornful, defensive) what really happened was quite different. I was in the park last night. I was reading a book and having my dinner and she was there and she sat down with me and she started to talk. Well, the conversation was very difficult and so to keep things going I started to talk about this book I was reading. (getting more animated) Well she got up and she grabbed the book from me and threw it down on the ground and she pulled me to my feet and she walked me into the woods, into the clearing, the one that I just described before, and there she sta-CENSORED . . . I'm gonna stay in my room with the door locked. I'm not going out. I'll avoid her completely.

Actually, um, (woman becomes more flirtatious, confident, macho) I went to the park last night because I knew she'd be there. Well I've always been attracted to her you know. So I ah, I start following her into the woods, yeah. And she looked real annoyed when she saw me following her but I kept on walking beside her telling her CENSORED . . .

Actually, (woman becomes playfully sullen) I didn't even go to the park last night. I stayed here in my room and I read this book. It's about violence and seduction. Oh yeah I really got off on it. Well I like (cough) . . . I like being alone. It's better this way. At least then there is none of the pretense of closeness, none of the frustration of trying to be close but finding only walls . . . (static snow fade back to Little Richard [Pryor] singing).

In this deeply disorienting vignette in which the parody of Little Richard frames the personal confessions of a seemingly deranged lesbian, we find the *Pryor Show* at the apex of its avant-gardism. By suppressing the erotic portions of the heroine's narrative, the vignette not only surreptitiously invokes Pryor's ongoing struggle with television censors,[20] but also proffers us a parable about closeted desire—decades before the activist artistry of Ellen DeGeneres or Rosie O'Donnell claimed their place in common American discourse. For the protagonist to progress through different accounts of the sexual encounter (willful seduction, rape, willful seducer) only to proclaim them the product of her own confabulation—itself inspired by a fictional text and her deep sense of social alienation— foregrounds the trauma inflicted upon a subject when society deems her desire profane, non-normative, and unrepresentable.

Moreover, the sympathy that the woman's narration elicits from the audience then is asked to be extended to Little Richard, whose effeminacy, gender-ambivalent comportment, and flamboyant excess have caused whispers, and here, can thus also be read (as Pryor's representation seems to do) as symptoms of the rock pianist enduring a sexual repression similar to that of the lesbian raconteur. Additionally, we can't eliminate Pryor implicating himself as commiserating with the woman and the rocker, whether it be in terms of sexuality or love, since he in his memoir confessed an insatiable need for "love and attention" (28) throughout his life and also admitted a brief love affair with a transsexual man.[21] In short, the complex ingenuity of Pryor's sketch places no limits on where the vectors of empathy may travel. This dynamism gives clear proof that Pryor was preoccupied with more than just the liberation of black voice and desire.

Such a progressive aesthetic, even though it kept Pryor's pro-black sentiments subtle and at times inconspicuous, could not survive the incessant carping of the network censors. The siege the station directors laid upon the show was surprising, since the medium had proven itself open to more artistic gumption and black participation from the beginning of the decade. This posture resulted in the premiere of Flip Wilson's show in September of 1970 (for which Pryor wrote and acted), Lily Tomlin's daring, self-named venture in 1973 (in which, in the dramatic sketch entitled "Juke and Opal," Pryor played the host's drug-addicted love to a perfection that helped both performers garner Emmys),[22] Pryor's own occupation of the guest host position for the renowned *Saturday Night Live* in 1975, and the classic miniseries based on Alex Haley's masterpiece, *Roots,* in January of 1977. This recent history made television appear to be an "unanticipated land of opportunity" (135) in which "one week of truth could blow people's minds . . . and [produce a] revolution in the way everybody [thought]" (153). Due to the censors' penchant for safe, unprovocative programming, however, the forum ultimately failed to measure up to Pryor's idealism or accommodate his artistic ambition. The creative straitjacketing by network officials, the subsequent disappointment from being controlled, and the desire not "to sell out completely" (153) led the artist to default on his agreement with NBC to produce a season of ten shows (which explains why only the *Special* and the four episodes remain extant). Pryor's gentleman's pledge to host a number of future specials to compensate for the aborted episodes also never materialized. The comic fled the experience with a healthy dose of cynicism, grousing to reporters:

> The problem with the censors is that they don't like for people to communicate. I think it is on purpose and very political. I don't think they are naïve enough to believe they're protecting what people see. I think it has to do with anybody and anything that communicates a reality and might disturb or wake people or relate, I think they try to stop that anyway they can.[23]

Embittered by the industry's limits, Pryor re-routed his industry and ambition toward Hollywood film, never to return to the small screen in a sustained fashion again and making it easy to accept his words above as an eternal condemnation instead of a temporary one. Despite the spleen of such criticism, its doubtful that Pryor, wholly aware of life's dynamism and its capacity for change, would have predicted history to repeat itself less than thirty years later in the form of another African American comedian of Midwestern roots fleeing the industry, its censors, and its sizable profits in a desperate attempt to protect his muse and political sensibilities. Regardless of whether experience made of Pryor an augur, lightning did indeed strike a second time, albeit not for the same reasons, in the winter of 2004.

"I Don't [Want] Black People to Be Disappointed in Me . . .": On Chappelle's Commitments beyond Comedy

Certainly much had changed in the decades between the retirement of the *Richard Pryor Show* and the birth of *Chappelle's Show* in September of 2003. Pryor was praised for "the literal emancipation of African American humor" and the "breaking with blacks' long standing tradition of subterfuge and concealment of inner-community customs."[24] By the time Dave Chappelle breached the televisual landscape, the manumission for which Pryor was congratulated was thoroughly complete, if not passé. Pryor's successors, such as Eddie Murphy, Whoopi Goldberg, Adele Gibbons, and Chris Rock, not to mention the situational comedies of *The Cosby Show, A Different World*, and *Martin*, transformed black comedy from a foray into a tradition. In fact, arguably one of the most formative features of the postmodern epoch is the paradoxical increase of black media visibility alongside the persistence of black social marginality. Engendered by formal desegregation and affirmative action initiatives, the black public sphere experienced a fracture along class lines that turned the middle class into a stratum of ghetto fugitives. Lingering hegemonies of whiteness persuaded the burgeoning and mobile black bourgeoisie to suppress their cultural backgrounds for the purposes of successful assimilation into the professional mainstream. Black cultural practices thus remained situated in the racialized enclaves of the preceding apartheid era, with the sole quixotic hope of gaining exposure by means of the proletariat's self-insinuation into the performance cultures of the American public sphere, namely the over-mediated entertainments of comedy, music, and sport. This media hyper-presence, enabled by the stupefying explosion of outlets, particularly the birth of cable and fledgling networks vying for stability (including Fox and UPN), has produced the vexing irony of blackness (virtually) seen and (socially) unseen simultaneously. Thus Dave Chappelle's charge, if he was to make of his comedy a pro-black politic, was not to expose the cultural periphery, but to do as the stand-up version of Pryor once did: he was to *explain* and *adjudicate* it; offer his own personal assessments of the amount of credence American audiences should give to the various samples of blackness the media brought before them. In short, he was to keep it as real as he could. Chappelle defected from his own program, the journalistic record suggests, because the authority of his adjudicative role, what Mark Anthony Neal calls "a rigorous form of self and communal critique," the very trademark of the post-Soul artist, appeared to be undermined not only by the comic's executive collaborators, but by his own comedic practices themselves.[25]

The details of the controversy are well known because so few people willfully walk away from their own professional and economic success. The show was brought to a halt by Chappelle's untimely departure from network studios in the middle of producing the third season—work for which he would receive over $50 million in compensation. The handsome salary was awarded the comedian for a number of reasons; among them was that despite claiming as its broadcasting home the modest cable network Comedy Central, the show was the top-ranked program among males 18–34 years of age without being a sports program.[26] In addition, its edgy racial humor grew the network's black audience, without alienating, but instead by expanding, the channel's traditional white audience.[27] Most importantly, the show's ability to tickle men across racial lines produced lucre: the first season's episodes sold a television record 2.8 million DVD copies and projections showed that the second season would generate an even larger bounty.

Unflattering rumors attempted to explain Chappelle's terrible business sense. The more scurrilous cited an overactive party schedule, increased or decreased drug intake, or psychological breakdown. Tamer speculations pointed to a salary-induced performance anxiety or creative struggles with program and network executives. When he finally returned to American public life, after a retreat into relative anonymity in Durban, South Africa, Chappelle brought gravitas to the discussion of his hiatus by attributing his self-imposed exile to his own realization that he was being "socially irresponsible" and that such behavior was being "deliberately encouraged."[28]

The comedian sees the discomfort that occasioned his flight through the prism of a particular incident. Chappelle taped a sketch that jocosely represents what social psychologists Claude Steele and Hazel Markus have identified as "stereotype threat": the anxiety that besieges an individual when s/he is faced with the prospect of fulfilling an unflattering stereotype of one's race.[29] In the piece, the comedian costumes himself as a blackface Negro Minstrel, which, in being reduced to the size of a mystical pixie, heckles the normal version of Chappelle about choosing a fried chicken dinner for a meal on an airplane. The pixie gesticulates and comments to the very peak of hilarity, but as Chappelle confides to *Time* magazine reporter Christopher John Farley, the performance may have been *too* funny for the comedian to continue working with the cast. Farley writes

> [A]t the taping, one spectator, a white man, laughed particularly loud and long. His laughter struck Chappelle as wrong, and he wondered if the new season of his show had gone from sending up stereotypes to merely reinforcing them. "When he laughed[,"] [Dave says,] "it made me uncomfortable. As a matter of fact, that was the last thing I shot before I told myself I gotta take f—— time out after this. Because my head almost exploded."[30]

From this discrete episode of excessive white laughter, the ever-intuitive comic gleaned what cultural studies scholars took years to admit: "that the way people use television is subjective."[31] Due to the fact that every subject, says Lawrence Grossberg, is a nomadic wanderer, whose being and affect is constantly shifting and never fixed, it is impossible to pin down exactly the reasons that certain parts of a text interpellate an observer. Quite simply, a person has myriad and complex reasons why s/he identifies (or not) with a show.[32] Having reckoned with the harsh truth of this reality and accepted partially its potential horror (that because of the contingent nature of people's identifications, one's audience may not espy one's intended meaning), Chappelle conceded in momentary defeat, "there is a line of people who will understand exactly what I am doing. Then there will be another group who are just fans."[33] I find it terribly interesting that the comic has resorted to the language of in-group in an attempt to verify his audience. The remark is redolent with ideas of particularity and authenticity, pointing to a viewer whose insight into Chappelle's designs is somehow immanent in the viewer her/himself. The remainder of this essay presumes its author's standing among the privileged cognoscenti, who see in Chappelle's work an undertone of black nationalism hiding in plain sight. Though evidence of this sentiment rests in the ideo-logic of some of the show's most ingenious sketches, there is material in Chappelle's biography that hints at the comedian harboring such political sensibilities.

For example, Chappelle's rearing was marked by a solid tutorial in the black protest tradition. The comic is the son of two professional intellectuals who came to adulthood during the sixties and seventies, the decades of American dissent. The father, who is deceased, was a professor of voice and opera at Antioch College in Yellow Springs, Ohio; the mother, in contrast, continues to serve Prince George's Community College (northern Virginia) as a professor of African American Studies—itself a scholarly tradition with radicalism at its origin. Those even marginally savvy about the politics of the institutionalization and production of knowledge and society's lingering incredulity toward black intellect would concede that to establish a standing as African Americans in the American academy is a racially resistant act in itself. Yet the Chappelles did not merely model political restiveness in their career choices, but also used black protest materials to create the ambience for their son's upbringing. The comedian reflects on this aspect of his background with NPR's Terry Gross:

> In the household I grew up in, my parents were somewhat, I don't how to explain it but over our mantle place there were pictures of Malcolm X, you know. I listened to Dick Gregory records growing up. I listened to the Last Poets. I mean, there were books all over the house and I was always reading stuff, so like, you know, people like Frederick Douglass, these guys' pictures were on my walls when I was growing up.[34]

Surrounded by a provocative balance of literary and popular protest culture, the young Chappelle would have had to actively resist these ideas in order to eschew their influence. Yet if his parents' active and subtle mentorship failed to sufficiently inculcate the comedian with these sentiments, the socio-historical context of Chappelle's formative years, I contend, was certain to endow philosophies of black protest with credibility and personal meaning.

His parents' divorce had Chappelle split his youth residing in the two aforementioned regions. He spent his elementary school days in Washington, D.C., and his middle school years in rural Ohio, only to return to the District, particularly the neighborhood of Capitol Hill, for his training at Duke Ellington School for the Arts. There, according to one observer, "the kids preferred Shakespeare to semiautomatics."[35] Present in Chappelle's rearing was a sense of security that Pryor never enjoyed for sure; yet the former was in no ways insulated from the potential dangers of black urban life. Returning to an enclave in which the majority of the black residents "didn't have any contact with white people outside of [those whites] being authority figures," the young

Chappelle was befuddled by the speed with which his old neighborhood had fallen prey to the ravages of the drug trade. He explains,

> Crack came out while I was gone. So I saw like the before and after picture. I had to piece the crack epidemic together . . . trying to figure out how everyone has all this gold and expensive stuff and then I was like "oh, ok, everyone is selling drugs." I knew so many people in the beginning like in my freshman year in high school that were selling drugs, I can't even imagine how many people were using them. The crack epidemic was crazy man . . . all the inequities were just under-lined.[36]

Chappelle's account of his D.C. neighborhood's stark transformation from community to drug emporium is laced with lament, suggesting that the change left deep impress on the memory of the aspiring comic.[37] Yet the comedian witnessed not merely the degradation of the environment, but his neighbors' sometimes rage-filled response toward being the drug-industry's victims. Their protest was manifest in church action, community health organizations, and neighborhood watches on the ground. Through the airwaves, however, black frustration was registered by what Jeffrey Decker and Charise Cheney regard as "nation-conscious hip hop."[38] Populated by the likes of Public Enemy, KRS-One, and Ice Cube, this strain of the art form "functioned as a vehicle for disseminating political discourse" that aided beleaguered black urbanites across the country at the time to cognitively assimilate the geopolitical implications of the drug economy and the racialized misery it produced.[39] By casting the suffering of the postindustrial ghetto as a black problem that warranted pro-black solutions, these artists "reinscribed the cultural nationalist Afrocentric idea in rap music."[40] Cheney particularly locates the emergence of political "raptivists" in 1988, the year Chappelle returned to Washington for high school, began his fledging career as a professional at Garvin's Comedy Club, and suffered the continuation of Republican rule as Reagan gave way to the first George Bush. I am encouraging, then, that we take seriously this cultural context—the colonial predicament of D.C., the crack epidemic, the first Bush presidency, the Afrocentric parents, and the protest music—as seminal to Chappelle's comedic aesthetic, especially since it provided the sociopolitical backdrop in which that aesthetic was first forged. To do so would poise us to reckon with the sense of history with which Chappelle spoke when he declaimed in his series's first show, "I am a huge fan of the hip hop music!"[41] It would also lend credence to the idea that upon recognizing that his continued collaboration with his own series deeply endangered the nationalist undercurrent of his comedic muse, Chappelle elected to perform "the clumsy dismount" by which he left the show and the millions that it promised.[42]

Chappelle offers a subtle glimpse of his nationalist sympathies in the very first sketch the series features. By swiftly driving a polished automobile through the streets to a fast-paced urban music beat, the comedian uses the opening segment to quote what has become the standard aesthetic for sports car commercials. The sketch, however, adds a Hollywood logic to such a compact narrative. The commercial occurs twice, as if to suggest the imperfect take of the first version and the revised, more acceptable take of the second. The first features the comic in the car with a dancing white woman at his side. The pops and locks of the latter hardly titillate and hearken back to an urban dance style—breakin'—whose appeal is more a product of nostalgia than of dance fans' contemporary appreciation. Chappelle registers his disgust with the woman's unsexy datedness by kicking her out of the car. The camera cuts in a fashion that allows the commercial to restart itself, this time with the comedian chauffeuring a black woman in the speedy vehicle. It is immediately clear that the provocative jiggling of this woman appeals to Chappelle much more. He exclaims, "Now that's what I call dancing!" To make his preference clear, however, the car drives onto a desolate street of the city where, by chance, the first woman continues her rejected dance moves in isolation. Chappelle drives the car rapidly over a puddle close to the woman, drenching her with the dirty water of the pavement's surface.[43] The commercial concludes with the black woman peeking her head out of the speeding car's window while her butt bounces in the face of a smiling, driving Chappelle.

Possibly obscured beneath the economic and misogynistic imperatives that have made striptease the preferred style of public female dance may be the racial preference articulated in the sketch. Indeed, the black woman appeals to the car-handling Chappelle because her performance seems more directed at him and his desires (In fact, in an attempt to demonstrate the wide breadth the series will grant his comedic prerogative, Chappelle shows an after-sketch clip of the black women's breast popping out of her sleeveless, V-neck blouse during one of the sketch's tapings). But it is difficult to dismiss the possibility that the very blackness of the booty-dancing passenger broadens the woman's appeal to the comedian (the sketch could have easily had either woman perform the more provocative dance). In short, the preferred woman not only intimates Chappelle's partiality to sexual socializing among racial similars, but also stages the subordinate, sexualized status black women are to have in such encounters. Such female subordination has historically served as tacit precondition of any nationalist project.

Chappelle's comedic nationalism and corresponding discomfort with coalitional politics can be brought into sharper focus, I believe, if we also read the opening sketch of the second episode both as an elaboration of his political disposition and as aesthetic methodology. The second show begins not with a sketch, but revealingly with a stand-up segment (which is live, more personal—more real, so to speak) in which Chappelle meditates on the impossibility of "a young black dude" expressing publicly his thoughts and feelings. He closes his commentary on the matter with the remark, "The only way people would listen to the stuff I think is if a pretty white girl sang my thoughts." The audience soon becomes aware that Chappelle's contemplation of his own expressive freedom is preface to an actual white woman singing aloud his otherwise unspoken worldview. His satiric disclosure here of what he alleges are typical black male suspicions, complaints, tastes, and dislikes are startling:

> Crack was invented and distributed to intentionally destroy the black community. AIDS was too.
> The police never looked for Tupac and Biggie's murderer.
> Fuck the police.
> O.J. didn't do it.
> On second thought, yeah he did.
> Gay sex is gross. Sorry. I just find it to be gross. Unless, of course, they're lesbian.
> I like lesbians.
> I like lesbians.
> All Chinese people look alike.[44]
> So do white people.
> Pretty much anyone who isn't black, looks alike to me.
> I want to stick my thumb in J-Lo's butt.
> I wouldn't mind sticking my thumb in this white woman's butt either . . .
> And now it's time to collect ad revenue for Comedy Central
> Revenue they don't share with my black ass.

Showing little of the fledgling timidity that might come with embarking upon a new creative enterprise, Chappelle seems to suspend the political ambiguity characteristic of his satire in favor of franker commentary. Through Chappelle, we seemingly gain insight into the street sentiments of the hip hop generation, one that apparently harbors deep suspicion and resentment of government leaders and police, one that disdains black public figures who embarrass the race, one that abjects gay male sexuality while fetishizing lesbian eroticism, one that has difficulty reckoning with the subjectivity of non-black people, and one that is open to socializing with these non-black Others only if they are female and heterosexually available. Though most certainly its kin, this is not the ideological vision that animated Pryor's comedic enterprise. Instead, the political posture assumed here is heteronormative, racially intramural, aggrieved by past injustice, and unempathetic toward other socially marginalized identity groups who yearn for the acceptance and respect of the broader American society.

Yet, as the segment's prelude intimates, the contemporary public sphere is not amenable to the free and unharnessed expression of this impolitic black masculinity. Thus the white woman who serves as Chappelle's ventriloquial stand-in does not merely make this soliloquy more palatable and entertaining, she also signals the expressive structure through which Chappelle's comedy is to pass if it is to gain expression at all. His incendiary politic will be somehow feminized and whitened in order to remain media-acceptable. The objectification of women, the frequent deployment of pothead and scatological humor, or the brutal mockery of blackness by way of the very stereotypes he aspires to explode, may all contribute to the containment of the nationalist resentment that colors his comedy and enable audiences, as Bambi Haggans ventures, "[to] laugh at one part of the joke and leave the critique to the side."[45] Thus, in a manner similar to the comedic concession implied by the introductory sketch of Pryor's own aborted series (Pryor wore a flesh-colored body suit that gave the appearance that he sacrificed his genitalia to having a show on NBC), Chappelle confesses here the blanching self-castration he will willfully undergo to give his politics voice, even in its muted form. The exposition of the second episode, then, is a latent artistic manifesto that avows all the ambivalent comedic principles that will organize the entire series.

Equally striking for how Chappelle's nationalist sympathies may be buried beneath the buffoonery of his comedic practice is a sketch featured in the second episode of the second season entitled "The Racial Draft." Modeled on the televised selection process professional sports teams use to secure new players to join their ranks, the sketch features an arena peopled by delegations from five of the six phenotype groups that European Enlightenment wrongly understood as races (indigenous Americans are conspicuous in their absence). Their mission, as Chappelle's verbal preface explains below, is to decisively defrock interracial celebrities of their racial ambiguity. The comic reasons:

> You know, what's cool about being American is that we're all mixed up. I'm talking about genetically. We all got a little something in us. Right? And in some people there's more than others. And that's when we get to arguing. For instance, my wife's Asian, I'm black, and we argue about which half of Tiger Woods is hitting the ball so good. Derek Jeter is another guy like that. Halle Berry is somebody else. We got to stop arguing about who is what. We need to just settle this once and for all. We need to have a draft. That's right, I said it.

In addition to being uproariously funny due to how the sketch players lampoon the selecting process, the drafters, and the draftees (Chappelle plays a sportscaster, Tiger Woods, and the white drafter), the bit reveals *Chappelle's Show*'s perspicacity toward the function of race in contemporary society in addition to disclosing the deep anxieties that produce and inform the comedian's sublimated nationalism. First, the draft hyperbolizes the non-subjective nature of racial identity. Race here is not an identity intrinsic to and elected by the subject, but one determined by the often whimsical visual observations of an impersonal crowd.[46] In short, we don't get to say who we are; others do. Second, the sketch crassly reveals race's function as a social commodity. Starting with the extractive and racializing labor processes of slavery and imperialism and extending to affirmative action and diversity initiatives in the present day, race has dictated the terms in which social advantages and disadvantages have been bestowed upon people and institutions. Here, rather than spectacularizing how a person may reap the rewards of a timely racial identification, the draft highlights how the reputation of a race itself may benefit from being associated with (or selecting) a person of value. Implicit in the black delegation's choice of Tiger Woods is the hope that his affiliation with blackness will deepen others' respect and admiration for it. Third, the segment dramatizes the metonymic manner in which race functions in the mass media in particular. The draft "prospects" are not randomly proposed or anonymous. They are instead pop-cultural luminaries who enjoy the fame and fortune that comes with such prominence. The sketch shows how often audiences and media turn these figures into racial icons, renowned parts of a particular racial whole.

Tiger Woods doesn't represent merely himself, but all the people who allegedly share his racial classification.

The sketch suggests, however, that the level of angst Woods experiences as a non-white, monied athlete in racial demand is comparable to that of the politically minded Chappelle, who seems to see in Woods and other multiracial pop icons an ambiguity that antagonizes the racial boundaries necessary for his latent nationalism. Amidst a milieu in which "racial divisions are becoming more complex, harder to understand, more challenging to discuss," Chappelle's prefatorial desire "to settle [identities] for once and for all," and thus calcify the racial lines, seems marked by an eerie sincerity, especially since the drafted icons speak to anxieties particular to pro-black African Americans in this hybridizing epoch.[47] Woods, for instance, is not only seen by some to use his multiracial identity to absent himself rhetorically from anti-racist efforts in the pop culture arena; he has also fed the concern about mixed-race and black males selecting whites as their romantic partners. The Jewish delegation's selection of Lenny Kravitz, the son of black actress Roxie Rooker and her Jewish husband, stands as the embodied spectre of the surprising (and maybe unwelcome) interracialism behind the revered and arguably pro-black situation comedy *The Jeffersons*. Elian Gonzalez, the Latino contingent's selectee ("so that white people won't try to claim him again," the delegate explains), references the citizenship scandal surrounding the former Cuban boy refugee, which is certain to conjure up thoughts of blacks competing with immigrant Latino labor for jobs, the Republican Party's desperate drive to recruit Latinos into its ranks, and the internecine power struggle between blacks and Latinos in the city of Miami.[48] Both the Jewish and Latino draftees are particularly striking because rather than being selections that appear more in keeping with their own putative ethnopolitical interests, they both appear much more to be haunting icons of black (Chappelle's) political imagination and memory.

Worries about Republicans of color certainly explain why Colin Powell and Condoleeza Rice become acquisitions of the "white" delegation. These two black political luminaries symbolize the ever-present possibility of a black body politic becoming so diverse that some of its members may affiliate with organizations that actively antagonize black socioeconomic opportunity. The Asian delegation's tapping of the Wu-Tang Clan—the black rap group that has weaved a distinctive artistic style out of appropriating aspects of Asian culture—seems to signal more Chappelle's own fetishistic fantasy of acceptable ethno-racial boundary crossing than the "serious" political choice of Asian Americans. As Chappelle is married to an Asian woman, it is reasonable to read out from the sketch the comedian's partial desire to adopt and be adopted by Asian culture. In short, the racial draft, like the slave auction of yesteryear, is a rigged marketplace that commodifies and shuffles iconic subjects in the interest of producing a racialized political advantage. Its failure to include non-black political hopes and fantasies in its comedic narrative reveals the artist's race-specific investments to be insufficiently malleable in incorporating any type of political coalitionism.[49]

The nationalism that sets the imaginative ceiling for the "Racial Draft" is also manifest less subtly in the material iconography of the show's studio. Particularly befuddling to this essayist is the lack of lay and academic attention paid to the semiotics of the show's iconographic frontispiece. Emblazoned on the in-studio monitor during every show is a large white "C" (which is to visually signal the comic's last name and the formal title of the series) set against the backdrop of a red, black, and green rectangle. The symbol clearly borrows its colors from the flags of the African countries that share them and signals Chappelle's ideological kinship with the domestic Afrocentric movement that came to prominence in the 1980s. The banner almost hangs in the air like a flag itself, suggesting that the studio hosts an imagined community that brings "foreign" and insurgent comedic material into the homes of mainstream Americans.

The Afrocentric symbolism does not end with the series's escutcheon but also creates an ambient environment for some of the more memorable sketches of the program. For instance, in the acclaimed game-show spoof entitled "I Know Black People," the entire set is awash with the aforementioned colors as a ethno-racially diverse assemblage of contestants competes over its competence in black culture. The décor strikingly suggests that, at least in the show's imagination, these are the display colors necessary to convey blackness as the primary item of concern. Moreover, the colors suggest quite literally the contestational posture of the comedian, who, according to his pre-sketch prelude, gained inspiration for the skit from being told by a white person what aspects of his comedy most effectively (or not) served African American political interests. By installing Chappelle as the Alex Trebek–like arbiter of black truth while accoutering the set with the racially coded color scheme, the sketch reinstates Chappelle as the Afrocentric authority over blackness, thus enabling him (and the black community he envisages) to close ranks against non-black Others who dare to claim more credible insights into black political well-being.[50]

The nationalist propensities extend from sketch narrative and settings designed to foreground pro-black politics to small fragments of speech in sketches that intimate such leanings. From seemingly innocent statements such as "this is why black people don't have nothing," after one black personage shoots another at the close of a dice game, or "sir, my blackness will not permit me to make a statement like that" when asked to agree that O. J. Simpson killed his wife at a mock jury selection hearing, or the more explicit appeal he directs at performer Wayne Brady in a spoof of the movie *Training Day,* "black actors, man, we just need to unify," Chappelle repeatedly invokes racial commonality as a disciplinary force on social behavior. In the comedian's view, identity precludes black-on-black crime, mutual legal incrimination, and professional individualism, all in the interest of enhancing black sociopolitical standing within the United States. These micro-proclamations demonstrate an insistent commitment to the political goals of only one community.

For the subtlest, yet most shrill expression of the comedian's neonationalist sympathies, we must resurrect the spectre of hip hop that, I argued earlier, organized the artist's sensibility as a neophyte comedian and continues to shape his muse. Haggans is right to notice that there is something peculiar about the genre of hip hop that Chappelle elects to feature in his show. Calling it "a significant contribution," the critic lauds the program for creating "a space for diverse forms of hip-hop," and, leaning on the insights of Herman Gray, attributes the show's success in "generating identifications across racial lines" to its hip hop features.[51] Yet by missing the difference between that which is *diverse* and that which is *alternative,* Haggans understates and mischaracterizes the political intervention Chappelle makes through his selective incorporation of hip hop artists and music into his program's content. All of the musicians, from Mos Def to Erykah Badu to De La Soul to Kanye West, can be aptly characterized, as Devin Gordon and Allison Samuels have done, as performers who have consciously "bypassed the bling and booty set" of their profession and who, in different ways, "reject the get rich and fuck-the-world nihilism that ultimately brought gangsta rap to a dead end."[52] Noticeably, rappers and musicians who have sullied themselves with the genre's less progressive side have often found themselves the subject of his satire—R. Kelly, Lil' Jon, and 50 Cent most famously.

Evidence that the show's relationship with hip hop is governed by a very deliberate editing process can be found in the musical segments of Snoop Doggy Dogg and Dead Prez. Since his debut on Dr. Dre's commercial juggernaut "The Chronic" in 1992, Snoop Doggy Dogg has progressively distinguished himself as the poobah of hip hop's hedonistic underside. His pimp persona and consequent peddling of verbal misogyny has facilitated the artist's migration into other salacious entertainments, such as hosting an episode of "Girls Gone Wild" and producing his own pornographic video. Despite this ignominious resume, Snoop does grace the stage of *Chappelle's Show* in the second season's tenth episode. But rather than perform a more recent song from his oeuvre, one certain to be in keeping with his myriad indulgences, Snoop reprises the movie anthem "One Eight Seven" (1992), a song of passionate protest against police corruption and the urban constabulary's oppressive surveillance of black neighborhoods during the first Bush presidency.[53] That Snoop needed to reach back almost fifteen years to find a piece in harmony with Chappelle's aesthetic signals how high race-based protest ranks on the comedian's artistic agenda.

Yet if the containment of the pimp-rapper's decadent proclivities did not convince audiences of Chappelle's political sentiments, the inclusion of Dead Prez on his docket of televised performances was certain to do so. The Florida-based rap duo has consciously fashioned themselves as legatees of the nation-conscious strain of hip hop, frequently peppering their music with agitprop encouraging Afrocentric revolution. The group was already slated to feature in the still-birthed third season wherein they were to perform their deeply inflammatory track "It's Bigger Than Hip Hop." Donning sports jerseys in the aforementioned Afrocentric colors with the word "Panthers" emblazoned on their fronts, the musicians perform a song that is one long and shrill lyrical preachment about repudiating hedonism and fostering revolutionary change through music. The verses leave little to be interpreted:

> I'm sick of that fake thug, R&B-rap scenario, all day on the radio
> Same scenes in the video, monotonous material
> Y'all don't hear me though
> These record labels slang our tapes like dope
> You can be next in line and signed; and still be writing rhymes and
>   broke
> You would rather have a Lexus? or justice? a dream? or some
>   substance?
> A Beamer? a necklace? or freedom?
> Still a nigga like me don't playa-hate, I just stay awake
> This real hip hop; and it don't stop till we get the crackers off the block
> They call it . . . hip hop

In addition to calling into question the aesthetic value of the music, the video images inspired by it, and the impact of both on its consumers, Dead Prez's diatribe against the culture is particularly interesting because of its implied spatial cleansing of white people from the hip hop land-scape ("it don't stop till we get the crackers off the block"). Charise Cheney, in her work on the sexual politics of nation-conscious rap, explains that theorists of nationalism have often disqualified movements in African American political culture as true nationalist phenomena because they lack attachment or grounding to land or a nation-state. Cheney's critical treatment of nation-conscious rap labors diligently to disabuse us of the notion that hip hop cannot be understood as national-ist without a nation. My argument about Chappelle's work has done much to demonstrate my agreement with Cheney's contention. Yet, it is possible to see Dead Prez's commentary here as providing some relief to talk about African Americans as exceptions to nationalist thinking. De-spite the fact that there is no black nation in sight, the rap group uses a *spatial conceit to express racial exclusivity, progress, and protection.* More importantly, they do so publicly, here, enjoying the full breadth of Chap-pelle's imprimatur. It is also crucial to consider that *Chappelle's Show* has featured this song as its anthem, having the initial chords open every episode of the series.[54] These facts strongly suggest that though the co-median's desires for a post-racist society are inspired by a sincere hu-manism, those desires have at their foundation an investment in the collective liberation of African Americans.[55]

What I have been arguing here, then, is that Chappelle's loosely veiled nationalist animus, when juxtaposed against Pryor's more coali-tional comedic praxis, in some way signals the possibility of an impend-ing historical foreclosure in black cultural politics. The elder comic, performing in the twilight of nationalist revolt, and the secure winds of a broadening democracy, could sideline pro-black politics gracefully, espe-cially since television executives virtually mandated such suppression. Pryor's politics unwittingly anticipate the political bind in which black anti-racism finds itself in a now globalized, post–Civil Rights America. In fear of charges of political myopia or reverse racism, African Ameri-cans cannot agitate solely for black rights, but must demonstrate a politi-cal ecumenism, that is, a coalitional affinity, in order for any of their grievances to be seriously heeded. Ironically, it this ecumenical posture and its ability to obscure black needs by means of their subsumption under those of Others, that has in part hindered any significant black political successes in recent years and has contributed to some devastating losses (i.e., affirmative action, welfare, privatized incarceration, whitening of mainstream television programming, continuing production of racist mythology in the American media). Chappelle's comedy seems to respond to this pressure by asserting the protest voice languishing beneath more than two decades of political multiculturalism.

In addition, Chappelle's self-orchestrated emancipation from the binds of his own television show thrust some of the most celebrated aspects of the post-Soul aesthetic into crisis. It was not so long ago that proponents such as Trey Ellis celebrated Reagan-era black avant-gardism that ignored the "demand[s] [of] propagandistic positivism" made on their art, often by other African Americans.[56] "They cared too much about what white people think," diagnosed the eminent film auteur Spike Lee, about what occasioned the aridity and failure of some of the black aestheticians that preceded him.[57] In pulling back from his irreverent airing of black stereotypes in the public sphere, Chappelle resurrects the politics of respectability as a viable artistic practice. His retreat not only rejects the idea of profit at any cost, but it also supports the notion that the whitelike gaze might matter, and matter crucially. By leaving fifty million dollars on the bargaining counter, this post-Soul artist raises the possibility that for black cultural success in the era of postmodernity, resisting the seductions of capital, succumbing to creative conservatism, and retrenching one's political ecumenism are the last hopes for black people to keep it real—and that these choices, as much as we hope otherwise, are certain to produce our deep regrets.

NOTES

1. My title is inspired by two sketches of that title in the *Chappelle's Show* series. One shows the unfortunate consequences of a woman trying to affect the comeuppance of a crank telephone caller, the other shows the violent demise of a man who uses an unnecessary machismo to defend the honor of his girlfriend. Both scenes seem to equate "keeping it real" with unleashing repressed anger upon one's adversaries (in short, "not going out like no punk"). Chappelle explains that reality is kept hidden for a reason and that we all should pick our spots (when we keep it real). Both Chappelle and Pryor seem to have done so by walking away from their respective television series—a point I explain in the body of the essay.

2. Richard Pryor with Todd Gold, *Pryor Convictions, and Other Life Sentences* (New York: Pantheon Books, 1995), 17.

3. Oprah Winfrey, "Why Dave Chappelle Walked Away from Fifty Million," *The*

Oprah Winfrey Show, 3 February 2006, interview transcript (Chicago: Harpo Productions, 2006).

4. Jean-François Lyotard, *The Postmodern Explained* (Minneapolis: University of Minnesota Press, 1992), 5. Here, Lyotard ventures that the job of the postmodern artist or cultural worker is not so much the object that s/he produces but to question the rules and categories that make the object an acceptable artistic production. In short, the postmodern is a meta-practice; a self-reflexive meditation that in being so challenges what makes something artistic.

5. Henry Louis Gates, *The Signifying Monkey* (New York: Oxford University Press, 1988), 47.

6. I use the term "whitelike" here in an attempt to nuance myself away from binaristic thinking and account for non-white viewers who may read black performative practices in a way that resonates with white supremacist ideology. In short, a racist, denigrating gaze may be adopted from any identity position regardless of hue. The hegemony of whiteness makes this possible.

7. Mel Watkins, *On the Real Side: Laughing, Lying, and Signifying—The Underground Tradition of African American Humor That Transformed American Culture, from Slavery to Richard Pryor* (New York: Simon and Schuster, 1994), 528.

8. Bambi Haggans, *Laughing Mad: The Black Comic Persona in Post-Soul America* (New Brunswick, N.J.: Rutgers University Press, 2007), 5. Haggans pulls the quotation from Mark Anthony Neal's *Soul Babies: Black Popular Culture and The Post-Soul Aesthetic* (New York: Routledge, 2002), 3.

9. Trey Ellis, "The New Black Aesthetic," *Callaloo* 12, no. 1 (Winter 1989), 237.

10. Richard Pryor with Todd Gold, *Pryor Convictions, and Other Life Sentences* (New York: Pantheon Books, 1995), 92. Future citations will be numbered in the text and made with all the appropriate angst that comes with the awareness that the memoir is an act of self-fashioning and feature truths told to aggrandize the self for its readers. That the text may be historically unreliable, I hope is tempered by deploying the writer's words for analytical, not hagiographic, purposes.

11. Haggans captures succinctly Pryor's multimedia political engagement with American popular culture in the following remark: "As seductive and popular as Pryor was with live audiences, his humor possessed a racially political quality which was foreign to network television" (*Laughing Mad*, 51).

12. Richard Pryor, *The Richard Pryor Special?* dir. John Moffitt (New York: NBC, 1977); *The Richard Pryor Show,* dir. John Moffitt (New York: NBC, 1977).

13. Harold Cruse, *The Crisis of the Negro Intellectual* (New York: William Morrow, 1967), 466.

14. Not yet adequately documented in the annals of African American comedy is the virtuosic Paul Mooney, who in addition to having his own renowned stand-up career, can claim writing credits for three of the most distinguished black comedy shows in television history: *The Richard Pryor Show, In Living Color,* and *Chappelle's Show.*

15. Watkins, *On the Real Side,* 240.

16. W. J. Rorabaugh, *Berkeley at War: The 1960s* (New York: Oxford University Press, 1989), 76.

17. This same political disavowal is executed in a sketch from the television series, entitled "The 40th President of the United States." In the sketch, there are several moments in which Pryor as the U.S. president demonstrates by his answers at a press conference that he is quite sympathetic to black political concerns, from reducing unemployment to expanding the pool of black professional quarterbacks. At one point, he even responds to the Islamic greeting of one black reporter with "Walaikum a Salaam." This performance of racial solidarity, however, is soon con-

tained when the president responds without the appropriate remorse to an inquiry about the frequency of him courting white women. The president confesses that he will continue these types of sexual pursuits "as long as he can keep it up."

18. Christine Acham, *Revolution Televised: Prime Time and the Struggle for Black Power* (Minneapolis: Minnesota University Press, 2004), 156.

19. For discussions of televisual drag see Haggans, *Laughing Mad,* 42–44.

20. See the chapter by Audrey Thomas McCluskey in this collection.

21. Interestingly enough, the affair occurred shortly *after* his return from Berkeley to Las Vegas. Pryor explains in his memoir: "I never kept [the transsexual Mitrasha] a secret. Mooney, for instance, knew I was fucking a dude, and a drop-dead gorgeous one at that" (130).

22. Hilton Als, "A Pryor Love," in *Life Stories: Profiles from The New Yorker* (New York: Random House, 2000), 383–402.

23. Acham, *Revolution Televised,* 154.

24. Watkins, *On the Real Side,* 563; 544.

25. Mark Anthony Neal, *Soul Babies: Black Popular Culture and The Post-Soul Aesthetic* (New York: Routledge, 2002), 120.

26. "Funny Business: Dave Chappelle and crew shoot—Comedy Central scores!" *Entertainment Weekly,* 20 and 27 August 2004.

27. Alan Hughes, "Funny Money," *Black Enterprise,* December 2004.

28. Winfrey, "Why Dave Chappelle Walked Away from Fifty Million," 6.

29. Hazel Rose Markus, Claude M. Steele, and Dorothy M. Steele, "Colorblindness as a Barrier to Inclusion: Assimilation and Nonimmigrant Minorities" in *Daedalus* 129, no. 4 (Fall 2000): 233–259.

30. John Christopher Farley, "Dave Speaks," *Time,* 23 May 2005.

31. Winfrey, "Why Dave Chappelle Walked Away from Fifty Million," 7.

32. Lawrence Grossberg, *Dancing in Spite of Myself: Essays on Popular Culture* (Durham, N.C.: Duke University Press, 1997), 133.

33. Ibid., 8.

34. Terry Gross, "Dave Chappelle," *Fresh Air,* National Public Radio, Washington D.C., 2 September 2004.

35. "Just Say Yo," *People Weekly,* 9 March 1998, 67; Jonathan Rosyln, "Stand Up Guy," *Washingtonian,* July 1996, 58–59.

36. Gross, "Dave Chappelle."

37. One could go as far as to say that Chappelle's comedic imagination is wholly structured by his lingering grievance he has against the late Reagan-Bush era. In the second episode of the series, he dedicates his unforgettable sketch about "crack fiend" Tyrone Biggums to the Reagan-Bush administration—a gesture that clearly indicts that administration for the myriad social ailments caused by the crack epidemic. For scholarly treatment of the psychological implications of racial grievance, see Anne Anlin Cheng's *The Melancholy of Race* (Oxford: Oxford University Press, 2000).

38. Jeffrey Louis Decker, "The State of Rap: Time and Place in Hip Hop Nationalism," in *Microphone Fiend: Youth Music and Youth Culture,* ed. Andrew Ross and Tricia Rose (New York: Routledge, 1994).

39. Charise L. Cheney, *Brothers Gonna Work It Out: Sexual Politics in the Golden Age of Black Nationalism* (New York: New York University Press, 2005), 2.

40. Ibid., 12.

41. Dave Chappelle, *Chappelle's Show,* dir. Andre Allen and Bill Berner (New York: Comedy Central, 2004).

42. John Christopher Farley, "Dave Speaks," *Time,* 23 May 2005.

43. In the audio commentary that Chappelle and his co-writer Neal Brennan included in the DVD collection of the first season, the two noted that the initial plan

for the sketch was to have the driver run over the white female dancer rather than merely douse her with standing water from the street. Network executives felt that this more violent censoring of the woman's unsexy style was an excessively harsh statement to make.

44. Those familiar with Chappelle's biography are aware that the comedian is married to an Asian woman, a fact that certainly puts my claims about the artist's nationalist sentiments to question. The sketch material, however, buoys my contentions because of moments like this one, in which Chappelle seems to under-recognize the particularity of Asian or Asian American subjectivity. In later sketches like the "Hater's Ball" or "The World Series of Dice," Chappelle creates his own Afrocentric version of the integrationist aesthetic by including one Asian male into sketch narratives set in racially homogeneous black cultural spaces. These gestures don't necessarily suggest a mutual intercultural mix of blackness and Asian-ness, but rather the incorporation and thus effacement of Asianness by blackness. Put another way, Asians are included in the aesthetic not on their own identitarian and cultural terms, but by becoming black themselves.

45. Haggans, *Lauging Mad,* 193.

46. My thanks to Michelle Elam for being the first to make me aware of Chappelle's remarkable sketch and confirming for me the importance of understanding racial identity as phenomenon adventitious to the subject.

47. Farley, "Dave Speaks."

48. The surprising invocation of Elian Gonzalez, since he is not "the" Latino commodity one would expect to be draft-eligible, leads me to speculate about Chappelle's ethnic background. Does the Francophone nature of his surname bespeak a Haitian heritage? If it does, it would add the differential treatment between Haitians and Cubans by the state to the list of political pressure points touched by including Gonzalez in the sketch.

49. The sketch "White People Dancing," in which Dave lampoons the types of instruments that move racial groups to dance (i.e., guitar/whites or drums/blacks), also seems inspired by the desire to maintain racial boundaries rather than de-materialize them.

50. This issue of who or what types of people have credible knowledge about black people recurs spectacularly throughout the series through the repeat appearances of the comedian Paul Mooney, who, in the sketches "Ask a Black Dude" and "Negrodamus," gains guffaws by frank displays of black erudition.

51. Herman Gray, *Watching Race: Television and The Struggle for Blackness* (Minneapolis: Minnesota University Press, 1995), 180.

52. Devin Gordon and Allison Samuels, "Fears of a Clown," *Newsweek,* 16 May 2005, 60–62; Owen Gleiberman, "In Dave We Trust," *Entertainment Weekly,* 10 March 2006, 42–43. I think it is important to question why, as opposed to other genres of music, hip hop has not been deemed creatively complex enough to earn the honor of sub-categories. In short, I see critical and descriptive use in conceptualizing some efforts as "mainstream" and others as "alternative."

53. "One Eight Seven," a duet with Dr. Dre, was the artist's first commercial hit and served as the anthem for a movie that itself pinned the prevalence of the drug industry squarely on the federal government's shoulders while meditating on the violence it caused between black people.

54. I would like to thank my colleague, novelist Kiese Laymon, for bringing this point to my attention.

55. Two other factors point to Chappelle's affinity to black nationalism. First, in September of 2004, Chappelle organized a massive outdoor concert featuring many of the alternative hip hop artists who have performed on his television show, making

a documentary out of the event entitled *Block Party* (2005). The concert was held in the predominantly black Fort Greene section of Brooklyn, New York. Second, as I noted earlier in the essay, the comedian chose Africa, particularly Durban, South Africa (home of the International Conference on Race in 2001), to be the destination site of his escape from the show. Both gestures suggest Chappelle's desire to grant his nationalist sentiments a spatial grounding, particularity with localities populated by black majority.

56. Ellis, "The New Black Aesthetic," 238.
57. Ibid., 237.

II.

Biography

8 Jump Street!

JOSEPH NAZEL

"If you're born black, you come from Jump Street. I wonder if the doctors don't mess with you when you're born. And diseases!—especially if you're poor in this country. You live around rats and roaches and you survive those bites and don't get rabies when everybody in the world gets rabies, and you don't get brain damage from eating the lead paint. You come up and go to school and in spite of them trying not to teach you anything and destroy your character, you hold on to it and try to have your principles about you, and you learn all their stuff and hold yours and you're a proud black person walking the street. It's amazing! It knocks me out! It makes me cry."

Jump Street for Richard Franklin Lennox Thomas Pryor was North Washington Street in Peoria, Illinois, on December 1, 1940. Peoria was a town of 105,000 souls, the population swollen over the years by a rag-tag group of escapees from the Deep South. Seeking freedom from the racist practices in the South, the hopeful refugees looked northward and rushed the Mason-Dixon Line, pushing past the great Cotton Curtain which they were sure was the only thing separating them from a more human and prosperous reality. They got tricked.

Some found North Washington Street in Peoria. For others there was Lenox Avenue which knifes through New York City's Harlem. There was Filmore Street in San Francisco. Central Avenue in Los Angeles. Main and Division Streets in Biloxi, Mississippi. Howard Street. 116th Street. Beale Street.

The streets were the same, charged by the same energies, choked by the same miseries. But that was the beauty of the experience—sometimes. It created the blues.

The street transcended reality and became a symbol for the vibrant culture that sprang from the masses of blacks who huddled on the banks of the rutted arteries. Paule Marshall introduces the symbol in her work, *Brown Girl, Brownstones:* "Fulton Street . . . was clamorous voices, hooted laughter and curses ripping the night's warm cloak; a welter of dark faces and gold etched teeth; children crying high among the fire escapes of the tenements; the unrelenting wail of a blues spilling from a bar; a man and a woman in a hallway bedroom; a drunken woman pitching along the street; the sustained shriek of a police siren and its red light stabbing nervously at faces and window. Fulton Street on Saturday night was all beauty and desperation and sadness."

The street did not respect class or education. It was fashioned as a place to tuck black folks away and out of sight. Whites did not differentiate between black folks. They, like their streets and neighborhoods, were all the same. "Respectable tenants," writes Ann Petry in her 1940s novel, *The Street,* "in these houses where colored people were allowed to live included anyone who could pay the rent, so some of them would be drunk and loudmouthed and quarrelsome, given to fits of depression when they would curse and cry violently, given to fits of equally violent elation. And . . . because the walls would be flimsy, why, the people, the bad people, the children, the dogs, and the god awful smells would all be wrapped up together in one big package."

Street people who made their way in the streets, were not the same as those who lived on the street, their thoughts on that day when they would escape the street, escape the *niggerness* associated with the street, the blues, crime, drugs. The lives of all who lived in, or on, the ghetto streets throughout America were all "wrapped up together in one big package." Their common fate was due to a similarity in condition. It was a forced similarity, visited on the "packaged" people by outsiders.

In the streets a black man learns what it is to be a man, a black man, not born nigger, or to be nigger. Nigger is a learned-in absurdity. Nigger is carefully and brutally orchestrated into the language, into tradition, into law and into reality by white folks using exclusion, poverty, undereducation, and even murder to insure that the process takes place or takes its toll. It is in the streets beyond his own street that he really feels his *niggerness* most of all, if he has not found some identity he can hold onto in his own streets.

Black militant H. Rap Brown, who managed to shake macho Americans with his call for black people to arm and protect themselves, said, "The street is where young bloods get their education. I learned how to talk in the street, not from reading about Dick and Jane going to the zoo and all that simple shit. The teacher would test our vocabulary each week but we knew the vocabulary we needed. They'd give us arithmetic to exercise our minds. Hell, we exercised our minds by playing the Dozens."

Life in the streets was based on a different set of rules, different goals. "It was hard," Pryor said of his early years in the streets. "They (parents) did the best they could. They taught me stuff that the average person doesn't get to learn, like real morals and honesty and dignity. You have to have that if you're going to live in the streets. Your word is all you have."

What kind of morality can be found in the streets? Is it simply a reversal of definitions? Bad is now good, as African writer Dugmore Boetie sees the ghetto, "the skeleton with the permanent grin? A live carcass bloated with grief and happiness. Where decency was found in filth and beauty hidden behind ugliness. Where vice was virtue and virtue a vice. A Black heaven glowing with sparks of hell."

Pryor says of Peoria, "some of the neighborhoods, they called them 'bring your hat' neighborhoods 'cause they bring your hat to you. You go down there with your hat on and then later they hand it to you with your head in it . . . It's on the weekends a lot of that shit happens. People get drunk and it's like a pressure cooker, and then there are the fights."

Still, Pryor could tell an interviewer, "I see God in the streets. He's in me and around me."

Where is the morality?

"I used to be the neighborhood baby," Pryor explained to an interviewer for *Ebony* Magazine. "This one would take care of me while that one was out of town and like that. Then my grandmother started taking care of me. I always felt," he goes on, "I was the child protégé of the neighborhood because they wouldn't let me get into stuff. No dope! I first smoked a reefer when I was twenty-years-old. I was that kind of child. They just seemed to help me all the time."

Is it possible that Pryor is leg-pulling when he boasts about his family? "We were *affluent*—had the largest whorehouse in the neighborhood." And certainly Pryor is stretching the truth when he brags, "My grandmother. She was the madam. We had three on one block—313, 317 and 324 North Washington. My grandmother was the rule, the power base, a very strong woman."

If true, that would account for some of the characters and experiences that have entertained and shocked Pryor audiences. If not true it wouldn't discount the authenticity of Pryor's material because it is known that his grandmother owned and operated a pool hall in Peoria, up until her death, a recreation room for pimps and hustlers. But Pryor insists that the whorehouse was a very real part of his life, along with other hardships.

"I just saw some hard things in my life that I hope my kids don't have to see; my father fighting my mother, my being in the whorehouse . . ." But Pryor feels no shame.

"On the other hand, I wouldn't change it. I think you live your life and there's something very, very special about it."

Pryor saw beauty in a wino trying to straighten out a young junkie: "Boy, you know what your problem is? You don't know how to deal with the white man. I do, that's why I'm in the position I am in today." Maybe the irony is not intentional on the part of the wino who Pryor has allowed to show impotence in his failure to control the traffic on his *own* street, in his own neighborhood. Does it matter? Does it soften the sting of the tragic underlying truth?

"I always have a tendency," says Pryor, "to lean into the underlayers and tones of what people really are feeling."

Does Mudbone, the wino, feel his impotence? Has he recognized that he is considered a failure? Does he agree? And if he does see himself as a failure wouldn't that nullify anything he might say as being simply ramblings? Not for Pryor.

"Everybody got some good shit in 'em, you know, we *do*. I believe people good."

Is Pryor searching for an out? Is he trying to justify some of his eccentricities by weighing them against a good that is in all mankind?

"I mess up a great deal in my life," Pryor says. "But I do an enormous amount of good work that supersedes all the bullshit I go through."

More probably Pryor's perception was determined by the lessons he learned under his grandmother's care and in the streets themselves.

"My grandmother," said Pryor, "always told me, 'Son, one thing a white man can't take from you is the knowledge.' You take some sixty-three-year-old cat on the street, ugly, spit coming out his mouth, he's still got something you can't have. You can't say he didn't see that gutter or he didn't drink this wine. That is the knowledge."

The "knowledge" taken one step further, organized by a creative hand, becomes the art, the culture, the history and hopes of a people. It is what makes life "something very, very special."

The knowledge is translated into the language of the people and is thereby preserved and communicated in a more beautiful form by the artists.

"The language of the Negro," according to writer Sarah Webster Fabio, "is classical in the sense that it never gets too far from concrete realities, from the 'thingy' quality of objects, persons, places, matter perceived." Fabio explains further that "Negro . . . is a language—largely unassimilated and unlettered—which cuts through, penetrates things as they are reflected in spirituals, blues or jazz lyrics to a core of meaning eliciting a soulful response, to a moment of realization of what it means to be a human being in a world with a stranglehold on this awareness."

It was in the streets that Pryor learned to speak. He seldom reads but has noted that he remembers everything, including the mental and physical nuances of what is said to him. It explains his ability to capture, so quickly and easily, those living persons who give body to his humor, his art. Lawrence Levine observed, "Black humor . . . presupposed a common experience between the joke-teller and the audience. Black humor, too, transformed personal expression into collective expression. Black humor, too, functioned to foster a sense of particularity and group identification by widening the gap between those within and those outside of the circle of laughter."

While Pryor's humor, black in content and context, does not appeal readily to white sensibilities, the art of it transcends the uneasy feelings and reaches that level of universality when all parties are unmasked for what they are. Pryor has become a universal artist, though many would deny that anything black could ever have a universal impact.

Pryor's art, like black music, can easily reach out to others because of its very visual quality which combines with vocals which are qualified by tones, sounds that communicate without use of the spoken word. It is truly the language which has come from the streets. And that language is spoken and acted out with a series of nods, movements of the face, eyes, and hands, vocal inflections which take away all doubt as to what is meant. The language, like Pryor's comedy, must be seen and heard at the same time in order to be fully understood. A movement of the eyes can change the entire meaning of a word or phrase. A change in pitch can be a warning, even in the most innocent of conversations.

Part of Pryor's act is a routine where he says, "I feel," without much feeling initially. But in a matter of moments, using the same "I feel," his change in inflection and facial and body movements transform the word into a living piece of art that expresses pain, pleasure, agony, a series of emotions carefully orchestrated by Richard Pryor. It is universal because it is universally understood. It is universal not because it looks exactly like art forms or statements from other cultures but because it serves the same *function*. A foot does the same job no matter the color.

"Niggers just have a way of telling you stuff," said Pryor, "and not telling you stuff. Martians would have a difficult time with niggers. They be translating words, saying a whole lot of things underneath you, all around you. That's our comedy."

More to the point it is reflective of all arts which came out of the black experience—blues, jazz, even the literature, though Amiri Baraka (Leroi Jones) would disagree, at least where literature is concerned.

". . . the absence of achievement," writes Baraka, who was a thorn in the side of both the black middle class and the white establishment, "among serious Negro artists, except in Negro music, is that in most cases the Negroes who found themselves in a position to pursue some art, especially the art of literature, have been members of the Negro middle class, a group that has always gone out of its way to cultivate *any* mediocrity, as long as that mediocrity was guaranteed to prove to America, and recently to the world at large, that they were not really who they were, i.e., Negroes."

Poet Langston Hughes echoed Jones, writing that "this is the mountain standing in the way of any true Negro art in America—this urge within the race toward whiteness, the desire to pour racial individuality into the mold of American standardization, and to be as little Negro and as much American as possible." The underlying assumption is that in order to be "American" blacks must mimic whites in thought, word, and deed. This was something that street people objected to, rebelled against. It was this kind of rebelliousness that was *learned* into Pryor through his association with those blacks who made up that body.

Pryor is reluctant to give too many details about his early life, in the streets, in the whorehouse. It is what he calls his "real stuff" which he protects with the passion and concern with which one would watch over the family jewels. But there is no doubt that Pryor, like most black young men facing puberty in the late forties and early fifties, knew what it was to hang on the corner. Corner boys knew where the action was. At least they watched, listened, muscle-flexing as they "began to smell themselves good," as the old folks say.

On the corner young blacks got the message of who they were, who they might have been and might be. It was on the corner that they heard the blues "talkin' shit" and "teachin'" from the dark, smoky innards of bars. On the corner they saw the world, as they knew it, and all its nuances. It was a living encyclopedia that kept an account of history through song and a rich folk poetry, toasts, which comprised the oral tradition that kept things *alive.*

The oral tradition is a very personalized way of communicating thoughts and ideas.

The Dozens, toasts, jokes were all part of the oral tradition and were games street corner boys got into to pass time. "It's like niggers train in a different way," said Pryor. "Like, they don't have no theater groups, but niggers train on the corner, you know what I mean? Like when you hang out bullshittin', and singin' and shit. I mean, them cats trainin' for when they get their groups together."

Pryor would have been exposed to the stories told by pimps, hustlers, and gamblers. He would have been exposed to the toasts which bragged of black victories over whites, passed on information, or simply entertained. The signifying monkey toast is one of the better known, revolving around the antics of a fast talking monkey who cons a lion into fighting an elephant:

> The monkey told the lion one bright summer day,
> There's a bad motherfucker heading your way.
> He talked about you brother, put your sister in the shelf,
> The way he talked about your mother, I wouldn't say to myself.

The lion is forced to defend himself and his against the slurs of the "Dozens" playing elephant without challenging the signifying monkey's accusations. It ends in disaster for the lion, who finally says "quits."

The "signifier" becomes the target of the angry Lion.

> Said, "Monkey, I'm not kickin' your ass for lyin',
> I'm kicking your hairy ass for signifyin'."

But the quick-thinking monkey is up for the challenge, his mind working against the lion's brawn, first failing in a teary appeal to the lion's sympathy, then attacking the lion's macho:

> The monkey said: "Let me get my teeth out of the grit and
> my balls out of the sand,
> and I'll fight your ass like a *real* he-man.
> So the Lion stepped back to the end of the curve,
> 'cause that was the boldest challenge he'd ever heard.
> But faster than the hand or the human eye could see,
> the monkey was back in the coconut tree.

Bruce Jackson did a great deal of research into the street toast and concluded in his book, *Get Your Ass in the Water and Swim Like Me,* the toast is a kind of street theater, a theater involving only one performer at a time. People who can say the lines but cannot act them get little opportunity to perform, because they are boring.

Jackson adds further, "The street corner world includes those who make it with brawn and those who make it with brains, and a very few who make it with both."

Pryor found out early that he wasn't a street-fighter. "I would always get degraded in a fight. Yeah, I wanted to win them all, but the dude would make me back down and I would always feel like a coward. I'd go home and say, 'Nigger, if you are a coward then stay out of those situations and you won't have to worry about it.' Then I'd find a little something to make me feel cool."

Pryor admitted that he once "used to take a lot of drugs—to experiment, to find out who I was. Mostly I did it to accept the fact that I was no street-fighter." In that respect the streets of Peoria's black community were much the same as the other streets in ghettos around the United States. They were angry places. Places where a man, or a woman, could get killed, sometimes, over the slightest provocation. When you could not run—even "cool run," like Richard—you had to learn to survive, or be broken. Pryor learned that early. His characters reflect that realization. They know their limits. Many of them constantly, though slyly, challenge those limits at every opportunity.

It was through humor that blacks challenged those limits and taboos imposed on them. The humor was biting, showing a situation for being absurd, yet there was an undercurrent, the recognition that pushing the limits too far could lead to an ass whuppin', or worse. Here we find the essence of Pryor's sharp humor. It cuts both ways, like a swinging pendulum, punishing both, unmasking all the participants in the tragicomedy. There is nothing more tragic or funny than Pryor's confrontation with the reality of the awesome power of the police in his role as Oilwell, who asserts that he is "six-foot-five, four hundred and twenty pounds of *maaaaaaannn!*"

The assertion is always applauded by all within earshot. The act is a defiant one. A show of strength. But there are consequences which have to be faced. The act could be suicidal. Confrontations with police are often degrading.

"Boy, you hit me with that stick I'm gonna bite your dick! They'll be some bloodshed. I ain't bullshittin'." Or Jesse who would fight the cops.

Cop: You kids stop having so much fun and go home.
Jesse: I ain't goin' no place.
Cop: We've got ways of making you move.
Jesse: Yeah, well they'd better be some good ones.

The defiance would lead to a battle with 30 cops who issue Jesse what is referred to in the streets sometimes as a very "righteous ass whuppin'."

It was a bitter victory for Jesse. And it is still a victory, even though he is viciously beaten. For Pryor's people the victory comes in Jesse's willingness to stand his ground no matter the consequences. He becomes the absurd heroic figure who is celebrated in his defeat. No one expected things to be otherwise, though in the back of their minds, way back so as not to be a pressure, they hoped that Jesse would win out, for them all. Pryor is no Jesse or Oilwell. He gave up that hope when he claims to have been "unmasked" for the coward he supposedly was by a stern, "Nigger! Unball your fist!" Pryor backed down!

Oddly, though, he hasn't backed down from much since. He found, like most other brothers who once *do whopped* with the "corner brigade," that there were many more ways of getting over and surviving life in the streets. Being cool, quick-witted and using his keen perception to put things together, Pryor survived, as the Signifying Monkey did, with guile.

"We used to have good sessions sometimes," Pryor said of the verbal contests, "I remember once I came up with a beaut, man, I killed them one day. We was doin' it all day to each other, you know. Bang-bang— 'Your shoes are run over so much, look like your *ankles* is broke,' and shit like that. I called the motherfucker 'The Rummage Sale Ranger,' you know what I mean? 'Cause that's where he got his clothes. That was a knockout, I saved that one for the last, that ended it."

Like the Dozens, the word games, the jibes and jokes, were not intended to draw blood. They were intended as insulation against the depression that came with the realization that the joke-teller was in the same boat as the butt of his joke. "Under the mask of humor," says Gershon Legman, psychologist, "our society allows infinite aggressions, by everyone and against everyone."

It was the tool most often used by slaves who found some satisfaction in humor that sliced out at their oppressors without any fatal consequences. Still, there were fights. Pryor became a master of the art, learning how to overcome the obstacles he faced, so that he wouldn't have to run. In the late forties and in the fifties, there really wasn't any place to run. His ancestors had already run from segregation in the South to meet a more subtle kind in Peoria. But for all of Pryor's energy it is doubtful that this talent would have developed beyond the level of the streets and small time bars if not for the encouragement of one Juliette Whittaker, supervisor of the Carver Community Center in Peoria.

The Carver Community Center, like most of its kind, were buffers provided by the white community. Part of their function was to limit gang fights, supposedly due only to idleness. Richard Wright saw the sometimes folly in them and wrote, "They were paying me to distract . . . with ping-pong, checkers, swimming, marbles, and baseball in order that he might not roam the streets and harm the valuable white property which adjoined the black belt." But Wright did not damn the "clubs and ping-pong as such," pointing out that "these little stopgaps were utterly inadequate to fill up the centuries-long chasm of emptiness which American civilization had created . . . I felt that I was doing a kind of dressed-up police work, and I hated it."

Juliette Whittaker took her work seriously and helped Pryor direct his energy. At age twelve Pryor made his first appearance at Carver Community Center. He played the King in the Center's production of *Rumpel-stiltskin*. The role became a trademark routine when Pryor took to the professional stage.

In 1977 Pryor returned to Peoria and in a show of everlasting gratitude presented Juliette Whittaker with the Emmy statuette he won for writing a Lily Tomlin special. Pryor hadn't forgotten those who helped him. It is a trait that shines through all the jive that often clouds the mystique of the man. But the early years were not always street-corner fingerpoppin', Dozens games, and basketball. There was school. And though school, before the May 17, 1954, legislation that was supposed to knock down *separate but equal* educational institutions, was quite different, the difference was hardly a positive one.

Pryor's initial exposure to the school system was as a Catholic. "I went to Catholic school for about three weeks," Pryor told David Felton of *Rolling Stone,* "and then somebody said that my mother worked in a whorehouse, you know, so I got kicked out of school. It was a drag, 'cause that was the only school I was gettin' good grades in. They were very polite! It's not enough that he's a nigger, but you see . . ."

Pryor's mother, Gertrude, was a Catholic and Pryor was born in a Catholic hospital, quipping, "I was born in St. Francis Hospital—I was meant to be a Catholic, you know. That was pretty hip to be born in a hospital in Peoria. Most cats was born at home, in the kitchen." The remainder of his school career was spent in the public school system in Peoria. Probably a good thing for the Catholic Church. Pryor's sensitivity and intensity might well have led him into the priesthood. Given Pryor's atti- tudes and approaches to things, the Vatican would have had its hands full.

Allegedly Pryor was put into a class for the mentally retarded be- cause of his hyperactivity. Absurd? Of course! But it was reflective of the times. Teachers were not expected to be sensitive to the children of the darker herd that crowded into the cities. And even those few who were sincerely concerned about educating their charges found it difficult, at times, to communicate because of the very real cultural gap that sepa- rates the black community from the white community.

Pryor would have a rougher time of it. He would have faced the school system that had not heard of the still un-inked *Brown vs. Topeka, Kansas School Board.* All studies of the time were directed at finding out just why *they* supposedly could not compete with their white counter- parts. Even some black escapees supported such "victim-directed" dis- sections that were designed to support the assumption that blacks were either inherently inferior to whites, or that they were inferior to whites because of the long years of slavery and poverty and racism that kept them separated from mainstream America. In any case, liberals and racists seemed to agree on one thing: black folks, at least most—Roy Wilkins was cool—were inferior *but it really wasn't their own fault.*

Pryor had established a "rep" as a prankster. It is no doubt that this show of embryonic genius was probably misread by those who still had not accepted blacks as possessing a distinctly black culture, even though they were interacting with the larger group. Pryor was expelled at age fourteen for hitting a science teacher. Did the confrontation come out of a need for better communication? It's hard to tell. But it is certain that by then Pryor had begun to feel his *niggerness,* or at least the ill-fitting jacket of niggerness that was being forced on his still growing mind and body.

"When I was a little boy," said Pryor, "I was in love with this girl in my class, and I brought her a scratch board. You know, one of those gray cardboard things you draw on, and then you lift up the plastic and the picture's gone? The next day her daddy comes to school and says, 'Don't you dare give my little girl a present.' When I told my father he just shook his head. You see, nobody had told me about racism, but he knew!"

Pryor's father, Leroy, owned a construction company in Peoria. As a young adult Pryor is said to have driven a truck for his father. It would be difficult to guess at the elder Pryor's reasons for not telling his son about racism, though it is a subject which is more difficult to explain to a youngster than is the whole matter of creation and sex. There is a logic to sex, a simplicity that follows. Where is the logic in racism?

Maybe we can find the answer in Pryor's art. Or at least get an overview of the chaos, racism, that hit Pryor without warning, a jolt that all blacks have faced. Pryor would have had to find some way to deal with it humorously. The wino who gets blamed for a break in the levee in Lawrence County provides a clue to how some parents, probably Pryor's, approached the whole subject of racism.

In defense of himself under the charge of allowing the levee to bust, the wino said, "Shit, can't a nigger in the world hold back no water when it want to go!" And explaining why he didn't run through the water to warn the people he says, "They was gonna find out about it soon enough."

All black children find out about racism "soon enough," which is often too soon. And many black parents, especially those who have escaped from the South, where training is started much earlier, avoid the subject in hopes that they will never have to address themselves to the degrading aspects of their own participation in or lack of power over the madness.

"I was ready to cry as a kid," Pryor said, and explained that he, like all kids, saw things simply, without color. "I didn't think about color—just feelings. My heroes at the movies were the same as everyone else's. I wanted to be John Wayne too. I didn't know John Wayne hated my guts." Bubbles burst quickly. "That's the way I see kids," said Pryor. "I just get fascinated talking to 'em, 'cause it'll be honestly sweet, and whatever they say is innocent. They deal with real shit."

Pryor survived it all; the whorehouse, the streets, the public school system. And a great deal of credit must be given to his grandmother Marie Carter Pryor Bryant who was the guiding force in Pryor's life, the "rule" which had to be obeyed. Much of Pryor's defiance must have come from the independent Marie Bryant. If in fact she actually owned a chain of whorehouses, it would be proof that she lived in defiance of all the rules and regulations set to keep her in check. Still, all information seems to show that she refused to allow young Richard Pryor the same latitude, forcing him to conform to certain restrictions.

Pryor's mother died in 1969 but it was Pryor's grandmother who had taken over his upbringing long before. Pryor recalled his mother: "My mother went through a lot of hell behind me, because people would tell her, 'You don't take care of that boy.' She always wanted me to be somebody and she wasn't the strongest person in the world. But I give her a lot of credit. At least she didn't flush me down the toilet like some do."

While he was understanding of his mother's plight, he more than adored his strong-willed grandmother. In 1977 he bought her an expensive, ranch style home in Peoria. But she was only to enjoy the home for two years. Marie Bryant passed away in 1979, tearing some of the heart out of her adoring grandson.

Pryor was overwhelmed with grief at the passing of the one person who could still exercise some modicum of control over the so-called unpredictable Pryor. He had cancelled all of his concert dates when the seventy-nine-year-old, still-active businesswoman was felled by stroke. He spent his time near her, and was with her when she died at 6:30 in the morning in Methodist Medical Center in Peoria. Miss Mexcine Pryor, an aunt of the humorist's, was reported to have said of Pryor, "He just stood there shaking like a rag doll. He was just crying and talking, 'Mamma! Mamma! Mamma!' He had a grip on her hand and they couldn't pry him loose without a struggle. They couldn't get him out of that room and when they did, he broke and come right back in there.

"When they pulled him out of there and took him down to the lounge, that's when he really broke down. I tried to console him and he cried: 'Everything I've had and everything I've got is gone. My mamma's gone. I just loved her, I loved her, I loved her. Mamma, I did everything I could for you. Everything! I prayed, and I prayed. Mamma, I prayed so hard. I didn't even know I could pray."

While alive Pryor's grandmother saw to it that he graduated from Central High School where it is said that he lettered as a cool running halfback, and as a center and forward in basketball. There may still be some doubt as to the authenticity of reports by Pryor that he actually lived in a whorehouse. Pryor may well have concocted the story to further enhance the rebelliousness of his art as symbol. There is no doubt that Pryor loved and respected his grandmother, and, but for her, the Pryor story might well have taken a quite different course.

NOTE

From Joseph Nazel, *Richard Pryor: The Man behind the Laughter* (Los Angeles: Holloway House Publishing, 1981), 19–38.

9 The Politics of Being Black

John A. Williams and Dennis A. Williams

Curiously, most of Pryor's white fans discovered him in the mid-1970s, when he was pounding out film after film, and his concerts and club dates grew to monstrous sizes and numbers. It was bicentennial time, that period of reflection and celebration of two hundred years of American-style democracy, which Pryor marked with his album, *Bicentennial Nigger*. In the final monologue the comedian recounts the travails of Afro-Americans and concludes the list of wrongs with: "I ain't never gonna forget," lending an overtly political note to the album (which won him another Grammy) and perhaps even acknowledging his awareness of his own political influence.

Pablo Guzman of *The Village Voice* wrote that "the heart of Richard's appeal is that he is a *political* force."

> "That's right: politics, not mere entertainment, is what Pryor's always been about. The politics of being an Everyday African Male in America. . . . After all, Richard's comedy has always been both subversive and revelatory."

Silver Streak not only helped to make Pryor the "crossover" star—it helped to make him, unofficially, of course, but nevertheless palpably, a leader.

At no time during their bleak and circuitous sojourn in the American wilderness have black people been without a voice urging them to keep on keeping on. Sometimes there were several; sometimes they argued about the direction to take and how, but there was always a voice, and there was always laughter. The laughter was dark and removed. Those white people who had designed the wilderness knew that if the situation was reversed, they would not have been able to live, let alone laugh.

Even so, if a voice was to be heard, it was to be the preacher's voice; preachers most readily spoke the language the trail wardens understood —meekness and piety. The voices that were not raised purely and completely to God, but were instead leveled at the wardens, were ignored or silenced. Still, from out of the dark, the voices kept sounding and not the least among them were the voices of the funny men and women who made people laugh in the Saturday sessions at the barbershop or hairdressing parlor, in the mean bars and meaner street corners, in church basements where choirs gathered before marching upstairs to services, or out in the sharecropped fields.

The black funnymen like Bert Williams and George Walker were first heard loudly, speaking through their own voices, during the 1920s, when W. E. B. Du Bois edited *The Crisis* and Marcus Garvey had run afoul of both the government and the elements of the black population that did not like him or his Back-to-Africa movement.

In the 1960s and early 1970s there existed side by side black militancy, black piety, black academic rationalism, black political realism, and black humor—and all were converging on the system in flank and frontal assaults. It did seem that way, and later, in some of the high places after things had been whipped back to near normal, it was learned by many of those in the several movements that the overcoming had been closer than any of them had ever realized, that the voices had not only been heard, but feared as well; the murders indicated that—whether they occurred in Mississippi or Soledad Prison, at Kent State or Jackson State, in Newark or Watts or Detroit. The Nixon administration's "Garden Plot" contingency plan for rounding up dissidents was the proof.

And Richard Pryor's voice stabbed the ferment with sardonic "I-am-reaching-into-my-pocket-for-my-license-'cause-I-don't-wanna-be-no-motherfuckin-accident!" hysteria, and let every cop know that black (and some white) people understood precisely what was going on. "If," Bill Cosby said, "Richard isn't doing anything more than just letting black people have a hero in the monologue, a hero who kicks the white cop's ass, for that release, then Richie's a bad cat. And he makes them all bad cats. He's not trying to draw people out; he's just telling them what's in his mind." What had been on Pryor's mind, though, was fame, how to become famous doing what he did best. He would say in 1976, "I want people to be able to recognize me by just looking at a caricature of me that has no name on it. I want to be great, and you can recognize great people like Muhammad Ali and Bob Hope by just looking at a nameless caricature and say, 'That's him, that's Richard Pryor!' Then I'll be great."

It seemed he always knew that shocking people would attract their attention, and in the early 1970s there were many things to distract people's attention away from Richard Pryor, who was moving briskly along the trail upward, becoming ever more prominent. The events surrounding his rise at this time included the recognition by many white Americans that the term "nigger" was demeaning. Crackers who beat up Freedom Riders and burned their buses used it; the men who murdered James Chaney, Andrew Goodman, and Michael Schwerner used it. In the film *To Kill a Mockingbird* (1962) we *knew* Gregory Peck was a good guy because he *didn't* use the term while defending Brock Peters on a bogus rape charge in the Deep South. Of all the pieces of luggage in the racist baggage car, this term was the easiest to unload. To do so cost nothing. The times demanded that the term be stamped DO NOT APPLY IN PUBLIC. Private, in-house use was another matter, of course. One did have to be more careful. When force or control is present, one does not employ derogatory ethnic designations to those who have the force or control. Not wise.

Black use of the term has been consigned to the psychological shelf labeled "self-hate." The location may be apt, but the first step to eliminate that and to control one's destiny is to determine the name by which you shall be called. No one else can really do that. (The experience is not confined to Afro-Americans alone; all over the world people and places have been named by adventurers who came from someplace else. The word, Egypt, for example, is not "Egyptian" but Greek.) Dick Gregory's book, *Nigger* (1962), purported to take the sting out of the term.

Pryor's use of the word in concert with others that were biologically *not* related to race brought a familiar shock to black people. It made some of them uneasy. Some complained, others had reservations about the comedian and his lack of "black pride." It was like hearing a language that might be spoken only at home being shouted through the streets. "Oh, he's disgusting," people said. But they watched and listened without missing a beat, equally fascinated and repelled because there were so many things to work through to get to where the comedian himself assumed it was all right to call people by something other than their rightful name. Was this the return the black middle class was getting for its investment in a Richard Pryor vogue? Why were the white folks as delighted with him as they were? Sure, he spoke golden truth—but did he have to say *nigger* so much?

James Alan McPherson wrote: "[Pryor's] scenes are sprinkled liberally with this gem, so much in fact that some black people have complained he is damaging the image of the group by moving the word from the pool-halls and barbershops back into public usage. The word 'nigger,' however, has never gone out of style. The movie industry and some whites opposed to busing have done far more than Pryor to keep the word alive."

Whatever uneasiness some black people were feeling, there were some white writers like Mark Jacobson who were of the opinion that "Using the word 'nigger' was the masterstroke. It aced him [Pryor] out of the mainstream, plus it made it quite clear where his racial allegiance lay. Everyone knows white people are not allowed to say that word."

And *Time* joined the chorus that seemed to be all white when it agreed that it was a nifty word, cleverly used by Pryor to mean something other than what it had always meant:

> When Pryor says it, it means something different from what it did through too much of America's history. Depending on his inflection or even the tilt of his mouth, it can mean simply black. Or it can mean a hip black, wise in the ways of the street. Occasionally nigger can even mean white in Pryor's reverse English lexicon. However he defines it, Pryor is certain of one thing. He is proudly, assertively a nigger, the first comedian to speak in the raw, brutal, but wildly hilarious language of the street.

"Nigger" is a word, a term, that concretizes an idea, a concept, a historical entity, a designation of the caste and class to which black people have been assigned. It did not matter that when Pryor used it, it became like punctuation. At other times when he uttered it, the word dripped with contempt. It was the bear trap of history, with six razor-sharp teeth: n-i-g-g-e-r. Maybe Pryor was asking people to work their way through the pain, the memories, to conclude that this word was only a word.

Black publications, however, did not excuse its use; their writers did not attempt to rationalize or psychoanalyze it; for them the word was what it was, and that was precisely why so many white people stopped using it publicly. They didn't have to. For there was a voice "re-zounding" in larger and larger clubs to bigger and bigger audiences in the 1970s, and it pronounced "nigger" like a machine gun. It was Richard

Pryor's voice. White people had found a black man who could call other black people "niggers" for them. [*Richard Pryor is funny*] Funny, yes, and he always called white people white people or white folks.

There were many times, however, when Pryor while using the term deftly switched from his own persona to another—a white authoritarian person (a stock voice-character in his repertoire). His audiences learned that he was then speaking (and acting) in a way that was perceived by blacks to be accurate; that he then projected a collective white mind-set in regard to blacks. The classic example of this change in projection is the skit "The New Niggers" (. . . *Is It Something I Said?* 1974):

> . . . Got all the Vietnamese in the Army camps an' shit takin' tests an' stuff, learnin' how to say nigger [*laughter*] so they can become good citizens. [*laughter*] But they got classes—you know—they have—[*authoritarian voice*] "All right, let's try it again, troops."
>
> "Nigguh! Nigguh! Nigguh! . . . Nigguh! Nigguh! Nigguh! Nigguh!"
>
> "Eh, that's close. If you get your ass kicked, you know you made it." [*mild cheers, loud, long applause*]

(A dispute between Korean grocers and black customers erupted in New York City in early summer 1990, when one of the grocers was accused of beating a black woman. The Koreans said she had been shoplifting. She denied the charge. The New York media pounded its drums; pickets and anti-pickets appeared in the street before the Korean shop. In the end, the woman said she did not remember which of the Koreans had attacked her, and witnesses appeared for the cameras in support of the grocers. The dispute probably is reflected a hundred times a week between Asian Americans and African Americans in those cities where the Asians have established businesses in the black communities.)

"His [Pryor's] vocabulary," wrote Janet Maslin in *The New York Times* eight years after "The New Niggers," "noticeably lacks the word 'nigger,' which was formerly one of its great staples." It was, indeed, and when the wisdom came, after the 1980 fire, few whites were using the term publicly. Before this time, with his multitude of voices Pryor *did* expose the word, pried open its nuances as used between black husband and black wife, between white and black (male, female), and between black and black (male). But one black college professor, who loved all the Dionysian displays, found that Pryor's use of the word still rankled.

He said, "When I was young I went to see Jean-Paul Sartre's *The Respectful Prostitute*. That was the first time I'd ever heard 'nigger' spoken out in a very public place. I was angry that I'd paid my money to go and hear that, and I am still angered when I hear Pryor—I am also puzzled that he seems to get such a positive response whenever he uses the word in those things he does."

The voices of leaders should show some constraint, but that depends on the kind of leader people need at a particular time; sometimes they need all they can get their hands on at the same precise time. We know that Dick Gregory all but gave up his career, not to be a leader but to serve. That, however, almost automatically makes one a leader, in the black community, anyway, if a person gives up a highly lucrative career in order to work with the people. Cosby is a role model for many black people. Neither Gregory nor Cosby flayed their audiences with "nigger."

It is possible that, during his Berkeley stint with "Broadway" Brown and the other writers, it occurred to Pryor that here was Cecil Brown, following the lead of Gregory, actually using the word on the cover of a book! Indeed, Pryor once introduced Brown to his audience, called him —not a writer—but a novelist, and mentioned the title of his novel, *The Life and Loves of Mr. Jiveass Nigger.*

In *Richard Pryor—Live! in Concert,* the comedian introduced a for-mer leader, Huey Newton of the Black Panthers, and in *Live on the Sunset Strip,* the camera rested momentarily on the Reverend Jesse Jackson. Pryor's politics have always reflected an awareness of racial injustice. This made it all the more difficult to understand why he used "nigger" for so long, unless it was to shock; certainly it cannot have been to make white fans smug. And "greed," too, must be eliminated as a reason, for he was fast approaching the point where he would have "enough money for a black man to live on forever."

In time he would say that it was his trip to Africa that made him realize that the word should no longer occupy a place in his public vocabulary—and that would be a good show-business rap. Fans re-sponded to the announcement with whistles, cheers, and applause, be-cause they understood, however dimly, the political ramifications of the statement.

It was not that his fans always misunderstood the manner in which Pryor employed the term; the use was always two-leveled: black people using it against (the preposition is apt) each other, *perhaps* as a reflection of a long, ingrained self-hatred, cast onto a fellow, that had been taught by the American experience in subtle and not so subtle ways. Using it made you—maybe—feel just a little bit better about yourself, as in the stunning skit of "the Wino and the Junkie" (which has a couple of levels itself).

The second level, obviously far more political, had to do with Pryor's crawling into the white psyche (or the ones that dominate society) and using "nigger" the way they do. And even if they did not, in Pryor's view, *speak* the word, they thought it, and Pryor gave those thoughts the voice all black people heard.

Still, it was the public shock that gnawed at so many black fans, together with a lingering sense of betrayal. It was like having a brother on the Civil Rights Commission who was supposed to do you some good, only the brother turned out to be Brutus' best teacher. Most people did not care about the levels of use of the term; they only knew what they heard and what it had always meant. For Pryor, the easy, frequent use of the word may have started at home.

In the skit "Have Your Ass Home by Eleven" (*That Nigger's Crazy*), the comedian relates a "conversation" with his father about going out at night, with the deadline for return at eleven. The father addresses his son as "nigger!" just about every five words. On the same album, the description of the commonplace ritual of sitting down and eating dinner is laced with the word. If, once again, Pryor's life is his act, what he brought from home was—some people think—peculiar baggage. A generation of black people concluded during the 1960s and early 1970s that the name *could* hurt, but it seemed to have taken Pryor far longer to understand its devastating effect on Afro-Americans.

Pryor told *Ebony's* senior editor Lerone Bennett in 1982 that he went to Africa and discovered there were no "niggers" there. Bennett reminded Pryor that the comedian once said "that using the word took the sting out of it."

Pryor responded: "Yeah, I told myself all those lies. . . . It can't make you feel good, because when the white man calls us that, it hurts, no matter how strong we try to be about it. There's pain [in that word]. . . . I feel funny when I see black men and black women in positions of power use it."

So he had, by the time of *Live on the Sunset Strip,* "grown" (one of his favorite terms) enough to publicly announce that he would no longer use the word "nigger."

However, he made no such vow to give up the Black English he'd used so effectively in his monologues. The appearance of Black English on the national scene coincided with the international emergence of the French-speaking Caribbean and African writers' philosophy of Negritude—which owed its beginnings to Langston Hughes and the Harlem Renaissance. Negritude was the philosophy of extraordinary pride in all aspects of black culture wherever in the world it might be found, but particularly Africa. In the 1960s, black writers—especially poets—often went back to the streets for inspiration and reaffirmation of the validity and vibrancy of black life. Black college professors, newly hired on at prestigious universities, often would finish a class on the British Romantic Writers, or American Literature to the Twentieth Century, then retreat with a black colleague and begin "talkin' the talk."

The double negative flourished in writing as well as in speech, an example of which is Pryor's "I don't wanna be no accident!" The intransitive verb, *be*—to exist not only in actuality, but also in a specific place and time—became the hippest way to use the verb *am.* "I be walking" was more powerful—and picturesque—than "I am walking." Two or three words were converted to one: "What is happening?" yielded "What's happening?"—which was finally rendered as "Zappening?"

Professor Geneva Smitherman of Wayne State University, through her talks and writings, became one of many defenders of the use of Black English, but there were many educators who opposed it. White teachers who favored the use of Black English as a way of getting ghetto kids to express themselves were looked upon with great suspicion, because everyone *knew* you had to speak White English to get any kind of a job, and maybe some white educators were running a game on the students. This battle was raging long before James Baldwin observed in 1979 that "People evolve a language . . . to describe and thus control their circumstances, or in order not to be submerged by a reality they cannot articulate."

Richard Pryor articulated extremely well in Black English, his voice rising and falling, his body flailing about as he acted out what it was he was saying. "Richard Pryor," Cosby had said in 1970, "is perhaps the only comedian that I know of today who has captured the total character of the ghetto."

In the 1970s, Black English became "Talking Black," the hip way to communicate, and Richard Pryor helped promote and legitimize it. His boyhood mentor, Miss Whittaker, approved, observing: "If he is portraying a man in the street, then he's got to do what a person like that does and says."

The question for Pryor in the mid-1970s was whether he was going to be a movie star or a comedian. Despite the attractions of movie money, there would be fewer chances in film for him to be the force he was in performance, because the script would not always be his. Most people knew by this time that the Richard Pryor on the screen was not the person they knew on stage.

On stage, Pryor might have been to his contemporary audiences what Charlie Chaplin was to moviegoers over a half century ago. Hannah Arendt noted that Chaplin "could not fail to arouse the sympathy of the common people who recognized in him the image of what society had done to them." Pryor did some Chaplin-like skits.

Many of the "common people" who empathized with Chaplin's portrayals have themselves become oppressors, but they raised, for one reason or another, a generation whose sensitivities seem to have been, in the 1960s and 1970s, alert to political and economic inequities based on race, and Pryor, therefore, may have been a contemporary version of the Chaplin figure in the way Reggie Jackson updated Babe Ruth.

As the underdog, Chaplin usually managed to achieve the small, timorous revenges of the common man, but these were tacit recognitions that the powers could grind him into dust if only endowed with his luck and cleverness. There is no victory for Pryor's characters, even Mudbone. Steve Allen recognized that "What almost all of them [Pryor's characters] have in common is a pathetic tendency to try to disguise or manipulate the facts of their own experience by pure talk, what the Irish would call blarney. . . . In bringing such men and women to the attention of his audiences, Pryor is much closer to literature than to traditional nightclub or concert comedy."

Whether literature or concert comedy, Pryor's characters were aggressively black, even if they were victims. And we recognized the characters, just as we recognized Chaplin's. Pryor's characters were often pompously black, hot-air balloons wafting about in capricious winds trying to avoid the needle that would prick them, blow them apart. Pryor is as black as Woody Allen is Jewish—and as cynical.

In his best comedy, Allen laughs at himself, at his mostly ineffectual attempts to best a world that has stereotyped him as a schlemiel. That he sometimes triumphs is the classic rags-to-riches plot. On the other hand, Pryor played to the knowledge that one must conceal weakness, camouflage vulnerability with bravado, as in "We bad, we bad." The sham is immediately recognized. Fans of all kinds understand where power resides and the ways in which it can be exercised.

Aristotle said comedy was built on ridicule; one attacked some "defect or ugliness" within a system as well as within a person, within the self, within one's people and one's society. Such was the function of Pryor's scathing ridicule. He laughed at himself, his people, his country. He pinioned the black preacher to a bulls-eye of a target when he mounted what was his most horrifyingly hilarious skit in his "Bicentennial Prayer" from his album *Bicentennial Nigger,* in which the preacher alternately soothes his congregation and then rages at it:

> I'd like to say to the crippled peoples that come here—can't you find another church to go to? [*laughter, oooos*] Goddamn, come in knockin' shit down [*laughter*] 'n' breakin' up furniture 'n' shit. . . . [*laughter*] Learn how to crawl!! Shitttt. [*laughter, ooooos*] An' you deaf and dumb motherfuckers, you motherfuckers that can't talk, we don't need ya here! [*laughter*] All that whoo-whoo shit, kiss my ass! [*laughter*] They got schools for ya to go to. [*laughter*] Go learn how to speak, goddamn it! [*laughter*]

Chaplin, of course, did not and could not use such comedy—to trip up a pursuer with his cane seemed to have been enough, given the time when Chaplin performed. To pose defects against religion (or more accurately, some purveyors of it) is a loaded double-barreled shotgun. Pryor's skit did not shock us as much as scatter all our fine sensibilities to the wind. And yet we laugh, and Aristotle is again proved right, as Richard Pryor demonstrates once more his stated theme that "those cats in church were jive."

If Chaplin and Woody Allen are understated, and Bill Cosby is supercool, and Redd Foxx blase, Pryor took an entirely different approach; hyperbole was his thing, exaggerating for understandings other than credence. The monologue above was a hyperbolic romp: We know that even the most unsavory preacher is not likely to conduct himself in this manner in the pulpit.

It is the nature of black comedy to be hyperbolic, for expressions are needed that will more precisely highlight black life in the United States. Sometimes the hyperbole is sexual, at the root of things that are so bad they almost defy description from a white point of view. The hyperbole of the language in the two-voiced skit "The Wino and the Junkie" offers two statements that give the term new meaning.

The Wino has told the Junkie that he knows nothing about women, and the Junkie responds that he does indeed and that he had a woman: "Bitch was so fine I wanted to suck her *daddy's* dick! Izzat fine enough for your ass?" When he has a tough time at the employment office, the Junkie reflects on the female clerk there and says, "Ugly bitch—I seen better faces on a iodine bottle." This last, of course, deals with concrete "ugliness," yet, an unattractive person can no more do anything about the way she looks than can a person who is black. Thus, the tradition of hyperbole, older than Stagolee and Shine, was continued by Pryor in the presentation of American comedy.

The United States has attracted or had brought to it a greater variety of peoples than any other nation since Rome. Each incoming group brought its humor and its comedy, and employed them as it underwent ridicule from groups that had preceded it. No group was more vilified for the ugliness and defectiveness assigned to it by its oppressors than the Africans. Laughing at the powerless was easy and habit-forming. Thus in the United States we have had the redskin joke, the nigger joke, the greaser joke, the spick joke, the Mick joke, the Kraut joke, the chink joke, the kike joke, the dago joke, the Jap joke, the Polack joke, and so on. However, the laughter at the under-group did not alter, did not lessen, the victimization by the more powerful.

Why then should a black comedian like Pryor be immune to the tradition that has washed over, indeed inundated, almost every American? He wasn't. He simply took that tradition to its basest level, and in discussing the "New Niggers" reaped the laughter, from deep within the belly, that always seems to ride with our fears upon which we so easily place stereotypical concepts:

> An' if you ain't done it, be careful if you get some Vietnamese pussy, Jack. Right? Cause they got a VD scare the shit outa penicillin. It be up there waitin' for penicillin, Jack. C'mon up in here, peni—yeah, we got sumpin' for your ass, c'mon up in here. Git a big knot on your dick. . . .

This monologue (like a few others) not only elicited wild laughter, it produced uneasy silences, rising crescendos of "oooo-ooooooooooooooos," as if to say, "Boy, you ought to be ashamed of yourself," but, in the end, it was the laughter that rocked the club or concert hall.

It is not that sex has ever been far from the collective American mind. It was always there, partially concealed in innuendo. Another generation found it in the endless round of traveling salesmen jokes. In the black community (upon which many whites fixed much sexuality anyway), discussions and considerations of sex were always more overt than among whites. And black preachers in these tales and discussions and jokes (along with icemen and coalmen and milkmen) were a favorite target—which is to say, given American history, that black leadership from the pulpit was accepted with a grain of salt. Pryor exposed the relationship, and his audiences agreed with him—otherwise they would not have been falling out with laughter. There was that recognition.

By the same token, white churches and their leaders were viewed by Pryor as pretty pallid stuff, some evangelists being as much charlatans as the black preachers. Much of Pryor's work, in any case, consisted of drawing comparisons between the two groups in sex, manners, and politics; in addition, there were the "private" skits that dealt with his family and himself. ("Who is Richard gonna talk about *tonight*?"). More as with Chaplin than with Allen, Pryor's figures were universal; Allen's are definitely New York or Hollywood chic, not much in between. Perhaps Pryor's comedy would not have been so successful without the range and variety of his intonations, which he matches up with not only the character of the moment, but the mood of the moment.

There were times during a monologue, as in the classic "The Wino and the Junkie," when audience hilarity stopped cold and Pryor's voice sank, bringing his audience with him. Winding down into self-pity, the Junkie says, "I'm sick, Pops. Boy, can y' help me? My mind's thinkin' about shit I don' wanna think about . . . I can't stop the motherfucker, baby [*sighs of sympathy*] . . ." The Wino's response picks up the monologue, moves it back into high humor. But Pryor had the audience, his eyes glistening momentarily with tears that did not brim over, as he trod the edge of things most comedians—even the black ones—have not dared to.

"Acting out" has always been an integral part of black comedy; the straight stand-up could be stifling; the genes cry out not only for movement, but for other characters, other voices, for black consciousness is a collective experience. Perhaps the touchstone for the "other voice" was Cosby's "Noah." Doing a dialogue—two characters building a skit—of course takes skill and some knowledge of how to use the mike, and the body. At this Pryor's mastery was clear in skits like "Dracula," the "Faith Healer," "Eulogy," Mudbone in "Little Feets," and other dialogues.

All this is a far, far cry from the days when Pryor did "poop the ship" jokes, or one-liners that began with: "Did you hear the one about . . . ?" Or told hecklers that he was being paid to make a fool of himself, what was their excuse? There were times when he reached so deeply into the psyche of his black audiences that he *did* become that charlatan preacher. The response then was as if a giant awoke; it was more a roar than applause. And there were those times that hark solidly back to the ancient call-and-response which plays over the comedy like a durable backdrop:[1]

"Mudbone was born in Mississippi. Tougaloo." From out of the audience a female voice calls, "Where is that?" Pryor responds: "Tougaloo? It's near Woomaloo."

The roar comes again. There is no "Woomaloo" but Pryor met the challenge, and the roar is praise for his quick thinking. If he asked for an amen, he got it, the roof trembling on its moorings. In the 1970s and 1980s, many in his audience, black and white, thought themselves victims on some level. And Pryor displayed the victim, complete with hip language and bravado, along with something else—the probability that, when people became aware of their common victimization, they might do something about it.

Sex, genitalia, body functions, and human smells were Pryor's major metaphors for just about everything—including politics. Sigmund Freud would have been interested in the comedian because of the extent of his sexual references, which evoke the gods Min and Dionysus. Preceding them, as evidenced by the 15,000-year-old Venus of Willendorf statuette (as well as other finds), sex and genitalia in ancient cultures were highlighted. The Willendorf Venus is all buttocks (*steatopygia*), hips, belly, and monstrous breasts, like the Pryor character, Miss Rudolph. Erect phalli on small replicas of ancient Egyptians, and the wall reliefs and friezes in India that display an astounding variety of sexual gymnastics of thousands of years ago, attest to the natural public place of sex and genitalia in everyday culture. This changed when the Europeans invaded the southern latitudes, bringing along their missionaries to "save the savages." Sex of all kinds was herded into the closet and remained there until relatively recently when, having forced its way out—at least partially—it was excused because society had become "more permissive."

Whether by instinct or design, Richard Pryor arrived at precisely the proper moment to project what is truly the human comedy, and the fact that it has been widely accepted must surely mean something. "I've never seen anyone walk out on his act," Cosby said. Maybe Pryor's fans understand better than most how commonplace sex is in their lives; that it is nothing special, that it just has its place.

"You can't talk about fucking in America, right?" Pryor told an audience. "People say you dirty. But if you talk about killin' somebody, that's cool. I don't understand it [*from the audience: Amen!*] myself. I'd rather come. I've had money and never felt as good as I felt when I come, when you're gettin' the nut—especially if it's a girl." [*Audience howls*]

For Pryor, the most pathetic man was the one who couldn't have an orgasm—the miserable role he once assigned to Richard Nixon. And a revolting spectacle was evoked when he later conjured up Ronald Reagan as "a penis in a suit." On the other hand, an erect penis was hyperbole in Pryor's terms, an image reflecting the highest admiration, as in the way Sugar Ray Robinson used to fight. ("That Sugar fight so good, make y'dick hard. Sugar *git* in a motherfucker's ass. Ask Jake LaMotta.") Pryor worked sodomy in metaphor: When he was sentenced to his ten-day term, he told his audience in a monologue that his pants were down around his knees and that he asked the judge "not to stick it in too far." Why, he wondered, do cops, when they arrest you, demand that you "spread your cheeks?" He suggested that in jail you ran the risk of having to "give up the booty," or being sodomized. "Didn't nobody fuck me no place," he boasted, because he kept everyone laughing "to keep their minds off the booty." On it goes: "the air that gits in there" when you're making love, the failure to get an erection and how you react. He had found a common denominator that people seemed to understand, because they laughed, howled, screamed—and didn't walk out.

There was a lot about fighting in Pryor's material, some of it between men and women. But in many of his stories, he affirmed, as in the cliché, that after fighting, making love was groovy. Being in love, however, was condensed to a metaphor wherein a man does not want his woman to have sex with another man once he has found one (pussy) "that fits!" A stranger would "stretch it outa shape." The comedian's women were "bitches," for the most part, females without names, but curiously, his sexist terminology was overshadowed by the fact, repeated in several monologues, that his women invariably triumphed in their encounters with men, like the wife who leaves her husband, declaring that had his penis been two inches longer, things might have worked out. Another character, Big Irma, was bad, tolerating no foolishness; as was the Playboy Bunny who had Pryor the narrator talking like a child before she gave it up. And when Pryor did skits built around his family, the mother gave quite as good as she got. In portraying marriage, the husband trying to psych out his splitting wife was finally reduced to angry tears and threats to get her to stay. In Pryor's comedy, women put out their cigarettes on him as he stood at the elevator of a women's hotel waiting to get picked up. A fantastic-looking woman, who was into body-building, bedded down with him, and he discovered that no sex was involved, only "cosmic communication." Women were usually the winners in intersexual conflict.

Chaplin's characters were shy; Allen's usually stumble onto a good thing; Pryor's males made the hip moves; they were cool and bombastic by turn, but down deep they were losers in relationships with women. If they were unable to make love, then they had to fight them. And if they didn't have to fight, they were cuckolded, like Mudbone, who came home from work to find the toilet seat *up* that he had carefully nailed *down,* in order to trap his woman in an infidelity. "Ain't no bitch in the world piss with the toilet seat up," Mudbone says.

Pryor's exploration of the basic extended to additional cloacal analyses. Bad smells intrigued him—of feces, urine, vomit, unwhiskeyed bad breath, perspiration, whiskeyed bad breath, flatus. But good ones did too; one woman character, a friend of Mudbone, did have "breath as sweet as Carnation milk." Watching and listening to a Pryor performance, in many ways—especially in the use of language that described bodily functions—must have been the way it was sitting through a play by Aristophanes. None of the "bad" words the comedian used derives from the Greek. Indeed, very few even possess Latin origins, unless one uses the polite forms (urinate, defecate). Most of the words are from the Middle English (fuck, ass, bitch, piss, shit) and one of his favorites comes out of Swedish/Icelandic: pussy (the vulva of a mare). This is the language America speaks, not on television (except for cable channels like HBO), but increasingly in film; not in church, but more and more in other public places. It was always there and sometimes we use it. But not like Pryor. Lenny Bruce had used profanity to shock, but Pryor had woven this language so thoroughly into his work that it seemed peculiar when he did not use it. (As when he did a monologue on "The Tonight Show" that omitted the language he would insert in the same monologue on the concert stage.) For people who still had reservations about certain words, Pryor was the bad boy for them; they lived uncomfortably through his language and exploits that were detailed in his monologues. English the language may be, but black people tend to carry the African aptitude for tonality to it, so that one intonation can mean one thing, while another can mean quite something else. Pryor did this exceptionally well and thus he provided a learning experience for those who thought that "bitch," for example, had only one meaning.

The character Mudbone, like Gleason's "the Poor Soul," or Sid Caesar's young man at a dance, or Chaplin's underdog, or Allen's schlemiel, was enduring because it reflected the experience of a life of small tragedies. He was Pryor's greatest achievement in characterization. Probably based on his Grampa Tommy, Mudbone in many ways was also Pryor himself. Everyone tolerates an old man who mixes bombast with shreds of wisdom and also tells immensely funny stories. The character not only was a vehicle but a shield from behind which Pryor could attack anything, anybody; Mudbone could be the left hook; Pryor himself the right-hand cross. But a comedian once explained that "If you've got yourself a character and you're working through him and the routine bombs, you can always tell yourself, 'Well, *I* didn't bomb. The character did.' Helps protect the ego."

In Mudbone, Pryor arrived at a father figure, a man who had done nearly everything and survived, the character who reminded the comedian that "You don't git to be old bein' no fool, see. A lotta young wise men, they deader'n a motherfucker, ain't they?"

In one monologue from *Live on the Sunset Strip,* Pryor even split his persona, having Mudbone go to work on Richard Pryor himself. "I knowed that boy . . . see. He fucked up. See, that fire got on his ass and it fucked him up upstairs. Fried up what little brains he had. . . . 'Cause I 'member the motherfucker—he could make a motherfucker laugh at a funeral on Sunday Christmas Day. But, y'know what happened? He got some money—that's what happened to 'im—he got some money."

There was more money to be made in the movies, but the movies would not allow Pryor to be as great a movie star as he was a comedian. No way. The movies made Charlie Chaplin, and they extended Woody Allen's talents, but they would almost certainly do nothing like that for Pryor. Yet he always wanted to be a movie star—a term which was correctly jabbed into place with Peter O'Toole's line in *My Favorite Year* ("I'm not an actor, I'm a movie star"). Yet, Pryor continued to expend just as much energy working on his comedy and preparing for concert tours. Why? Probably because he knew that in his own comedy he had full artistic control. He wrote the material or oversaw what was written; he approved staff, the technicians—he had, we assume, the final word. He could set his own pace, which appeared to be murderous, or he could quit before the end of a tour.

All these he couldn't do in filmmaking or television production, where control is firmly in the hands of others. *They* said "yes" or "no"; "jump" or "stay." From 1976 to 1980, when he again teamed up with Wilder, Pryor appeared in nine movies, none of which showcased him to great advantage. He made money, got good reviews, and starred in two of those films, *Greased Lightning* (1977) and *Which Way Is Up?* (1977), neither of which did more than to say for his career that he "needed the money."

In the United States (and probably elsewhere), being in the movies (or on television, the poor man's silver screen) has always symbolized success, whatever one's previous career, or however well-known an artist has been in other media. Sometimes the change in careers works out. But handling two careers at once is a problem, and Richard Pryor had a problem.

NOTES

From John A. Williams and Dennis A. Williams, *If I Stop I'll Die: The Comedy and Tragedy of Richard Pryor* (New York: Thunder's Mouth Press, 1991).

1. Perhaps an even more vivid example is in *Bicentennial Nigger,* through the Preacher character: "We're celebrating two hundred years of—of white folks kickin' ass [*applause, roars, cheers*]. . . . How-elsn-ever, we offer this prayer, and the prayer is: How long will this bullshit go on? [*applause, roars, cheers*] HOW LONG?

10 "He Wasn't Afraid to Get Naked in Front of People"

MICHAEL SCHULTZ REMEMBERS RICHARD PRYOR

Audrey Thomas McCluskey

Audrey T. McCluskey: Hello, Michael. Thank you for finding time for this conversation about Richard Pryor, with whom you had a working relationship over the years. Can we begin by having you talk a bit about your own extensive and pioneering career as a film director first, and then how you became involved with the late comedian? I recall that started out in theater . . .

Michael Schultz: I did. When I decided to get into this crazy business there were no role models. Gordon Parks had not appeared on the scene, nor Melvin Van Peebles. To a young guy in college asking, "Is it possible for me to do this?" I didn't see any examples. But in the midst of my collegiate confusion, and not knowing really what I wanted to do, I spent a lot of time in the movies. I was in a college town— Madison, Wisconsin—where you could see movies that you couldn't see in Milwaukee, where I grew up. Movies by Fellini and Bergman, and Zeffirelli and Antonioni. I said, "Wow! This is amazing." I had never seen storytelling like that. I said to myself that I'd love to be able to tell stories like that in that way, not necessarily in the Hollywood way, about our people and our history and our psychology.

ATM: Was that when you decided to switch your major from engineering?

MS: Yeah, I was going to be an astronaut [laughter] until I got into calculus and realized that I was not cut out to be an engineer.

ATM: I heard that. Was this in the early 1960s?

MS: Yes. I graduated high school in '57 and my chief ambition was to be another Colin Powell of the Air Force [laughter]. I wanted to go to the Air Force Academy, fly jets, and be a general like Colin Powell. There were also no precedents for that, no role models for that, but that was my burning ambition as a high schooler and they were only going to take one person out of every state for the first Air Force Academy class and I was number two in the state of Wisconsin and the guy who was ahead of me decided to go. So they gave me as a consolation prize an appointment to West Point, but I realized I didn't just want to be in the military; I wanted to fly and that was my whole motivation. So I turned that down and said, "Well, if I can't fly jets in the Air Force, I'll fly rockets and I'll be an astronaut. I'll go to the moon." And then reality set in when I got to calculus: the thing that had kept me from being number one in the state was my math scores, which I didn't know at the time but I found it out in college. And then I kind of searched around trying to figure out what I really wanted to do and that's when I spent all this time in the movies.

ATM: Were you at all affected by what was going on in the country then—the beginning of the Civil Rights Movement?

MS: Right. Well, in the mid-'60s I was in theater school. I went back to a different college and got involved in the theater and was learning all of this great classic material: Shakespeare and Molière. Being completely absorbed in everything theater because that was the closest that I could get to film. And as I was doing this the energy to change was spilling out into the streets, but I felt that my mission was to really get good at what I was learning and make my contribution that way. By the mid-'60s—I went to New York in '64, and did participate in some of the marches on Washington, against the war and all of that, and traveled with fellow thespians like Jon Voight and Jennifer Salt, who was the daughter of Waldo Salt, the famous screenwriter. I spent most of my time perfecting my craft in the theater. My theory was that if I got to be a good director in the theater that someone would offer me a film. If I made a reputation as a director in the theater somebody would offer me a film and after my first Broadway . . . My Broadway directing debut, as a matter of fact, was a play called *Does a Tiger Wear a Necktie?* [1969] in which I cast Al Pacino as the lead role—his first time on Broadway—and my wife played the female lead—her stage name was Lauren Jones at the time. Pacino won for best acting that year. I was up against the director of *The Great White Hope* and he won that year but my wife and I and Al got nominated. My first play in New York was a play for the Negro Ensemble Company that dealt with the oppression of Mozambique and Angola by the Portuguese, so the stuff I was doing in the theater was very impactful and there was this blend of social activism and theatrical art that was inseparable in a way. I came from that school of thought: if you weren't doing something that made a difference in people's lives or made them think about how they were living and what their relationship was to their fellow man and to God and to themselves then you weren't really doing anything of value. So that was my theatrical training and after one of the performances of *Does a Tiger Wear a Necktie?* a producer came up to me and said, "Would you like to do a movie? I'm doing a movie of this off-Broadway play called *To Be Young, Gifted, and Black.*"

ATM: Of course, Lorraine Hansberry's *To Be Young, Gifted, and Black.* She was the brilliant, young black author of *Raisin in the Sun* and *The Sign in Sidney Brustein's Window* and several other plays, who died too young at age 34.

MS: Yes. I jumped at the chance, and said, "Yes, I'll do it." And I had read everything about making movies, everything I could get my hands on, but I had no film school training. It turned out to be the perfect segue for me to move from theater into film because it was a film about a theater person, of which I knew a lot.

ATM: You had quite a cast to work with, including Ruby Dee, Al Freeman, Jr., and Blythe Danner, Roy Scheider. Were you at all intimidated or were you just too young and ambitious to think about it?

MS: I was never intimidated [laughter]. If I had been the intimidated type, I would've been intimidated by just the sheer impossibility of trying to do this project in the short time we had to shoot it.

ATM: I could say that the rest is history. With that start, you went on to direct television shows, and, of course, to direct the cult classic *Cooley High* [1975]. That really put your name in lights.

MS: It did, as a matter of fact. When I came to L.A. I had been sent the original manuscript for *Cooley High* from a producer I had worked on another film in Atlanta. And I said, "You know, it's really not a movie but when I get to L.A. and get a chance to talk to the writer, Eric Monte, I'll figure out if there's a movie in there somewhere." So I met with Eric and realized that here was a young writer who was a really brilliant storyteller of anecdotes but not a screenwriter. So what I convinced the producer of was to let me work with Eric for a month and hire a stenographer and so I got Eric Monte to commit to me coming over to his house every day, five days a week, and not letting there be any distractions whatsoever and having the stenographer just listen to he and I trading stories about growing up. And she would type out everything and then I would look at it and I'd take the best stories and started to create a structure that eventually became the script. So that's how *Cooley High* was created.

ATM: Well, it's oftentimes compared to *American Graffiti* [1973], but it certainly didn't emanate from the same cultural context.

MS: No, not at all. As a matter of fact, the critics, you know, they always look at black material and try and compare it to something white because that's their frame of reference.

ATM: *Car Wash* [1976] was your next film. Is that when you met Richard Pryor?

MS: Yes. When I went to Los Angeles. I actually I met him in Los Angeles through a very interesting man named Clarence Avant. Clarance Avant is one of these quiet, powerful black businessmen in the music world—like Don Corleone of the music world. [laughter] And he was trying to get a movie made called *Timmons from Chicago,* which was a very amusing film about a black guy in Chicago who becomes President of the United States. And he wanted Richard Pryor to play the part, so I had read the script and they arranged for me to meet Richard and talk with him.

ATM: And this was in . . . Do you remember the year?

MS: Well, yeah, this was when I first came to L.A. so it had to be 1974. We never got the picture off the ground. . . . I didn't really understand Hollywood politics at the time and if I had I would've made that picture with Richard, but I turned the movie down when they wouldn't give me the budget that I knew it would take to make a good movie and so it never happened. But the upside of that whole project was I got a chance to meet and talk with Richard on a fairly deep level. Then I went off to do *Cooley High* and that was successful. Universal offered me this movie called *Car Wash* and I actually tried to get this famous preacher out in New York—Reverend Ike—for the role Richard had. But he turned it down.

ATM: Oh, yes. I remember Reverend Ike. He was a predecessor of the present crop of "show me the money" preachers. [laughter]

MS: Reverend Ike was the screenwriter's [Joel Schumacher] model for the character. I said, since we can't get Reverend Ike to play himself, Richard Pryor would be the next best actor to do this. Since it was a one-day part, Richard could do it between his other engagements. He kind of did it as a favor to me. So that was the first time that we actually worked together. I put him with the Pointer Sisters and kind of created that musical way of dealing with his character because I had conceived of this movie as a closet musical. We didn't tell people we were doing a musical but that's exactly what *Car Wash* was.

ATM: Did Richard mostly ad-lib the script? I understand that he was famous for that.

MS: The base of it was written out, but Richard always added or made the material his own. He was so funny, so brilliant, that I would just let him do what he wanted to do because he was [the] comic genius, not me. I didn't know anything about comedy, but I knew when something was good. [laughter] So he would throw in little ad-libs and stuff but the main concept was written.

ATM: You said before that when you first met him, the two of you had fairly deep conversations. Can you talk a little about that? I mean Richard was known not to really let many people get very close to him.

MS: That's true and actually he didn't let me get that close to him either, but in our early conversations . . . because I was really interested in something else that he was doing—he had written a western called *The Black Stranger*—and I convinced him to let me do it . . . everyone in Hollywood was afraid to do it because it was the black guy coming in as Gary Cooper, like in *High Noon* [1952]. The good guys were black and the bad guys were white. [laughter]

ATM: I wonder why that film was never made? [laughter]

MS: Yes, so there was no way that movie was getting done in that time period. But I really loved it and so we started talking about the power structure and how hard it was to get past that to be able to do the kind of material that we really knew there was an audience for but the Hollywood powerbrokers didn't and wouldn't do. Most of our conversations were about that. As a comedian he could basically do whatever he wanted to do as long as it made people laugh. So he would tell his stories that way, but when it came to doing it in a mass media film, there were all the gatekeepers that you had to get through.

ATM: Do you think that Pryor realized what he was up against?

MS: Oh, absolutely. Absolutely. Richard was brilliant, number one, and extremely sensitive, and, in a way, almost psychic.

ATM: How do you mean?

MS: Well, he could read what you were thinking before you said it, and I'm not sure if it was because of his keen insight and awareness of how people's body language and everything, but he would see where you were going and then make a comment on it before you got there. [laughter]

ATM: Do you remember any particular incidents where that was apparent?

MS: One of the things that struck me was when I took Steve Krantz to meet Richard. Steve Krantz produced *Cooley High* and he's a very interesting older Jewish guy, with money. When I was working on *Cooley High* Steve would come up to me and say, "What about your next movie? What would you like to do?" And I said, "I'm not really sure but there's so much interesting, brilliant black talent out here that I'd love to do something with the talent that we have." He said, "Well, like who?" I said, "Well, like Richard Pryor, for example." Well, he didn't know who Richard Pryor was.

He didn't know who Richard Pryor was, so I told him about *Lady Sings the Blues* [1972] because Richard had played the part of Piano Man and outshone everybody in the cast as far as acting went, I thought.

ATM: Without doubt.

MS: I kind of educated Krantz to who Richard was and he came back several weeks later with the idea; he said, "Have you ever seen *The Seduction of Mimi* [1972]?" I said, "No, I don't go to pornos." He said, "No, no, no. This is an Italian movie by Lina Wertmüller and I'll get it for you. I'll find out where it's playing and you can go see it and tell me if you think you can make an American adaptation of that with Richard Pryor in mind to play the Giancarlo Giannini part." And so I went to see the movie and sure enough it was a brilliant kind of comedy that had a lot of political content in it.

ATM: And he thought Pryor would be good just based on your description of him and your comments about him?

MS: Yes. And then I guess Steve had listened to some of his [comedy] records.

After I saw the film, I said, "Oh, Richard could play that part with his eyes closed." So we started to put together . . . *Which Way Is Up?* [1977]. And so then I took Steve over to meet Richard and it was one of the funniest meetings. The first thing Richard did when he saw Steve was comment on his Beverly Hills attire, from his Gucci loafers to his pants and everything. Richard had me almost on the floor [with laughter] and Steve was so embarrassed. And he thought Richard didn't like him, but Richard was just, you know, being Richard.

ATM: He was just teasing him.

MS: Exactly, exactly, but it was hysterical. And I had to pull Steve aside afterwards and said, "No, no, no. That's the way Richard is. It's not personal." But he dissected Steve's personality at once.

ATM: You worked with Richard on at least three films, including *Which Way Is Up? Greased Lightning* [1977], and *Car Wash*. Did you work with him in other films?

MS: Uh, yeah. *Bustin' Loose* [1981].

ATM: Oh, *Bustin' Loose,* with Cicely Tyson.

MS: Well, *Car Wash* was like a one-day thing and Richard came in and did his part brilliantly and that was so quick it was almost like a non-working relationship.

The first real working relationship was *Which Way Is Up?* and that movie was just a joy from the beginning to the end with Richard, because I designed it to allow the characters that he had done on his records, in his stand-up—Mudbone, and some of the other characters that he created—to embody themselves in the multiple characters that he played in that movie.

ATM: Including another preacher role. The one who seduces his wife.

MS: The whole concept was to take the characters that Richard had created in his stand-up and give them life in these alternate roles that he was playing.

ATM: Was he the first black actor to handle those multiple roles? Of course several black actors do it now, including Eddie Murphy, who is known for his multiple roles in *Nutty Professor* [1996] films . . .

MS: Oh, yeah. It was all copied off of Richard. As a matter of fact, Eddie Murphy's whole career was copied off of Richard.

ATM: I think Murphy would confess to most of that.

MS: I don't know who, in the white world, was doing multiple roles like that but it was definitely the first black film where a character played multiple roles and Richard did it brilliantly. He so loved the process of doing it, too. He was extremely happy [on the set] and was extraordinarily brilliant. My hardest job in making that movie was trying to keep the crew from laughing on the soundtrack [laughter] and keeping his fellow actors from cracking up. He would just come up with all this outrageous, wonderful stuff.

ATM: It sounds like you didn't have to do much directing.

MS: I didn't. It was like, "Okay, Richard. Go for it. Turn the camera on" [laughter]. "Okay, shut up, shut up!" [laughter].

ATM: So as long as he was filming he was happy, and it was a perfect environment.

MS: Exactly. I think it was probably the one time in his career where he saw what movie making could be. That it was a collaborative, happy environment. It had its pressures but it was all about the work. And then he went from that to a terrible experience with Paul Schrader doing *Blue Collar* [1978].

ATM: What happened?

MS: Schrader's concept was to get the best work out of his actors by pitting them personally against each other. So he had Richard and Harvey Keitel . . . oh, what's his name? Oh, it just flew out of my head. The black actor . . .

ATM: Yaphet Kotto?

MS: Yaphet Kotto! Yeah. He had them at each other's throats—for real—in the movie to try and get performances out of them. And I think that going from the great fun experience of *Which Way Is Up?* to just hating the experience that he was having in *Blue Collar* . . . I think that's when he started up again doing drugs, but I don't know. I wasn't there. I just heard from him about how much he hated doing what he was doing. The next time I worked with him was . . .

ATM: *Greased Lightning*?

MS: *Greased Lightning.* No, actually, let's get this right for the history books. [laughter] While I was preparing *Which Way Is Up?* as Richard's first starring vehicle—he had always played second banana or side man in other movies he had done. But he decided while we were working on the script that he was going to do this movie for Warner Brothers called *Greased Lightning.* The story of Wendell Scott, the first black stock car driver.

ATM: Yes.

MS: Burt Reynolds had done a movie called *White Lightning* [1973] where he played an ex-con moonshiner, and so this was a complete non-comedic, straight dramatic role and Richard was intrigued by that. And I heard after the fact, "Oh, Richard's doing this movie called *Greased Lightning* with Melvin Van Peebles directing," and I said, "That dirty dog, he's supposed to wait for my movie!" [laughter] So evidently Melvin and the producer had some severe creative differences about making the movie and so either Melvin quit or they fired him and the movie came to a standstill. Well, Steve and I were going down to the set in Georgia to work on the script with Richard, you know, so while the movie was going good before they parted ways with Melvin. And so I knew a little bit about what was going on but not that there was any conflict there. So when Melvin left the scene, Richard called me up and said, "Would you come and take over this movie?" I thought to myself, "Oh, no. I do not want to . . ."

ATM: Jump into all that. [laughter]

MS: Yeah! Exactly. It was somebody else's movie, but I also don't want Richard to come out in a movie that bombs before he's in mine. [laughter]

ATM: Good thinking!

MS: Yes, so being totally selfish [more laughter] I said, "Okay, yes, I'll come do it." And Melvin was so gracious because he had a substantially black crew and was shooting in Georgia and they were all going to leave with him in protest against the producer—who really wound up being a pill—and Melvin said, "No, no. Stay. I want you to support Michael and Richard and do the best you can and make this movie happen." So that's how I got involved with *Greased Lightning,* so I really was the movie doctor on that.

ATM: Well, that was a good ending, especially since you and Melvin Van Peebles were supportive of each other in that situation. It seems to be a part of your whole way of doing things to be a conciliatory force for bringing people together. Working with Pryor you were saying how brilliant he was and you had no problems with him. Other people have had problems with him.

MS: I think the people who had problems with Richard were the people who didn't understand where he was coming from, what his concerns were. When we were doing *Greased Lightning* the only time I saw him have a problem was when he would see somebody else being mistreated by somebody else. Then he would go off the deep end, but he never had—as far as my working relationship with him—a problem, just to have a problem. If there was a problem, it was because he was always in trying to protect somebody else, or if he saw some injustice being done. I think those who had problems with him just didn't understand who they were dealing with.

ATM: How much of a revolution in Hollywood did Richard Pryor create?

MS: Oh. We wouldn't be where we are today without Richard's contribution, because he was the first talent to be able to bring a black audience and a white audience together in the same theater. At the time when Richard was coming up and when I was starting out, theater owners didn't even want a black audience to come into so-called "white theaters" because they thought it would scare their white patrons away. It wasn't as bad as a Jim Crow night when the black audience could only come on one night and sit up in the balcony, but the segregation mentality was still very evident around the country. There were theaters where black audiences went, and there were most of the rest of the theaters, where white audiences attended. When Melvin Van Peebles was doing *Sweet Sweetback* [1971], he could only get two theaters in the country to show his movie, which was a great thing for him because he wound up making most of the money as opposed to the studios making the money.

Now Richard, because of the honesty of his work and the fact that he didn't use street language just for the sake of using the language, set a new standard that both blacks and whites responded to. You see, he used [that language] for expressing what was going on in his life in a deep emotional way. It not only made people laugh but it really touched people, because nobody was really being that honest except for Lenny Bruce in his comic world. So Richard had a big white following as well as a big black following and he brought that from his stand-up comic act into the movie world—into his film roles. So I credit him to a large degree with changing the way that theater owners thought about bringing black audiences and white audiences together in the same theater. They finally had to concede that there could be a shared experience across the racial divide.

ATM: Do you think that this acceptance actually put a burden on him, in the sense that he was *the* man for maybe seven or eight years in Hollywood?

MS: You know, I don't think it became a burden until he got this deal with Columbia [Pictures], where he was suddenly able to green-light his own movies under a certain budget level. He wasn't really a business-man—he was an artist. He [depended] on other people to help him out in that arena and I don't think he chose wisely. Whatever the dynamics that were going on in his company—Indigo Films I think it was called—

ATM: Yes, it was.

MS: Well, things weren't really working and I don't think Richard knew how to handle it without the right people around him. His business manager at the time was not a good influence or a good person for him and took more advantage of him than gave him help.

ATM: I remember reading about it in *Jet* magazine. Very unfortunate.

MS: [It was] kind of like Don King to Mike Tyson. Anyway, I don't think Richard paid much attention to any of that. His prime concern was getting the best out of the comedy that he was doing. He knew what would make audiences laugh. He would work at that very hard; like a master sculptor he'd chisel away all the other stuff that didn't work until he got to all the punch lines. So it wasn't just off the top of his head, although he did have that ability to make it [look effortless].

ATM: Do you think that made him a better actor—I mean, the fact that he was a comic genius? Did that at all affect his acting ability? He was a good actor, but he was also in some very awful movies.

MS: Oh, the acting . . . I think primarily what influenced his acting more than anything was his real sensitive nature and his keen observation of human activity and his always push to go for the truth in what he was experiencing. So without even the first iota of acting training he had things that most actors didn't get until years of training, which was go for the truth, you know? Find out who the character is.

ATM: You had the sense that he didn't have any secrets; that he put it all out there.

MS: Right. Right. Absolutely. He wasn't afraid to get naked in front of people, and that's what made him so effective and so loved, because people looked at that courage and said, "Wow. I could never say that." And he made them laugh at the same time. It was an extraordinary gift.

ATM: There was also a tragic dimension to Richard Pryor, wasn't there?

MS: Well, of course, which we all saw later. But I never saw it while working with him. I mean, when I did—I worked with him on *Bustin' Loose.*

I was busy shooting something else, so I didn't know that much about *Bustin' Loose,* but I found out later that it was a project that he had conceived of and got people to [support it] and Universal to do it. But at the same time, because he had enough power at that time to get done, what he didn't have [was] the people around him to protect him. Because there weren't that many African American behind-the-scenes people, like producers. There were no producers that I knew about. Oh. Bill Greaves, actually, they brought in from New York, who was a documentary producer.

ATM: Yes. A great one.

MS: Yes. But Bill didn't know the Hollywood system. So they surrounded Richard with people who were first-time movie people. They had done television and all that, so the DP was a first time. The producer was a first time film guy, and the director was Oz Scott, who had never done a movie before but had done some really good theater work, and the result of the movie was that it was unreleasable. Then Richard went on to do some other movie . . . and then he burnt himself up. So I think the problems that he was having on *Bustin' Loose,* plus, he was deep into the drug habit again and that's when he set himself on fire, freebasing, and suffered tremendous burns across forty percent of his body and people thought he was going to die. Well, he's sitting—he's laying—in the hospital wrapped up in bandages and actually he's learning—by listening to the people who are sitting at his bedside thinking that he was dying—who his friends really were. He found out that they were very few.

ATM: He tried to deal with some of that in *Jo Jo Dancer: Your Life Is Calling* [1986]?

MS: Yeah, yeah. But he learned about the people that he had surrounded himself with. And I don't know where I was—off shooting somewhere—while all this was happening, so I never got to visit him in the hospital. But later on, when he told me that he had started to heal and he's still wrapped up in bandages and Universal had this movie on the shelf called *Bustin' Loose* and when they heard that he wasn't gonna die, they called him up in the hospital and said, "Richard, will you finish the picture when you get well?" [laughter]

ATM: Wow!

MS: Yeah. That's Hollywood.

So he probably mumbled "yes," you know, through the bandages, and he called me sometime after, when he had recuperated and rehabilitated, and asked me if I would come and do the re-shoots on the movie because Universal was willing to spend more money to solve the problems of the film and get it into release. So I go look at what was done and I thought it was a kind of impossible task, because it was pretty bad. I said, "Okay, Richard. I'll do it if they'll let me re-shoot half the movie. That's the only way to make it." So I got involved and did it. They wouldn't let me re-shoot half of it, but they let me re-shoot enough of it and I rehired the original writer that Richard had fired under stress. The kids in the movie were two years older and so they looked different. Richard had suffered these burns and he looked very different from when they had originally shot the film. But like doing a jigsaw puzzle, I would shoot some of the things that they hadn't shot and re-shoot things that were not well done, and rewrote and added stuff to make the movie make sense.

ATM: Were you satisfied with what you produced at the end?

MS: At the end of the process, yes.

ATM: And was Richard satisfied?

MS: You know, I think he was, but he told me at the time before we started shooting—I went to visit him in Hawaii; he had a very peaceful home there in Maui. When I was deciding whether or not I was going to do it. He told me that after suffering the burns in his accident and rethinking his whole life and what he had done, he said, "You know, I realize that this movie stuff is not very significant and I really don't want to do it anymore."

ATM: No more films?

MS: No. At that point in time he didn't think it was valuable enough to spend his life doing. He wanted to finish that movie because it was a labor of love for him. He created the idea, so he had a stake in seeing it at least come out and see the light of day and reach audiences, but he was disillusioned with the whole process. I think the bad movies that you're talking about that he was involved in were all post–that period.

ATM: Post–*Bustin' Loose*?

MS: Yeah. And that they were movies that he did basically to make money.

ATM: Well where was his heart then if it wasn't in movies? Do you know or was it just an alienation that he had?

MS: I don't really know. He did *Jo Jo Dancer*—after that period—and I think that that was probably for him the highlight, because he was able to tell his story.

But the other things: *The Toy* [1982], whatever . . .

ATM: *Brewster's Millions* [1985]?

MS: Yeah, yeah. All of that stuff he was basically doing for the money. His heart wasn't in it and you could see that.

ATM: But as we think back about Pryor and his legacy, what comes to mind?

MS: I think he's probably the comic genius of the century. That he was the first person that made it okay for black and white audiences to share the same theatrical experience in the same place at the same time and that that was a huge, huge contribution. I think that he laid the groundwork for all these other comedians who have come behind him since, and they haven't reached the mark—that bar—that Richard set, but he made the opening for them.

III.

Reviews

11 Time Warp Movies

A REVIEW OF *SUPERMAN III* (1985)

PAULINE KAEL

When we go into the theatre to see *Superman III*, we know that whatever else happens we're still going to have the pleasure of seeing a man fly without an airplane and without wings. But when I (for one) came out of the theatre it was with the distinct feeling that if the director, Richard Lester, had been able to deprive us completely of this pleasure he would have done so—not because he didn't want us to have a good time but because he loses touch with the simple, basic elements of his material. For roughly the first forty minutes of *Superman III*, during which Richard Pryor as Gus Gorman, who has been a flop at every job he has ever had, discovers that he's a computer wizard, Lester provides an agreeable mixture of the grandiose and the everyday. Our expectations are aroused: he must have some tricks up his sleeve. And he does, but the scattered impulses behind the movie cancel each other out.

Superman/Clark Kent (Christopher Reeve), who grew into a touching character in *Superman II*, is presented here as a blank—he's whatever is needed to fit the gags. Clark Kent is a bore with a simpering grin, and Superman has been doing his good deeds for so long that the people of Metropolis are jaded and take him for granted. Clearly, he needs a change, but it doesn't come from within. Richard Pryor's Gus, who has used a computer to embezzle from the conglomerate he works for, is caught by the boss (Robert Vaughn) and ordered to work out the ingredients of kryptonite—the only substance that can destroy Superman. Gus isn't that much of a wizard, though; the computer gives him all the ingredients but one, and so he fakes it, and the green chunk he hands to

Superman, as if it were an award, is only near-kryptonite. It doesn't kill Superman; it demoralizes him, and he begins to perform dirty deeds.

What's strange about the movie is that the best things in it aren't developed, and what Superman and the other characters do doesn't seem to have any weight. Robert Vaughn's polished smarminess is scaled to television; his villainy doesn't fill the big screen, and when he tries to ruin the Colombian coffee crop or succeeds in stopping the world's flow of oil, Lester treats what happens so flippantly that nothing appears to be at stake. Vaughn's harridan sister and business partner—Annie Ross as the black-haired, witchlike Vera—might be something left in cold storage since the era of the Munsters. And a potentially amusing bosomy blonde, a floozy-intellectual named Lorelei Ambrosia (Pamela Stephenson), just sits around. Lester may think that these women are gags just in them-selves—there are no payoffs. And when Gus hands Superman the chunk of green near-kryptonite, Superman doesn't have any idea what it is—it's as if he'd never seen *Superman* and *Superman II*.

Despite the film's anti-mythic tone, it's entertaining (in the early part) when we see Superman perform heroically. There's a dangerous fire in a chemical plant, and the firemen have no water. Superman freezes a lake and flies it over the site; the fire melts the ice, which turns into rain and puts out the fire. This comic-book fairy-tale fantasy is funny and enchanting—this, in essence, is what we've come to see for the third time. But although Lester had a hand in the first film and directed the second, he steps on our reaction here—he doesn't give us time to be exhilarated. He keeps his light, objective touch, which at times is indistinguishable from directorial indifference. Too many scenes are treated as if they were just obligatory, and because of that air of indifference, verging on dis-dain, the movie's sight gags and special effects—even the biggest ones—aren't particularly exciting. The splashy scenes that we look forward to don't seem to show up, because Lester has devalued them; everything feels marginal.

So when the soul-sick Superman is being prankish or surly—putting out the Olympic torch or straightening the Leaning Tower of Pisa or punching a hole in a tanker and causing an oil spill—we don't know how to react to this lecher with stubble on his chin and a soiled-looking cape. A funky, sexy-sheik Superman could have audiences squealing with plea-sure, and a Superman with a vendetta against the world could be awe-somely neurotic, but the movie has no sooner suggested the possibilities than it drops them. (When he sits alone in a bar, boozing and exploding bottles by flicking roasted almonds at them, we get more of a sense of how dangerous—and attractive—Superman could be than at any other time. The bad Superman has burning dark eyes; he looks like an Etruscan warrior.) We're not intended to take what happens to Superman as a genuine psychological crisis; the picture even loses track of the near-kryptonite. We're not intended to care about the victims of his spite. We don't know what we're meant to respond to.

It's a real loss that Clark Kent is shunted offscreen during these sequences, because we miss him—we wonder how he feels about what's going on. (Is he suffering? Or has he turned bad guy and told off his fellow-workers at the *Daily Planet*?) At last, Superman's headachy conflict with himself becomes so intense that he splits into two: a scene that needs to be crazed and funny—if only because the two identities are already split in our minds, so that we've been waiting for Clark. But what we get is a conventional battle of the titans, like John Wayne and Randolph Scott pounding each other in a frontier saloon. The setting here is an automobile junk yard. Superman keeps throwing Clark Kent into grind-up machines and demolishing him; he kicks him unconscious, and Clark keeps coming back for more punishment, like Wile E. Coyote in a Road Runner cartoon. It isn't comic, though, and it isn't satisfyingly worked out, either, but there's at least some psychological resonance in this battling, and when Clark Kent triumphs the scene is affecting. (We've come to trust him more than we trust Superman.) There's nothing to redeem the film's final big brawl when the healed, integrated Superman, who is once again at the service of mankind, goes up against a monster computer that Gus has designed and Vaughn has had built. Like Luke in *Return of the Jedi,* Superman is repeatedly fried by zigzag bolts of electricity.

Lester hasn't gone back to the heaviness of *How I Won the War* or the disaffection of *Petulia,* and he doesn't do the obvious subverting that he did on his *Musketeers* pictures, but he undermines the mystique of Superman as an ideal father image and an ideal self-image. (Lester almost seems to think that he's letting the material subvert itself.) There's an idea here: that Superman is a victim of his own do-gooding and needs to be liberated—needs to discover that he has the same impulses and drives as other men. But this violates all the information we have stored up about him, which starts with the given that he isn't human—he's superhuman. We can accept the bad-guy Superman as a casualty of kryptonite, but the notion that when Superman is idealistic and helpful he's an asexual Mr.

Square violates our memories of what was charming about Christopher Reeve's performance in the first two films. There was deadpan wit in Superman's impersonation of the clumsy, inept Clark Kent; here he doesn't seem to be in on the joke. And it doesn't make any sense that when Clark Kent goes back to Smallville to his high-school class reunion, everyone except Lana Lang (Annette O'Toole), who, we're told, has always had a crush on him, treats him contemptuously. In the first *Superman,* the schoolboy Clark Kent was physically strong and he was always considerate and sweet—why would he have been unpopular? Lester wants us to see Clark as a nerd and Superman as a virtuous clod, but all that does is drain the mythic life out of the movie. By not allowing the people on the screen to be enthralled by Superman's flights and miraculous rescues, Lester puts himself in the position of pooh-poohing the movie's special effects, and pooh-poohing the hero. He robs the picture of its chance to stir the viewer's imagination. He may also (out of impatience, or a willingness to sacrifice story points to pacing) have truncated episodes—such as Clark Kent's reentering Lana Lang's life—which are left suspended. Annette O'Toole (who has an American-goddess profile) makes Lana's small-town-girl infatuation with Clark seem perfectly natural. She's the only member of the cast who appears to believe in her role yet stays in a comic-book frame. As Brad, the fifties-style jock who wants to marry Lana, Gavan O'Herlihy is believable, too, especially when he tells Clark Kent he hates him for being so nice, but O'Herlihy doesn't have the knack of comic-book style. The logistical horrors of directing actors around special effects that are put in later may help to explain why Lester can't give this movie anything like the visual shimmer of many of his earlier films. And those effects may also be part of the reason he can't give it his jazzy, leapfrogging editing style. *Superman III* doesn't have much of a look, and the editing clumps along. (When a movie is heavy on special effects, you don't get much for forty-two million dollars anymore.) But all those technical problems don't explain why Lester, who tosses off a number of lovely visual gags, also uses so many labored tricks, such as a forties-style montage showing the results of Gus's fiddling with his computer: it ends with a man at the breakfast table opening his monthly statement from Bloomingdale's and shoving a half grapefruit in his wife's face. Lester does better with a gag sequence—a chain of mishaps—that sustains life for us during the lengthy opening credits, but the sequence doesn't have anything like the zest of the similar gag at the start of Richard Rush's *The Stunt Man.* And this attempt to get the film moving is marred by the credits themselves, which come sloshing up from the bottom of the screen and disrupt the action.

Lester, and the scriptwriters, David and Leslie Newman (who have been involved in all three films), are working with an insane disadvantage: they're trying to fuse two incompatible or, at least, conflicting legends. Christopher Reeve isn't the star of *Superman III*. Richard Pryor is. He's the box-office insurance that the producers, the Salkinds, bought for four million dollars. According to the Newmans, they and Lester dreamed up the idea (along with everyone else who was planning a new movie). And so, of course, once Pryor agreed, the Newmans tried to shape the story around him. At times, it isn't clear whether the action we're watching is in Metropolis or in Smallville, and at other times the central characters are apparently wandering in various directions around the Grand Canyon. What makes the picture seem so addled is the need to bring Gus and Superman together. They never do get to have a dramatic confrontation, and they don't actually become enemies—or friends, either—but Lester keeps so much fringe action going on that viewers don't have a chance to question what Pryor and Superman, who don't even belong to the same era, are doing in the same movie.

There's no way that this clean-language, family picture could use the Richard Pryor who used to do a "Supernigger" routine (which was spun off Lenny Bruce's "Superjew"). When Pryor puts on a pink shawl in imitation of Superman's red cape, he's rather forlorn. What the film uses is Richard Pryor playing off his rich white master (Vaughn) in the scaredy-cat way that Mantan Moreland and other earlier, eye-rolling black comics did. Pryor's Gus isn't a villain; he only works for the villain. (And he does everything but steal chickens and have his hair shoot up straight 'cause he's 'feerd of ghosts.) He cringes and acts cowardly, and, yes, the audience laughs and finds him endearing. (Pryor as a computer genius doesn't ring any bells; I wondered why the moviemakers hadn't tried the ploy of using Pryor to wise up Superman, or as the demoralized Superman's tempter—that way he wouldn't have had to be so limp, and he and Superman could have had more scenes together.) Pryor doesn't give a bad performance, but it's a hesitant and bowed performance, as if he were trying not to be noticed. And it's a one-joke role. Gus's mind is so fogged in that he does everything he can to please his slimy master; it's pretty close to the end of the movie before he—ever so tentatively—shifts his allegiance. First, his boss totes him; then Superman (literally) totes him. He never does go out on his own. And when Superman is flying with Richard Pryor they look the way they do in the ads for the movie that show Pryor openmouthed and pop-eyed with terror. The romance is gone; the flying has become just another gag.

NOTE

Pauline Kael, "Time Warp Movies" (Review of *Superman III*), in Pauline Kael, *State of the Art* (New York: E. P. Dutton, 1985), 7–12.

Richard Pryor Live on the Sunset Strip (1994)

12

PAULINE KAEL

When Chaplin began to talk onscreen, he used a cultivated voice and high-flown words, and became a deeply unfunny man; if he had found the street language to match his lowlife, tramp movements, he might have been something like Richard Pryor, who's all of a piece—a master of lyrical obscenity. Pryor is the only great poet satirist among our comics. His lyricism seems to come out of his thin-skinned nature; he's so emphatic he's all wired up. His 1979 film *Richard Pryor: Live! in Concert* was a consummation of his years as an entertainer, and then some. He had a lifetime of material at his fingertips, and he seemed to go beyond himself. He personified objects, animals, people, the warring parts of his own body, even thoughts in the heads of men and women— black, white, Oriental—and he seemed to be possessed by the spirits he pulled out of himself. To those of us who thought it was one of the greatest performances we'd ever seen or ever would see, his new one-man show *Richard Pryor Live on the Sunset Strip* may be disappointing yet emotionally stirring. His new routines aren't as fully worked out; Pryor hasn't been doing the stage appearances that he used to do—hasn't, in fact, given any one-man shows since the 1979 film was shot—so these routines haven't been polished and sharpened, and they're not as varied. The material specially prepared for this film, which was shot at two performances at the Hollywood Palladium—is rather skimpy, and a lot of it is patterned on routines from the first. Pryor doesn't seem as prickly now—he doesn't have the hunted look, or the old sneaky, guilty gleam in his eyes. He says he isn't angry anymore, and he seems to have been strengthened—he's more open. This probably has something to do with the vast public outpouring of affection for him after his near-fatal accident in June, 1980, when (as he acknowledges here) the dope he was freebasing exploded and set him on fire.

Pryor must have realized that millions and millions of people really wished him well, felt grateful for the pleasure he'd given them, and wanted him to live. How does an ornery, suspicious man who brought the language and grievances of the black underclass onto the stage deal with acceptance? (This is not a problem that Lenny Bruce, who brought the backstage language of the tawdriest levels of show business onto the stage, ever had to face.) Pryor doesn't appear sweetened, exactly. Even in the films in which he has played Mr. Nice Guy to children or whites, the stickiness hasn't clung to him; he's shed it. And he's always come clean with the audience. Pryor's best jokes aren't jokes in the usual sense— they're observations that are funny because of how he acts them out and because of his inflections. He constantly surprises us and makes us laugh in recognition. He tells us what we *almost* knew but shoved down, so when we laugh at him we feel a special, giddy freedom. That hasn't changed—he isn't soft in *Sunset Strip*. He tries on some benign racial attitudes and then drops them very fast—that's how you know he's still alive and kicking. He's different, though. You may sense that there has been a deepening of feeling, that there's something richer inside him, something more secure.

At the same time, he's adrift as a performer, because he isn't sure that he's got his act together. And he hasn't. The pressure of a one-man show before a huge crowd and on camera must be just about heart-stopping if you haven't been working in front of big live audiences. And that first film made him a legend; he has the pressure here of an audience expecting history to be made. This film doesn't build the performance rhythm that the 1979 film did; it's very smoothly put together, but in a meaningless way—you don't feel that you're experiencing *Pryor's* rhythms. Is the editing bad, or were the editors trying to stretch the material to this eighty-eight minute length? (Why are there so many cutaways—at just the wrong time—to laughing, dressed-up people in the front rows? You half expect to see a star or two among them. It makes the movie feel canned.) Haskell Wexler headed the camera crew, and the color looks true and clear, and Pryor, in his scarlet suit, black bow tie and shirt, gold shoes, and a snazzy designer belt with a piece hanging straight down, is vividly close to us. But he has trouble getting going. He has hunches—he touches on things and you wait to see what he'll do with them. And most of the time he doesn't do anything with them; they don't develop into routines—he just drops them. Midway, he starts getting into his swing, in a section about his experiences during the filming of parts of *Stir Crazy* in the Arizona State Prison. He goes on to talk about a trip he took to Africa, and it's a scene—he can live it. He turns himself into a rabbit, a bear, a lion, a couple of cheetahs, and a fearful gazelle. You feel his relief when he does the animals; a lot of the time he has been looking for his place on the stage, and now he has something physical to do. But then there's a sudden break. Voices, ostensibly from the audience, can be heard. One of them calls, "Do the Mudbone routine," and, rather wearily, saying that it will be for the last time, Pryor sits on a stool and does the ancient storyteller Mudbone, who in the seventies was considered one of his great creations. And the movie goes thud. This section feels like an interpolation—it doesn't have the crackle of a performer interacting with an audience. It's almost as dead as what happens when Johnny Carson asks an aging celebrity to tell the joke he used to tell that always broke Johnny up. Pryor looks defeated, shot down. The sudden dullness is compounded by his sitting: we're used to seeing him prowling—accompanied, when the spots hit the curtain behind him, by wriggling shadows.

When he picks up his act again, he talks about freebasing, and the feelings he had about his pipe—it talks to him, and he becomes the pipe. We feel as if we were actually listening to his habit talking to him. And he builds up a routine about his wife and his friend Jim Brown telling him what cocaine was doing to him. But "the pipe say, 'Don't listen.' " And then he tells about the hospital and about Jim Brown's visiting him every day. He's a great actor and a great combination of mimic and mime; he's perhaps never more inspired than when he assumes the personality of a rebellious organ of his body or of an inanimate object, such as that pipe—or Jim Brown. This is the high point of the film. When he becomes something or someone, it isn't an imitation; he incarnates the object's soul and guts. But he doesn't have enough material to work up the rhythmic charge he reached before Mudbone. What he has in *Sunset Strip* is the material for a forty-minute classic.

The picture is full of wonderful bits, such as his demonstration of how he loses his voice when he's angry at his wife, and to those unfamiliar with Pryor's infectiousness and truthfulness and his unfettered use of obscenity, and to all those who missed his 1979 film, it may be a revelation. But the greatness of *Richard Pryor: Live! in Concert* was in the impetus of his performance rhythm—the way he kept going, with all those characters and voices bursting out of him. When he told us about his heart attack, he was, in almost the same instant, the helpless body being double-crossed by its heart, the heart itself, a telephone operator, and Pryor the aloof, dissociated observer. We registered what a mysteriously original physical comedian he is, and we saw the performance sweat soaking his collarless red silk shirt. (There's no visible sweat this time.)

If he fulfilled his comic genius in *Live! in Concert,* here he's sampling the good will the public feels toward him. Audiences want him, they love him, even in bum movies, and he appears to be experiencing a personal fulfillment. But he hasn't yet renewed himself as an artist: it may seem cruel to say so, but even the routine on his self-immolation is a pale copy of his heart attack. In the first film, there was a sense of danger; when he used the word "nigger," it was alive and raw. When he uses it here, it just seems strange. He's up against something very powerful: the audience may have come expecting to see history made, but history now is also just seeing Richard Pryor. He knows that he doesn't have to do anything. All he has to do is stand there and be adored. And he knows there's something the matter with this new situation, but he doesn't know how to deal with it.

NOTE

A film review by Pauline Kael, "Richard Pryor Live on the Sunset Strip" (1982), in Pauline Kael, *For Keeps: Thirty Years at the Movies* (New York: E. P. Dutton, 1994), 933–935.

13 Richard Pryor

THE REAL SLIM SHADY (2001)

ROB SHEFFIELD

Ever since age and poor health wiped out Richard Pryor, he's been stuck in his role as a revered institution of American comedy. But sainthood doesn't suit him, because the man's genius was his evil, evil mouth. We've seen a lot of shock comics come and go since his time, but on the new Rhino box . . . *And It's Deep, Too!,* his first real career summary, you can hear Pryor freaking the mike onstage in the Seventies, and he still makes Eminem sound like kid stuff. His voice hasn't dated, because it echoes everywhere in pop culture today—not just in comics like Chris Rock but all over hip-hop. At one point, he says, with a sigh, "The bitch was so fine, I wanted to suck her daddy's dick"—and for all these years I thought Biggie [Smalls] made that one up.

Why is this old guy still so shocking? Some of it has to do with his words, which remain hilarious on the printed page, but mostly it's his voice. Like W. C. Fields or Bob Dylan, he's a master at sounding out-raged, pitching his voice up to a spluttering frenzy and then—this is the hard part—tweaking the heat, a degree or two at a time, modulating his outrage into a multiple orgasm of vocal hysteria. *That Nigger's Crazy,* from 1974, was Pryor's *Bringing It All Back Home,* the album on which he found his voice—and like Dylan, he blew it up so loud that nobody's been able to touch him ever since. On fire with power music electric-revival pain, Pryor likes to rap about his real-life demons: He does drugs, he goes to jail, he immolates himself freebasing. But all the death and cruelty he sees just make him appreciate a cheap laugh for what it's worth, like when he tells a departing girlfriend, "Shit, I'm gonna find me some new pussy," and she fires back, "You had two more inches of dick, you'd find some new pussy here."

Pryor is funniest when he's riffing on his favorite topic, physical pain—the heart attack in his 1979 film *Live! in Concert,* the freebase memoir in 1982's *Live on the Sunset Strip,* the amazing "Acid" on *Bicentennial Nigger,* in which he samples the white man's drug and finds himself the only black man in space, re-enacting dialogue from 2001 and chanting, "I'm gonna die!" This stuff shouldn't be funny, but as Eminem understands, there's a reason we go to comedians to help us live with our primal fears of death, violence, and bodily mutilation—the same way we tune in to Road Runner cartoons to see Wile E. Coyote go over the cliff again and again. Pryor brings the pain, but he wears the scars himself, which gives him more moral heft than guys like Eminem. He doesn't pretend that any kind of morality is getting him or us off the hook—he just uses his grown-up compassion to get deeper under our skin.

For me, the Richard Pryor character who has done this job best over the years is the preacher, who, almost heroically, refuses to give any moral dignity to all this bullshit; instead, he insults the cripples, tells the deaf to kiss his ass, and warns the dead, "If you think we gonna bury you with them diamonds and shit on, you got another thin[k] coming." Then he asks his audience if he can get an amen. Needless to say, even after all these years, Richard Pryor always gets his amen.

NOTE

A review by Rob Sheffield, "Richard Pryor: The Real Slim Shady," *Rolling Stone,* 15 March 2001, 28.

IV.

Social
and Cultural
Criticism

The New Comic Style of
14 Richard Pryor (1975)

JAMES ALAN MCPHERSON

The handwritten sign on the door of the modest Hollywood Hills cottage is literary and more than a little self-conscious: "To avoid ill feeling and/or unpleasantness," the sign advises, "Please be aware of the fact that *uninvited* guests are not welcome at any time, whatsoever. To avoid rejection, please do not take the liberty of 'dropping by.' Sincerely and Respectfully, Occupant." On one level of reality, the sign says a simple "Go Away!"

Inside the cottage, seated in the living room before a color television set, the occupant at this particular moment is a totally unselfconscious, direct, and toothless old blues singer. "Say, boy," he drawls. One senses the rhythms of the Mississippi Delta, the pitch of the South Carolina Geechee, the musical patois of the Louisiana Creole. The face expresses all the wayward experience and wisdom of a full life. As the man talks, the sounds of a guitar and harmonica tuning up flow with the words from his drawn-in lips. "Your mama . . . she a Elk, ain't she? . . . Rode the goat? . . ." Now both the guitar and harmonica sounds fall into place within the lyrics of the old man's song. "Killed a guard in Lou-ez-ze-ana [*whine*]/Stabbed him *fiff*-teen times [*humm*]/Wouldn't of stab him so much [*whine*]/If he had of been a friend of mine . . ."

Suddenly the face releases its age, the puckered lips move outward revealing strong teeth, and Richard Pryor permits his real self to appear. "That's one I'm working on," he says, lifting a glass of brandy from the coffee table before him. "When I was a kid in Peoria, he used to sit out in from of Johnnie Mac's Barbecue Pit. The nigger had a goatee, he was toothless, and he had a guitar and a harmonica with tape on the end." Here Pryor mimics the sound of a mouth blowing comfortably into a . . . harmonica. For a moment, he seems to forget he has company as he concentrates intensely on perfecting the technique used by a toothless man playing the harmonica. Finally, he says, "This is it, right? They have their lips sucked a certain way?" To test the sound, Pryor begins to improvise with the voice, evoking a scene in which a bashful-sounding but obviously cunning Southern black man is trying to underestimate his skills at playing dice in order to outwit a group of Northern black men. "Oh, I gamble a little," the voice says. "Me, I a'mit that. Say, now, the two green ones I had befo', you ain't changed them now, did you? God-dong! 'Cause I know y'all slick up here." What becomes visible in Richard Pryor's face and audible in the old man's voice is a complete understanding of the assumptions which once structured social relations between Southern and Northern black people. Across the room, next to a picture window, small human faces laugh and applaud on a television game show. The sound is turned down. Richard Pryor dissolves his comic mask, looks at the television and laughs . . . "Mercy?" he calls into the next room. "Bring me a pair of socks."

"Long ones?" his housekeeper, Mercy, answers from the back of the house.

"Yes, ma'am." ha says.

A *very proper* Chicano woman brings the socks. Pryor puts them on and leans back on the sofa, sipping his Courvoisier. He is an ordinary-looking honey brown–skinned man, with a thick Afro and a thick black mustache curving downward toward the edges of his lower lip. The face gives the impression of never being comfortable enough to come to rest inside itself. His manner is almost shy. "I'm waiting to watch 'Zoom,'" he says about the silent television. "It's one of my favorites, along with the cartoons."

Despite his private manner, Richard Pryor is one of the most popular comedians of his generation, although he is largely unknown to the broad American public. Almost singlehandedly, he is creating a new style in American comedy, a style that some of his admirers have called "theater" because there is no other category available for what he does. His style relies on extremely subtle dimensions which must be observed and heard at the same time in order to be completely understood and appreciated. Indeed, there is no way his brand of comedy can be described in writing without the generous use of parentheses noting nuances in sound and facial expression. Mel Brooks, one of his admirers, has called him a comic of "outré imagination." *Rolling Stone* magazine has said that Pryor's comic style is "a new type of realistic theater," a theater which presents "the blemished, the pretentious, the lame—the common affairs and crutches of common people." Most black audiences love Richard Pryor. He appears before them at night clubs and in concerts, and there are occasional glimpses of him on television and in movies. But because of the particular nature of hit art, because of the materials on which he draws, Pryor will probably have great difficulty reaching the wider white public. Unlike most comedians, his comedy is heavily visual; and also, unlike most comedians of his caliber, Pryor cannot utilize television in his search for a broader audience.

The cause of his exclusion is Pryor's choice of materials. The characters in his humor are winos, junkies, whores, street fighters, blue-collar drunks, pool hustlers—all the failures who are an embarrassment to the black middle class and stereotypes in the minds of most whites. The black middle class fears the glorification of those images and most whites fear them in general. Pryor talks like them; he imitates their styles. Almost always, he uses taboo words which are common in their vocabularies. And he resists all suggestions that he modify his language, censor his commentary. As a result, Pryor's audiences have been limited to those who attend his night-club and concert engagements. These are mostly black people. When he does appear on television, it is only as a guest; and even then he is likely to say something considered offensive to a larger and more varied audience.

Although his routines seem totally spontaneous, his work has moved away from the stand-up comic tradition employed by comedians like Lenny Bruce. Pryor improvises, but his improvisations are structured, usually springing from within his characters. He seldom throws out one-liners just to haul in laughter, unless it is social commentary leading to the depiction of a character. Instead he enters into his people and allows whatever is comic in them, whatever is human, to evolve out of what they say and how they look into a total scene. It is part of Richard Pryor's genius that, through the selective use of facial expressions, gestures, emphases in speech and movements, he can create a scene that is comic and at the same tine recognizable as profoundly human. His problem is that he also considers certain aspects of their language essential to his characters.

"I couldn't do it just by doing the words of the person," he says. "I have to *be* that person. I see that man in my mind and go with him. I think there's a thin line between being a Tom on them people and seeing them as human beings. When I do the people, I have to do it true. If I can't do it, I'll stop right in the middle rather than pervert it and turn it into Tomism. There's a thin line between to laugh with and to laugh at. If I didn't do characters, it wouldn't be funny." Here Pryor pauses. "When I didn't do characters, white folks loved me."

There are many whites, however, who do admire Pryor. Like his black audiences, they seem to recognize he has completely abandoned the "cute" and usually paternalistic black comic images of the sixties, popularized mainly by Bill Cosby. Pryor's people are real and immediately recognizable by anyone who has had contact with them, whether in a black skin or a white one. He does not allow them to get away with anything. If it is true, as Henri Bergson has suggested, that laughter is a corrective, a social gesture that has as its purpose the punishment of rigid or inelastic conduct, Richard Pryor is giving a public airing to some of the more unadmirable styles of the urban black community and making his audiences recognize them for what they are. Any good comedian can do this, but it is Pryor's special genius to be able to make his audiences aware that the characters, though comic, are nonetheless complex human beings. "Watching Richard perform," said *Rolling Stone,* "is like watching yourself and all victims of human nature on stage; it can be painful and it can be exhilarating." The magazine calls this new comic style "the theater of the routine."

If "routine" means the passions and pains of ordinary people, Pryor definitely qualifies as an interpreter. His life has been rich in experiences which have allowed him to observe such people. He was born on Dec. 1, 1940, in Peoria, Ill., the stereotyped center of Americana. He says that his family ran whorehouses. His grandmother, a New Orleans Creole and a Catholic, was the owner. All kinds of people, including politicians, came within the range of Pryor's perception.

But possibly the stronger influence on him was his father, who, Pryor hints, was that very complex kind of black man given to operating by his own rules and within his own sense of reality ("Cut this stuff short!" Pryor recalls his father saying to the priest at his mother's graveside, while holding back tears. "It's cold out here!").

Pryor attended Catholic school, receiving all A's, he says, until the business activity of his family was discovered and he was expelled. Transferred to public school, he was put into a class for the mentally retarded because of his hyperactivity, and remained in classes for slow learners until his expulsion in the seventh grade for hitting a science teacher. Before he left school, however, a teacher encouraged him to act in skits at a local community center. In the meantime, he also hung out on the corner and worked in a packing house.

His career as a comedian began in the Army and continued, after his discharge, in small clubs in Peoria, East St. Louis, Youngstown, and Pittsburgh. In the early sixties, he worked his way east to Greenwich Village and Borscht Belt clubs in the Catskills, developing his abilities as an improviser. His materials at that time reflected the country's preoccupation with integration. Pryor admits to being influenced during this period by an early record by Lenny Bruce, probably the classic *I Am Not a Nut, Elect Me!* on which Bruce came as close as he ever would to making the transition from strict commentary later made by Lily Tomlin and Pryor. But Pryor's chief model at this time was Bill Cosby, who was the first black comic to reach a broad white audience. Pryor imitated Cosby, he says, because a white agent told him that Cosby was the kind of black man white television viewers would not mind having in their homes.

In the middle sixties, Pryor began appearing on the Ed Sullivan, Merv Griffin, and Johnny Carson shows, and eventually started working before predominantly white audiences in Las Vegas. During this period, he married and divorced several times, made a sizable amount of money, and developed a habit for cocaine. In 1970, he says, he experienced what might be called a breakdown on the stage of the El Aladdin Hotel in Las Vegas. He says he became frustrated because he felt the current of characters developing inside his head and could not "go" with them, restricted as he was to the expectations and tastes of a white night-club audience. He walked off the wrong end of the stage, leaving Las Vegas and encouraging predictions that he would never again hit the big time.

In 1972, however, Richard Pryor surfaced again, this time in the role of Piano Man in the movie *Lady Sings the Blues.* The comedian who had attempted to locate the comic vein in largely white audiences had been replaced by an actor capable of very subtle interpretations of his characters. In *Craps (After Hours)*, Pryor's second recorded album, he returned to the people and the comic situations he knew intimately. He still did commentary, but his approach was altogether different. Instead of remaining aloof from his characters, Pryor became them, moving beyond interpretation to total integration of himself and his materials.

Later, he played dramatic and comic roles in six other movies, including *Hit, Wattstax,* and *Uptown Saturday Night.* He wrote scripts for "Sanford and Son" and Flip Wilson, and, in 1973, helped write two television specials for Lily Tomlin. He won an Emmy award for this work. During the same year, he worked with Mel Brooks on the script for a movie tentatively titled "Black Bart," which became the highly success-ful *Blazing Saddles.* In 1974, just before the movie opened to mixed critical reviews and wide audience acceptance, Pryor was indicted for failure to file income-tax returns on $250,000 earned between 1967 and 1970. After plea bargaining, he was fined $2,500 and sentenced to 10 days in jail.

Shortly afterward, his third recorded album, the X-rated *That Nig-ger's Crazy,* was released; it promptly sold a million copies. He resumed making personal appearances, this time before predominantly black au-diences, in San Francisco, Detroit, Harlem, and Washington, D.C.

Returning to Los Angeles after months on the road, Pryor now seems determined to make another attempt to reach movie audiences, only this time not as a writer or a supporting actor. This time, he is writing his own film script, "This Can't Be Happening to Me." The sign on the door of his home, as well as his calm deliberation, suggests that he will allow nothing—hack work, fans, or interviewers—to interrupt his concentration on the script. Though he watches television in the late afternoon, the set runs without sound; and he will talk to a guest only until it is time for "Zoom" to come on.

Richard Pryor does not like to analyze his work, but he seems to have come to some firm conclusions about himself, his audience, and their standards. "I don't know what I do," he says simply. "I know what I won't do. I don't know what I will do. I turned down big money because I won't work Vegas and be that type. [Here he mimics the sound of a band playing a hackneyed introductory chord: da de dah *dah,* da de dah *dah* . . . 'Hi, folks,' the nervous voice of a stand-up comic says. 'Gosh, what a pleasure . . .'] I trust my audiences now. I worked the Apollo in Harlem. I was scared to death. Them niggers will eat you up if your—— ain't right. But they responded and I was fine after that, wherever I went. I worked Detroit, Chicago—everyplace the same. People felt good. And to see people laughing at each other and not being so serious, that made me feel good. The record people tell me now they can release my old work. I say, 'You can't release *nothing,* not under my name. You under-estimate them people that bought my last album. They didn't buy that to make me a million seller; they bought it because they liked it. And as long as I keep them liking, they'll buy. And when I stop, they won't.'"

He drinks from his Courvoisier and glances at the television before continuing. "The Mike Douglas Show" is progressing in silence. "See, there's a spotlight, and whoever stands under it, it don't matter to no-body. But I'm going to do mine right. Whenever they say, 'Richard Pryor,' they can trust me. Whenever I do a movie, I want them to say, 'Starring Richard Pryor? I'm gonna see that 'cause I know Richard Pryor gonna make us laugh. Bring the family!' There may be some blue words in it— they don't care. It's going to be funny."

What Pryor describes as "mine" is his ability to absorb and then re-create the lifestyles of the people around him. "I be listening to dudes talking, all over," he says, "in whorehouses and places. Everybody be talking the same kind of talk. No matter what city you go to, it's the same feeling, a universal feeling. That's what they be laughing at, themselves. They see themselves when I do a character. I noticed going around working for black people who're in a depression now, they all laughed at the same things wherever I was working. There's a kind of unity. In different cities, wherever I am, they be laughing at the same——, so I know we all know what's happening. I say, "Well, now, Huey [Newton] done went crazy. Whipped his tailor 'cause the pants was too long.' And they laughed all over 'cause they knew who I was talking about. They knew about all the niggers who died following after him, and here he is beating up a tailor."

Most people, black or otherwise, would find it difficult not to respond to some of the characters of Richard Pryor's humor. Among them are a philosophical wino who hands out advice to passersby, including Drac-ula and a junkie; the denizens of an after-hours joint; a meek blue-collar drunk who picks his weekly fight in a barroom, is beaten, then goes home to his wife bragging that he will make love to her, only to fall asleep; a pool shark named The Stroker; a braggart named Oilwell who showers policemen with muscular rhetoric; a white policeman named Officer Timson; a whore named Big Black Bertha; black preachers, hill-billies, and assorted minor characters—all of whom have individualized qualities. Not one is a stereotype. Their scenes are introduced from within them and conform strictly to the patterns of their individual experiences. Pryor presents them with such thoroughness and fidelity to their speech, gestures, flaws, and styles in general that the same charac-ters are recognizable to audiences in all parts of the country. Pryor's characters are human, and only that.

Even hillbillies tend to recognize themselves in Pryor's routines. "They'll come up to me," he relates. "They'll say, 'Man. I'll tell you. I mean that was really funny.' It's a strange feeling that transcends all that other stuff. They'll say, 'I know a guy just like that.' They mean it. You can see love for that guy in their faces."

It is significant that Pryor has considerable difficulty explaining this phenomenon. Instead, he slips easily into the character of a hillbilly, as if he would allow the man to explain himself. One recognizes immediately the truck driver, the service-station attendant, the man occupying the adjoining seat on the Greyhound bus, the lonely man on the next stool at the lunch counter. There is the smile with just a bit of condescension, the slightly conspiratorial eyes, the lips pulled in eight against the teeth, the nervous hitch in the shoulder signifying, perhaps, an uncomfortable intimacy. "Wal, buddy," the voice says, "you know that reminds me of the time Jed Tudd and I we uz daawn in El Paso—" the voice is flat and nasal, with just enough hesitation and hurry to suggest a friendly tension— "and a old boy—I never will forgit this—see, we uz loadin' manure on the back of a truck, and these boys come speeding down through there, and they just hit them brakes. *Goddam,* what a time! Just——spread all over the highway . . ."

No one really knows what makes us laugh. Henri Bergson theorized that the causes of laughter are external to ourselves, though existing within the context of what is human because laughter is dependent upon others for its echo. We know that we laugh at mechanical gestures, repetitions, inflexibility of character or language—any rigidity behind which we can perceive something human. To Bergson, laughter is a corrective which punishes the mechanical in human behavior. Freud sought for the source of laughter deep inside the chaos of man's unconscious self—a self from which, Freud said, the comic spirit erupted occasionally in a release of powerful impulses. These are two of the theories, but the source of laughter is still a mystery.

As Americans, we tend to laugh because laughter creates the illusion of unity and ease, when in fact we have never been unified or at ease. We laugh at the comic masks behind which we all hide in our endless searches for individual identities; for by laughing at the masks, we can laugh, with more emotional ease, at ourselves. This is why, as Constance Rourke has pointed out, the whole of the American comic tradition has been one of social criticisms. And vernacular humorists, from Mark Twain and the great political cartoonists to the best stand-up comics, have depended on an earthy level of language to provide resonance to their criticisms.

Viewed from the perspective of this American tradition, Richard Pryor is the first totally unselfconscious black comic to turn his perceptions—and language—on black people themselves. He forces them to look at their faults and laugh. Assured of their humanity, he holds up before his audiences patterns of behavior which have evolved into some-what rigid styles, and reminds them that they are only masks—and comic ones at that. His audiences laugh with him because they too know they are human.

Only Pryor knows his audiences well enough to do this. Only he could have made them laugh at the escapades of Huey Newton. Pryor's character Oilwell spouts braggadocio at policemen: "I'm Oil*wellll*, 6-foot-5, 222 pounds of *mannn!*" It does not matter that Oilwell is beaten up by the policemen. What matters is that Pryor's audiences can laugh at Oilwell's pretensions. When Pryor is onstage, his audiences shout, "Do Oilwell! Do Oilwell!" They have seen his style over and over. It has become mechanical and therefore comic.

In a Detroit theater recently, Pryor recalls, two black policemen came to his dressing room and reported they had just arrested a black suspect who used a line introduced by one of Pryor's characters in a comic routine: "I-am-rea-ching-into-my-poc-ket-for-my-li-cense." According to Pryor, one policeman said, "Don't you bring that to me! What you trying to do, a routine? Richard Pryor? Well, I'll do my part. Spread your cheeks! Put your face on the ground!" Then both policemen and the suspect stood there laughing with and at each other.

Pryor does not relate that anecdote without stating his ambivalence toward policemen. "They made me nervous," he says. "I was raised to hate cops. I'm sorry. We ran a whorehouse, and I was raised to not trust police. I know we need police, 'cause there are some niggers that'll pull the truck up to your house, and say, 'Give the furniture up! No, we's *taking* the furniture!' No, we need police. It's the police that you don't need that's in the way. But for these policemen to come to me was nice. And they liked me. See, the humanism in them hadn't been lost; it's just the job they had to do."

Part of Pryor's own humanism turns on the way he uses the word "nigger." His comic scenes are sprinkled liberally with this gem, so much in fact that some black people have complained he is damaging the image of the group by moving the word from the pool halls and barbershops back into public usage. The word "nigger," however, has never gone out of style. The movie industry and some whites opposed to busing have done far more than Pryor to keep the word alive. Also, and more impor-tant, there is a significant difference between Pryor's use of the word and the way it is used by whites to evoke an abstraction. When Pryor says "nigger," he is usually about to define a human type in all his complexity. It is to his credit that he is able to start with an abstraction and make it into a recognizable human being. If he does his work well enough, it would be difficult for even the most offended listener, white or black, not to say, "I've seen this man before."

Whenever the conversation reaches a point which requires Pryor to reveal more of his inner self than he would like to make public, he tends either to slip into a character or to laugh. The laugh is a rapid-fire, nervous chuckle, and one can hear within it the footfalls of a perceptive mind backing quickly away from the questioner in order to gauge the depth of the question's sincerity. But in matters touching his humanity. Pryor does not laugh and he speaks for himself, "It's love for them," he says. "I don't think you could do impressions of somebody you hate. If it is hate, it's some kind of admiration for something: the worst in the best, and the best in the worst."

He nods at the silent television. On the early evening news, there is a feature about Los Angeles people who visit homes for retarded children and the elderly. A mentally retarded white girl is on camera. "How do you hate that?" he asks. "'Cause she's white? You wish that on her?" A little black boy is bouncing a basketball to entertain a group of elderly white people. "Look at them old people," he says, "that old man sitting up there." The old man is smiling. The little black boy is smiling. "How do you hate that? 'Cause it's black? I wouldn't want to be like that. Can you imagine the hearts of people all tied up in hatred?"

As an example of what hatred does to an individual, he offers his own insights into the psychology of the white guards he observed while serving his 10 days in prison. He talks of how hate can extend into a guard's family life and affect his children. Step by step, he traces the psychological devastation from prisoner to guard to wife and children to the community. His descriptions are accurate and sobering. Then, to break away from this line of conversation, and to do so without laughing or slipping into a character, Pryor says, "Hey, has anybody ever written Santa Claus in June? Say, 'Dear Santa, how you doing? You all right, man? Here's a scarf. Wrap up. I know it's cold up there. How's the wife and kids?' Nobody thinks of that," he says. It is obvious that he is now eager to see "Zoom" and the cartoons.

What is it at the basis of Richard Pryor's comic style that enables him to enlarge his characters even while we laugh at them? Recognizable immediately are the speech styles of the "boys on the block," black preachers, blue-collar workers, policemen—all the types likely to be found in urban black communities. But when introducing them in comic scenes, Pryor does some very subtle things with their language. Expressed within the sounds of certain words are ideas which help define each character and expand the comic situation. The pomposity of a black preacher is suggested by the extra emphases on certain words ("I first met God in 1929," Pryor's preacher says, "outside a little hotel in Baltimore . . . and the voice got mag*niff*-ficent and *whooly* and re-*zounde-dah*"). The egotism of the character Oilwell rings through the broad sound of his self-definition ("I'm Oilwell. 222 pounds of ma*annnn*!"). The intransigence of a street-corner tough is incorporated into his lingo: "I ain't goin' *nowhere*. He go'n to mo*oove* me!" (The idea of a pushing contest is incorporated into the sound "mo*oove*"; it expresses resistance to forced removal.)

Richard Pryor is very sensitive to such subtle shadings of pitch and inflection. "Niggers just have a way of telling you stuff and not telling you stuff," he observes. "Martians would have a difficult time with niggers. They be translating words, saying a whole lot of things underneath you, all around you. That's our comedy."

But Pryor's sensitivity to verbal nuance is only one aspect of his comic style. The most important aspect, the one that makes his routines theater, is the almost unbelievable mobility of his face. His is probably the most expressive comic face since Chaplin's. It can express hundreds of subtle moods with very rapid shifts, making it impossible to see where one shading ends and another begins. Where did he acquire this skill? Pryor does not mind disclosing that he got it at the movies. "Cartoons are the art form of the movie industry I learn most from," he says. "They can do such things with cartoons. They can say such heavy things. Life now is a cartoon. We are cartoons."

Perhaps Richard Pryor is right. He is a child of the American movies, especially the animated-cartoon branch of it. Among major movie influences on his comic-style, along with Jerry Lewis, Fuzzy Q. Jones, Red Skelton, Pat Butram, Smiley Burnette, and Abbott and Costello, Pryor lists Porky Pig, Bugs Bunny, Baby Huey, the Roadrunner, Mickey Mouse, and the Little Rascals. As a youngster in Peoria, he spent many Saturdays watching matinees featuring as many as 25 cartoons, most of which accelerated the movements of humanlike animal forms by synchronizing them against up-tempo music. After more than 20 years, Pryor's face is trained to not miss a single beat in its union with the rhythms of his characters' speech. In his mind, he has integrated frame after frame of emotional nuance demonstrated by cartoon figures as they encounter seemingly insurmountable obstacles. In the forties and fifties, they were mere cartoons. In 1975, they seem much closer to the reality we see around us.

The final dimension of Richard Pryor's comic style is a moral one.

Mel Brooks has said Pryor possesses "almost Nietschean ideals of what is good, what is powerful, what is superior." While contributing to his humor, these same standards prevent Pryor from taking himself too seriously. He will not, for example, accept invitations to speak to young black kids about the dangers of drugs because of his past involvement with cocaine. "I feel like a hypocrite," he says. "As much cocaine as I snorted. The kids know that; they ain't stupid. All I can say to kids is, 'Know what you want to do.' I can *tell* them there ain't nothing happening in jail. You'll die, or be treated like a dog. If that's what they want, fine. I can't stop it."

Still, one senses that his imagination is drawn to the victims of drugs and that he has the most profound sympathy for such people. Because he must look, and because his imagination is essentially comic, he arranges what he sees, no matter how horrible, into comic patterns. He speaks of Harlem, of having seen there three blocks of junkies in Army jackets waiting under yellow lights for their contacts to arrive. His face registers the most profound sadness. In trying to describe the scene, he assumes, unconsciously, the voice of a movie director, and then the voice of an Army sergeant directing the movements of the junkies and their contacts: "Ten-hut!" he barks. "Roll up sleeves! Tie-*off*! Cookers-on! Ready-needles! Shoot-*huh*! Nod-*huh*! . . ."

For all of its appeal, Richard Pryor's comic style is not for everyone, although, watching him portray a character in a comic scene, one realizes that Pryor's people have always existed. In Elizabethan England, a period with a lower class whose manners and styles resembled some of those found in urban black communities, Oilwell might have been called Pistol, Big Black Bertha might have been called Doll Tearsheet or Mistress Quickly, the boys on the block might have been named Bardolph, Peto, Gadshill, and Poins. There might have been a sly old man, curiously resembling Redd Foxx, with the name Jack Falstaff. During that period, a genius who knew all levels of his society made a place for them in his historical plays. He produced great drama. Richard Pryor's is a different kind of genius. He knows intimately only one level of his society. But at least he is reminding us, in his special kind of theater, that such people still exist.

Watching Richard Pryor in front of his television, one senses that he is weighing very carefully the cost of his resurrection as a comic and the options now open to him. When "Zoom" comes on, he turns up the sound and sings along with its theme song. Mercy, the housekeeper, brings in hamburgers. Pryor says, "Thank you, ma'am." Then he looks at the television screen and says, "Kids' laughter don't it mess with you? They're so natural. They ask, 'Why?' That's the greatest kid question in the world. 'Why?'"

He studies the screen again. "I know all the tricks," he continues. "I assume that everybody does. But people like me because I won't use them, and if I do they can tell. I ain't never done that, and if I keep my pace I ain't never gonna be like that. I do like to work on television, but they say, 'No, we have to have laughter in there.' I say, 'Don't you think people are sophisticated enough to enjoy something without being told when to laugh?' The laughter is in yourself. If you don't want to laugh, you don't have to laugh; you could just be enjoying something. You don't have to laugh because somebody in the audience is laughing."

He finishes his hamburger quickly, looks around and smiles, and suddenly grabs part of a hamburger from the plate of his guest. It is a kind gesture. It says, I want to be friendly, but I also want to be alone. The gesture is much better than Pryor's exploratory laugh, and more gracious than his slipping into one of his characters. Richard Pryor is a young man from the streets of Peoria—a man whose skills have proved themselves marketable. He is also a keeper of the comic spirit for at least one level of American society. He may yet find ways to expand the range of his experience and the range of his responsibilities.

NOTE

James Alan McPherson, "The New Comic Style of Richard Pryor," *The New York Times Magazine,* 27 April 1975, 20+.

15 Jive Times

RICHARD PRYOR, LILY TOMLIN, AND THE THEATRE
OF THE ROUTINE (1974)

DAVID FELTON

I read the news today, February 9, 1974. . . .

A 71-year-old Wisconsin bachelor who forgot to pay his gas bill was found frozen to death at home after the gas company shut off his heat. In a futile effort to resist the one-degree February weather, the old man had surrounded himself with five shirts, several blankets, a hot plate, and a vacuum-cleaner motor. A spokesman for the gas company called it "a horrible tragedy" but denied the company had done anything wrong.

The FBI released composite drawings of three persons it suspects kidnapped newspaper heiress Patricia Hearst earlier in the week. The sketches of two black men and a white woman resembled so many persons in the Berkeley/Oakland area of California that police were swamped with hundreds of calls, most of them of little value.

In San Francisco, angry residents of the Bernal Heights area called upon street-sweeping supervisor Bernard Crotty at his tidy Sunset District home and asked him why his street was so clean while theirs remained unswept and filled with rotting garbage. Crotty slammed the door in their faces, later explaining to newsman, "I don't have my men do a better job out here. It's just that those people are dirtier."

In Washington, Navy Yeoman Charles Radford said he lifted private papers from Henry Kissinger and gave them to the Pentagon because "the government has to steal from itself to stay informed." He said that even though he sometimes felt guilty about spying, he did it to keep his job. "I just didn't want my record to have a black mark on it." Meanwhile Edward T. Schmults, general counsel to the Treasury Department, was asked why that agency had spied on F. Donald Nixon, the president's brother. He replied, "It's not unusual to put an individual under surveillance."

And in London, Wing Commander Graham Gardner, happy that he had just settled an argument at a Royal Air Force business meeting, slid down a banister and fell eight feet to his death. "It was a simple, almost childish impetuousness in a moment of relief," explained a friend.

. . . oh boy.

For months now rumors have been circulating inside and outside *Rolling Stone* about the imminent publication of a special "comedy issue." We've been besieged by advertisers, talent agents, and free-lance writers concerned that the picture of comedy we present be complete enough to include their self-interests. "When is the comedy issue going to appear?" is a question I've been asked almost daily, usually by the editor.

Well, as you will see, the rumors weren't entirely accurate. What follows is not a special comedy issue per se; it is not a roundup of comedians, or a survey of where comedy is today, or where it is likely to be tomorrow. That sort of thing is best handled by the *Newsweek/Time* boys who are so skilled at constructing compartments narrow enough for their ideas to fit snugly.

Nor, as it turns out, is this a special issue of any kind. Originally my plan was to write two stories with a common theme, about a new type of realistic theater—represented by comedians Richard Pryor and Lily Tomlin—that greatly expands the boundaries of traditional stand-up comedy and is particularly appropriate for the jive times in which we live. The plan was to present these stories side by side in one issue of the magazine, but ultimately I wrote them too long for that. To print them together would simply leave no room for any other articles—which was all right with me but not with several members of the staff who apparently felt their own work should be published if they were to continue posturing as professional writers.

So the solution was to present Richard Pryor's story in this issue and Lily Tomlin's next time. I'm sorry about the inconvenience and extra purchasing expense (you might try setting up a lending pool with an equally destitute friend), but I assure you it will be worthwhile to read both stories and to think of them as a unit. Richard Pryor and Lily Tomlin are not a comedy team, although they have performed together on television and seem to share a mutually high respect for each other's talent. Independently they have developed their art along similar lines.

Both are exceptional actors and mimes. Both are exceptionally funny and quick-witted. Both are astute observers of so-called reality—their private lives, experiences of friends and strangers, the news of the day—drawing from it material which they present onstage with a minimum of alteration. They don't tell jokes, they seldom indulge in hyperbole or commentary—traditional tools of most comedians.

Instead, they have introduced a version of comedy that goes way beyond laughter, certainly way beyond the escapist entertainment we are used to seeing in nightclubs and on television. It is real theater, a theater of the routine, the blemished, the pretentious, the lame—the common affairs and crutches of common people. Watching Lily and Richard perform is like watching yourself and all victims of human nature onstage; it can be painful and it can be exhilarating. Lily, musing on some very real characters from her past, put it like this.

"They were all like humans. Everybody had these incredible highs and terrible lows, everybody was afraid of something. They could be real petty and ugly, or they could be just real beautiful and uplifting and have wonderful little quirky moments where they made you laugh and other moments where you just hated them. And I saw that nobody knew anything. Nobody knew any answer to anything."

Although their attitudes toward comedy, and thus reality, are nearly the same, Pryor and Tomlin differ somewhat in their performing styles. Richard's act tends to be more spontaneous and free-form, whereas Lily's is quite formally scripted and varies hardly a word in any series of performances. For that and other reasons, I decided on rather different approaches to their stories, both involving experiments of sorts.

For some time I had wanted to play with a videotape recorder as a journalistic tool, in the manner one uses an audio tape recorder. Richard seemed a perfect subject, since his visual movements are so quick, spontaneous, and subtle. I think it worked OK, although really, there's no way he or Lily can be fully realized in print. That's why theater is such a turn-on, after all.

With Lily I have attempted a kind of journalistic play—in two acts, no less. Her interview was remarkable; it lasted 12½ hours and she performed the entire time, pacing about the room, acting out characters, gesturing, changing her voice, screwing up her face—a whole bag of tricks. So I gave her two roles, onstage and offstage, and wove them in and out of the story line. Thus Pryor's story sets up the argument about comedy and reality, and Tomlin's more or less illustrates it. That's my theory, anyway, and at least it gives me a chance to include a good deal of their material.

To show you how well these two people work together and how much they are changing the complexion of comedy, particularly on television, here's an excerpt from a sketch they did last year on Lily's second TV special, the one that won two Emmys. The sketch, written by Jane Wagner, performed without audience or laugh track, takes place during winter inside Opal's Soul Food Cafe. Lily plays Opal, the cafe's black proprietress. Richard plays Juke, a black junkie. Bill Gerber and Judy Kahan play two young, white community researchers who have just entered the cafe with questionnaires in their hands.

(BILL *and* JUDY, *wearing coats and business clothes, sit at a table.* RICHARD *sits at the counter in an Army-type field jacket.* LILY, *wearing a long blue dress and a pink cloth around her head, stands behind the counter. From the jukebox, Al Green sings "Let's Stay Together"*)

BILL: We'd like to ask you a few questions. They might prove to be interesting.

LILY: Oh, I imagine they will; I always find those questions interestin', don't you Juke?

(RICHARD *raises his eyebrows and nods blankly at Lily, as if to say, "Oh, yeah, sure, if you say so."*)

BILL: Say, this is a far-out menu.

LILY: I drew that pork chop myself.

RICHARD: (*Mimicking*) Far out, far out.

BILL: I think I'll have the, uh . . .

RICHARD: (*Gets up, walks toward* BILL.) Let me order for you . . . sir . . . allow me . . . (*grabs the menu from him*) . . . 'cause you new in the community; leave the menu, chump. Nobody gonna hurt you or nothin'. (*Sits down next to* JUDY *and shows her the menu with the pork chop on it.*) Hey, baby, check this out. Is she an artist?

JUDY: (*Slightly nervous*) It's very good.

RICHARD: (*Sing-song, to* LILY) And she don't look back (*chuckles*). Get this man some of your homemade potato soup. He'll like that.

BILL: OK. I'll have the potato soup.

LILY: (*To* JUDY) You want anything besides answers?

JUDY: Oh, well. I'll just have some tea, please, with some milk.

RICHARD: That's a good idea—hey, give me a bowl of tea . . . and a twist of lemon . . . and ten dollars.

LILY: (*Abruptly*) Ten dollars . . .

RICHARD: Cash money. I have some community affairs business to take care of, myself.

LILY:(*Upset*) You must think I'm crazy . . . come in here, insult my cookin', make sarcastic remarks, expect me to give you a Master Charge for lunch, I don't know what all else. (*She brings them the tea.*)

RICHARD: (*To* LILY) I love you. You should be more respectful of a man in my position. (*To* BILL) That soup's a knockout, ain't it.

BILL: (*Tastes it*) Hot!

RICHARD: Yeah, well it's got to be hot to be hot soup, turkey. That's a homemade recipe. She makes that from scratch, gives you. . . .

(*Suddenly* RICHARD *gasps, bends over in pain and clutches* JUDY's *wrist.*)

JUDY: You all right?

RICHARD: (*Groans*) I think it's the soup.

(BILL *pulls back and looks nervously at* JUDY, *while* RICHARD *tries to joke his way out of it.*)

RICHARD: No, it's the tea . . . no, it's the soup (*laughs and claps his hands*).

LILY: (*To* RICHARD) Will you take that one nerve you got left, get on outa here, leave the people alone.

RICHARD: Don't insult me and my date.

JUDY: (*Turns to questionnaire*) I wonder if you can tell me . . . have you ever been addicted?

RICHARD: (*Scowls*) What?

JUDY: Have you ever been addicted to drugs?

RICHARD: (*Hesitates, glances sheepishly at* LILY, *then at* JUDY) Yeah, I been addicted . . . I'm addicted now—don't write it down, man, be cool, it's not for the public. I mean, what I go through is private. (*Righteously*) My body is a temple. I mean, tomorrow I may be off the stuff, for all you know.

LILY: (*Disgusted*) Aw, shoot.

RICHARD: (*Laughs, then nervously rubs his mouth and chin*) I'm for real, baby. . . . I'm tired. (*To* JUDY) Uh, I have no dependents . . . self employed.

BILL: What are you going to do about your job?

RICHARD: I'm gonna marry your eyes. (*Everyone snickers.*) You got some pretty eyes. (*To* JUDY) How's your tea, dear?

JUDY: It's fine. Tell me, what do you think of your congressman?

LILY: Aw, just about what he thinks of me.

RICHARD: Yeah, she's a beautiful woman, she give them quickies. Dig, (*To* LILY) do that impression of Billie Holiday, momma.

LILY: Aw, no.

JUDY: (*To* LILY) Do you do housework other than your own?

RICHARD: (*Reaches over and grabs the questionnaire from* JUDY) Let me see this list, let me see the list.

JUDY: That's really highly irregular . . .

RICHARD: Let . . . me . . . see . . . the . . . list, tut, tut, tut. I have some questions. Who's Pigmeat Markham's momma? You dig? (*Starts writing on questionnaire*) Wilt Chamberlain the tallest colored chap you ever saw?

(*No one answers.* JUDY *adjusts her coat,* BILL *glares at* RICHARD, LILY *walks over to supervise.*)

RICHARD: Have you ever been mugged in the same neighborhood more than once?

JUDY: You know . . . I can't help but sense a certain amount of resentment, and I really don't think it's fair.

BILL: Excuse me . . . excuse me. . . .

RICHARD: What?

BILL: We don't make up these questions.

RICHARD: Gee, golly.

BILL: Try to understand.

LILY: (*Pats* BILL *on the back*) Aw, c'mon, try to understan', we do make up these answers. It's all right.

RICHARD: (*Hands questionnaire back*) Press conference is over. (*Mock news voice*) "Thank you, Mr. Cronkite." (*Gets up from the table*) Just playin', you know. Have a good time. Enjoy the soup, man, it's outa sight. You gonna pay for my tea?

BILL: Yes.

RICHARD: You're all right.

LILY: He don't have to pay for the tea, you didn't even use a tea bag.

(RICHARD *walks up to the counter, leans over and half whispers to* LILY.)

RICHARD: Let me have the thing.

LILY: (*Turns away*) No, baby, come on . . .

RICHARD: (*Pleading*) No, I need it.

LILY: Baby . . .

RICHARD: I got to take care of business. I'm gonna get busted if you don't gimme the bread. You want me to be out there in the street, trying to look in cars?

(*Reluctantly,* LILY *opens the cash box and hands* RICHARD *a ten.*)

BILL: You really shouldn't give him the money. You know what he's going to do with it, he's going to go out of here and just . . .

LILY: (*Defensive*) I know what he's gonna do with it, he's gonna go out of here and get me ten pounda potatoes. (*To* RICHARD) I like them little red new potatoes for my potato soup.

(RICHARD *hangs his head down for a moment, then turns to* BILL. *He sounds like he is about to cry.*)

RICHARD: Hey, man . . . that's wrong, you know. You wrong, man. I mean I ain't a bad cat or nothin', man . . . 'cause you hurtin' *me*. I wouldn't interfere in your life.

LILY: (*Comes up to* RICHARD, *buttons up his jacket and pulls the hood over his head*) Baby, look at this. If you don't get you a warm jacket . . . I'm tellin' you, it's cold outside.

RICHARD: (*To* BILL) I mean, I should dus' you off.

LILY: You got to bundle up, it's really cold.

RICHARD: I'm gettin' a coat.

LILY: This ol' light jacket . . .

RICHARD: I'm getting a coat. (*Starts out the front door and turns to* BILL) I'm civilized, man.

(RICHARD *leaves,* BILL *and* JUDY *quickly gather up their stuff, put some money on the counter and head for the door.*)

BILL: (*To* LILY) Excuse me, I'm sorry, I didn't mean to offend you, here's . . . that'll take care of the soup and the tea.

LILY: That's all right, I know where you comin' from, that's all right. You got some change comin'.

BILL: No no, that's all right, keep it.

(*As* BILL *and* JUDY *reach the door,* RICHARD *pops back in and the three stand awkwardly face to face.*)

RICHARD: Hold it, hold it . . . no, man, I'm tryin' to give you some advice. You got a black car?

BILL: Yes.

RICHARD: A family just moved in it.

(BILL *and* JUDY *scurry out, and* RICHARD, *laughing, walks over to the table and starts carrying dirty dishes to the counter.*)

RICHARD: Let me help you with this stuff. You know, I think I'm kinda crazy about you.

LILY: Thank you, baby.

RICHARD: You sweet. You a sweet woman. (*Picks up a coin from the table and gives it to her*) Looka there, a tip! (*Stands there for a moment, then pulls a bill from his pocket*) Here . . . here's your ten back. I ain't gonna buy no more potatoes. I'm gonna try it without some potatoes . . . I'm gonna try . . . I ain't shuckin' . . . OK? Now be cool. (*Leans over and she kisses him*) Take care of yourself.

LILY: OK.

RICHARD: All right? (*Heads for the door*) I'll think aboutcha . . . be glad when it's spring . . .

LILY: Yeah.

RICHARD: . . . flower! (*He leaves.*)[1]

The art and insight of Richard Pryor and Lily Tomlin represent an important new path for other entertainers to follow. As far as I know, they now share it pretty exclusively.

There are other comedians who act brilliantly—Jonathan Winters, Sid Caesar, Art Carney. There are others who deal with reality—Robert Klein, George Carlin, Albert Brooks. But few come to mind who can fuse both those creative talents into what approaches a philosophical statement.

Richard and Lily quite possibly have shown us a road to personal survival through times that turn harder and weirder by the day. For it doesn't take much insight to see that life at the same time grows more entertaining. Just think of what we've been through the last year or two. Crooks become leaders and entrap themselves. Revolutionary ex-convicts control whole newspaper chains. Distinguished actors sell snapshot cameras on the tube. And more than half the nation's people still suffer from an incurable disease that makes their breasts too large to be elected president.

Dare I mention Richard Nixon? Why not—I simply want to praise him. Certainly he was the most entertaining president in our country's history. How he enriched our vicarious lives . . . don't you miss him already? What drama, what mystery, what moves! . . . did you see the way he moved in front of that convention of national broadcasters? . . . when they asked him whether the press had been fair about Watergate, and he snapped back, "You expect me to answer that here?" . . . and his arms shot out and he did this great double-take? Don Rickles could take lessons from him. And what about the time he shoved Ron Ziegler?

Of course, he's made it tough for us to concentrate or get any work done in the last two years. In fact, only after he resigned did I become bored enough to finish these two stories. But I'll always be grateful to him for the way he enlivened our culture, our cocktail conversation, our language—shit, when he said shit, the *Los Angeles Times* printed shit. On the front page! Nixon and the SLA have advanced newspaper language ten years.

As far as I'm concerned, Nixon should stop moping about San Clemente in solitary confinement and get seriously into show business . . . maybe host a talk show, or do some movie cameos. Wouldn't he have been great in *The Three Musketeers*! . . . he could've played eight roles. At the very least he could always sell snapshot cameras on the tube.

The point is, survival in the future won't mean breathing clean air or eating three squares. We can forget about that. Survival will mean keeping our sanity and our sense of humanity. And the comedy of Richard Pryor and Lily Tomlin can do much to prepare us.

Lily says that nobody knows the answer to anything, and that's probably a healthy attitude. But there's a question which might help us cope. When our lakes become so polluted we can skate on them in the summer, and people are kidnapped for their nutritional value, and we're forced to share our drinking water with the creatures floating in it, and small, pimply nations are blackmailing us with nuclear warheads, and the music's over 'cause it can't be heard . . . our survival may depend on blind irreverence and the ability to laugh and ask, "Are you serious?"

What an exciting prospect.

NOTES

David Felton, "Jive Times: Richard Pryor, Lily Tomlin, and the Theatre of the Routine," *Rolling Stone*, 10 October 1974, 38–39.

1. "Juke and Opal" by Jane Wagner ©1973. Omnipotent Inc. Reprinted by permission.

16 Richard and Me (1994)

Nelson George

I was carrying my notepad, my tape recorder, and wearing my best beige summer jacket. Riding the subway into the city I studied my questions again and again. I was as nervous as a filly at the Preakness, and I had a right to be. I was going to interview Richard Pryor for the *Amsterdam News*. What could top that? What if the movie he was promoting, *Greased Lightning,* a biopic of black stock-car pioneer Wendell Scott, was as mild as skim milk? I knew he was the funniest motherfucker on the planet, had all his albums, and couldn't wait to laugh real hard during our time together.

But instead of the private interview I'd anticipated, I walked into a dining room with three tables full of journalists, all staring expectantly at the door. Check that: three tables of *black* journalists. Where the white press got private time with Pryor, the black press had been convened for a group grope, typical of how white publicity firms traditionally treat (or mistreat) African American media, even when they're dealing with an African American subject.

I settled in next to a friend from another black weekly, the *Black American.* He was as hyped as I about the interview prospect; he had as many questions as I did. Pryor appeared with a publicist and a bodyguard at the doorway. He looked like he'd just gotten out of bed and that his dreams had not been pleasant. The comedian was guided to our table. A plate of food was slid before him. Pryor proceeded to eat.

Being enthusiastic and young I peppered Pryor with questions. My friend from the *Black American,* not as young but equally enthusiastic, queried Pryor too. In lieu of answers Pryor stared, grunted, and generally generated a wave of nonverbal hostility. When his meal was finished and our fifteen minutes had elapsed, Pryor was escorted to table number two where two comely female writers awaited. Within two minutes the comatose comic had revived and the sound of women's laughter floated over toward the frustrated cinephiles back at table number one.

The publicist whispered that after Pryor finished at table number three we'd all get another crack at him. I was willing to wait. By table number three Pryor was wide awake and was jesting happily with a nitwit newsman from the local black FM station. By now I was fuming. My professional ego, quite fragile in my days as a rookie scribe, had been badly bruised. Moreover, I already had developed a profound intolerance of star eccentricities. The more Pryor cooperated with the other tables, including people I thought of as incompetent, like the radio guy, the more pissed I became. So I left.

I didn't think Pryor noticed, though later the *Black American* writer told me he asked, "Where was the *Amsterdam News* guy?" By that time I had pouted my way over to the subway. It was, for me, a missed opportunity. I wasn't self-aware enough to realize how much I wanted Pryor to acknowledge me. Shows how unprepared I really was. Why in the world would I expect the man who'd made *That Nigger's Crazy* or *Craps (After Hours)* to conform to interview niceties? That was never what this brother was about.

Nobody mentions this anymore, but Richard Pryor was once as notorious in the black community as Snoop Doggy Dogg or Luther Campbell. That he had the temerity to use the N-word in an album title back in 1974 was considered quite "negative" in the days when the idea of a monolithic "positive" black image was unchallenged. On the heels of sixties crossover icons like Sidney Poitier, Bill Cosby, and Motown, Pryor had another take on mass success. As rap did a generation later, Pryor reached whites with an in-your-face use of "nigger." His ghetto characters, scatological references, and florid profanity, hos, pimps, and junkies were early staples of his humor. Raw was his calling card.

Again, like subsequent hip-hoppers, Pryor developed both a loyal black constituency and a young hip white audience. Where Cosby and Sidney and Motown penetrated the American suburban mainstream, Pryor's rebellious spirit and drug fixations put him in sync with its white, often urban, counterculture. White Pryor fans had a lot of the same attitudes as those who'd helped Jimi Hendrix cross over as an icon, while his black fans were the young people for whom Redd Foxx, Moms Mabley, Wildman Steve, and the rest of the chitlin' circuit comics were either too old-fashioned or just plain too old.

Possession of *That Nigger's Crazy* back then was as crucial a signifier of hipness as Ice Cube's *AmeriKKKa's Most Wanted* would be in 1990. My friends and I would sit and listen to it, sipping beer or wine and smoking herb as if the album were as dense as *Stairway to Heaven* or Stevie Wonder's *Inner Visions.* Cheech and Chong's whole career was built on being smokable comedians. So to a great degree was George Carlin's. But the range of Pryor's genius defied being boxed in by druggies, black cultural nationalists, or cross-cultural hipsters of my persuasion.

That Pryor apparently lost his mind in Hollywood, like so many before him, is sad not simply in the way all human loss is sad; it was a tragedy of enormous proportions for African Americans. I've always considered Pryor one of the greatest African American writers. His characters were very detailed and always based on reality, yet surreal in a way you might find in books by Ralph Ellison, Zora Neale Hurston, or Chester Himes. His understanding of the pathology of the junkie and the allure of addiction (to cocaine, to alcohol, to sex) made him more than a funny man. As a performer Pryor not only did characters; he could also animate objects, breathing life into punctured tires, car engines, and seductive crack pipes.

My favorite character was Mudbone, a grizzled street veteran all too happy to dispense wisdom collected at the bad end of a bottle. In black lore winos are much more benign figures than junkies. Once fixtures in urban America, they were replaced menacingly in the seventies by heroin addicts as the community's street-corner tribe. In his famous "The Wino and the Junkie" routine, Pryor managed to capture that tragic transition in black culture where dope overwhelmed the community. Where the more folksy (and more romanticized) wino is still connected to his soul, the junkie's senses are so dulled that he can barely speak anymore, much less understand the wino's wisdom. There is no wisdom for the junkie— only a strange deathly limbo that will infect all around him or her.

"The Wino and the Junkie" is emblematic of the kind of multi-layered work that made Pryor's comedy so powerful. And it is precisely because of this oft-displayed brilliance that his film career was such a waste. Aside from the three concert films (*Richard Pryor: Live! in Concert, Richard Pryor Live on the Sunset Strip, Here and Now*), which capture the master in his element, his Hollywood work can by and large be praised only if you judge it in slivers. If you fast-forward your VCR through the crap that makes up *Critical Condition, The Toy,* and *Moving* you'll find a chuckle or two. Going back to his earlier work (the closer to his days as a pure stand-up, the less mannered were his performances) there are clips aplenty for a Pryor montage—Daddy Rich in *Car Wash,* Piano Man in *Lady Sings the Blues,* a manic con man in *Silver Streak,* and the pimp's comic sidekick in *The Mack.* For me the only two totally satisfying non-concert films Pryor made are the drama *Blue Collar* and the comedy *Which Way Is Up?*

Blue Collar was co-written and co-directed by one of my favorite filmmakers, the rigorously intellectual and often perverse Paul Schrader. He'd already written *Taxi Driver* and would go on to direct *American Gigolo, Hardcore,* and other films that depict men caught between decadence and grace. In *Blue Collar* Pryor plays a Detroit auto assembly-line worker burdened with kids, debt, and limited prospects. Along with his production-line pals, Harvey Keitel and Yaphet Kotto, Pryor steals cash from the offices of the corrupt union local. The powers that be within the union, company, and government deal with each thief differently. Kotto is murdered. Keitel is forced to inform for the feds. Pryor is purchased by the status quo and winds up a corrupt cog in the machine of the very enterprise they ripped off.

In Schrader's screenplay Pryor's character is an economic, not social, rebel. All he ever really wanted was to get into the system, not to destroy it. When offered a chance to sell out, to become the token black floor supervisor and do better by his family, Pryor jumps at it. There is a complexity to this man's strengths and weaknesses that Pryor totally understands. The hostility that smolders under Pryor's stand-up humor is given free rein in a character trapped between responsibility and desire. He goes from being a bedeviled man sitting in a cluttered living room with kids roaming about to a cold, sarcastic member of the establishment that once oppressed him. The role reversal is frightening. The great thing about Pryor in *Blue Collar* is that he doesn't become a classic Uncle Tom. He's a more contemporary, subtler manifestation of that archetype. He's no docile accommodationist. The anger of the underclass still boils within—but it is the anger to get paid.

Pryor depicts him as grateful to the white man. He simply becomes disdainful of those, white and black, who haven't played the game as well as he. In the film's final scene, Keitel and Pryor face off in a shouting match that resonates with, but doesn't unrealistically resolve, the class conflicts that underlie *Blue Collar.* Years later Pryor would be rightly criticized for playing so many wimpy insecure characters. But for this shining moment Pryor is as cocksure as he'd ever be. As a warrior for capitalism he leaps at Keitel with a fury his acting never displayed on screen again.

Which Way Is Up?, based on Italian director Lina Wertmuller's *The Seduction of Mimi,* had as its protagonist another sellout. Leroy Jones is a man whose life as a migrant worker puts him in the way of things— picketing strikers, lusty women, and Mr. Man, a mysterious power broker. Pryor is again a capitalist tool, but here the plot is completely subservient to the humor. *Which Way Is Up?* was the third of four Pryor films directed by Michael Schultz (the others were *Car Wash, Greased Lightning,* and later *Bustin' Loose*) and was the best of the bunch.

In *Which* Pryor defined the jittery, beleaguered fellow that became his standard on-screen approach. In addition Pryor essayed two other roles: he played a morally corrupt preacher, Reverend Lenox Thomas (Pryor's middle names), familiar from his stand-up act; and the father of Pryor's character who's the closest Pryor came to an on-screen Mudbone. Assertive, profane, and screamingly funny as this decidedly foul-mouthed Papa, Pryor made me sad to think he never dedicated an entire movie to this shrewd, crusty old man. *Which* is rife with silly sexual sight gags. One involves Margaret Avery, as Pryor's long-abandoned wife, who turns into a dominatrix to arouse her husband's desire, utilizing whips, chains, and a great big black dildo stuck in Pryor's butt to do the job. Marilyn Coleman plays a religious woman who's seduced by Pryor in her trailer home. The sight gag has the trailer bouncing up and down in time to their lovemaking (a gag used a few years later by director Carl Reiner and Steve Martin in *The Jerk*).

Which was hilarious and was enjoyed by most of the young black folks I knew. But it got mediocre-to-bad reviews from the mainstream press, and I know why. I first saw *Which* in a Universal screening room on Park Avenue with a collection of white New York reviewers. I was literally the only person laughing at many jokes. It was embarrassing to bust out with a loud guffaw only to hear it answered by a silence that announced I had bad taste. I split the screening room confused. I thought *Which* was damn funny. Yet all those movie pros sat stone-faced.

After *Which* opened I went down to Forty-second Street to a crappy little multiplex on the south side of the street. Squeezed into a narrow room with bad popcorn and a bunch of black and Puerto Rican kids, I roared even more than before—and this time I wasn't alone. The dildo scene rocked the house. Handslapping was rampant. People were still talking back to the screen about it two scenes later. Watching *Which* on the Deuce actually enriched its ribald humor. The film's faults were still apparent but those jokes flew.

After the movie, I stood at the Nedick's on Forty-second Street and Seventh Avenue (same one that's in *Shaft*) and pondered the difference between those two viewings. Pryor's stand-up humor, smart and deep, cut across all kinds of racial and social barriers. *Which* wasn't nearly as smart or insightful. It was, however, raw and visual and unapologetically working-class. It was the first time I'd really seen the gap between white critical opinion and black working-class taste so graphically illustrated. And it wouldn't be the last time.

Pryor was really the only African American film star whose career was spawned during the blaxploitation era and who continued on as a leading man after that tide had ebbed. His now legendary drug habit notwithstanding, Hollywood never lost faith in his drawing power in the seventies while consistently misusing his talent. It is also important not to absolve Pryor of his guilt for agreeing to prepackaged crap like *Superman III*, for which he was paid $4 million in 1983, and which he had to know was unredeemable at any price. Pryor's immense talent (and the cajoling of his black attorney David Franklin) earned him the most unique deal any African American has ever received in Hollywood. In 1983 Columbia Pictures head Guy McElwaine agreed to finance Pryor's Indigo Films to the tune of $40 million. That money was to be used to produce four movies including those that Pryor would write and direct. Pryor hired his main man, Jim Brown, as president and actress Shelia Frazier as head of development.

The good news was that young talent producers like George (*New Jack City*) Jackson and director-actor Robert (*Hollywood Shuffle*) Townsend got some early industry experience through Indigo. The script that eventually became Clint Eastwood's *Bird,* originally intended for Pryor, passed through Indigo as well.

The bad news is that Indigo never really got off the ground. The only films to reach theaters bearing the Indigo Productions logo were his third concert film and his directorial effort *Jo Jo Dancer: Your Life Is Calling,* an uneven effort that at least had the ambition of Pryor's stand-up to recommend it.

Indigo was a classic case of the Peter principle. The comic's success had earned him the clout $40 million represents. Yet nothing about Pryor's life prepared him for the responsibility of running a production company. What drug addict is suited to be a boss? In December 1983

Brown was fired. Within two years Indigo was history—just in time for a black film renaissance to emerge from the underground.

NOTE

Nelson George, *Blackface: Reflections on African-Americans and the Movies* (New York: Harper Collins, 1994), 39–45.

Hill Street Bullshit, Richard Pryor Routines,
17 and the Real Deal (1997)

Bob Avakian

> . . . I had a magnum, too, man. I shot one of them tires. P-voom! The tire said, 'O-o-oh, O-oh, Ooh.' It got good to me; I shot another one—P-voom—'o-o-oh, O-oh, Ooh.' And that vodka I was drinkin' said, 'go ahead, shoot somethin' else.' I shot the motor, the motor fell out the motherfucker. Motor said, 'fuck it!' Then the police came: I went into the house, 'cause they got magnums too—and they don't kill cats, they kill nig-gars.
>
> —Richard Pryor on shooting his car,
> from *Richard Pryor: Live! in Concert 1978*

Recently I was reading reports of police assaults on Black people and of Black people fighting against the police in Memphis and Miami. This called to mind a story I was told a while back. A rookie cop was riding in his police car with his veteran partner when a report came in that there was a Black man in the vicinity with a gun. As their car screeched around the corner, a young Black man suddenly appeared sprinting up an alley—into a dead end. "Shoot him!," the older cop screamed, "Go on, shoot him—it's free!"

"It's free!" Think about that for a second. "It's free"? In other words, here's a chance that gets a pig to sweating and salivating with anticipation —a chance to "kill a nigger" with the already provided cover that a Black male—*a* Black man, *any* Black man—was reported in the area with a gun. This is an opportunity too good to pass up; "Go on, shoot him—it's free!"

Well, in this case, the rookie was not ready for that—perhaps he was one of those rare ones who joins a police force actually believing the "serve and protect" bullshit—and that particular Black man did not die that day. But one of the most telling things about this whole incident is the fallout from it: The rookie cop had to resign. If he wasn't ready and willing—if he didn't have the proper attitude to do what his veteran partner was calling for, what came naturally to the seasoned "peace officer," what any pig in his place and in a pig's right mind would do— then there was no place for him on the force. It was *he*, the rookie who hadn't learned, and couldn't learn it seems, what it's all about—it was *he* who was the outcast and felt he had to resign.

Perhaps this whole story helps give an inkling of the answer to the question: Why do we call the police "pigs"? Perhaps it also puts in clearer perspective the comment of one of the main actors on the *Hill Street Blues* series, Daniel Travanti (who plays Captain Furillo), that as he sees it, one of the main purposes, if not the main purpose, of the show is to help give the police a more positive image, after the experience of the '60s, when many people came to call the police "pigs." Well, you can't say he doesn't lay it straight out—and *he* can't say he's not conscious of what he, and others, are doing.

But maybe they want to say that they're "making things better," they're "helping to promote communication and understanding between the police and the community" and so on and blah, blah, blasé, blasé. Well, bullshit! You don't "help make things better" by covering up and apologizing for the murderous role and vicious nature of the police. Or to say it more correctly, you only "make things better" for those the police really do serve and protect—the rich and powerful—those whose order the police enforce and whose laws they uphold. You don't help a mother protect her baby from flesh-tearing rats by "promoting understanding" between her and the rats—or portraying the rats as "human beings too, with the same hopes, fears, ambitions, joys, sorrows, humors, and desires as all other human beings"—just like the gang at the Hill Street Station. It's not true, and no matter how slickly it's packaged, no matter how much skill and talent of writing, acting, directing, and so on, go into it, that still can't make it true. Pigs are pigs. Of course, that's an image, a symbol—in the most literal sense they are human beings, but they are human beings with a murderer's mentality, sanctioned, disciplined, unleashed by the ruling class of society to keep the oppressed in line, through terror whenever necessary and as the "bottom line," as they like to say. Terror against the oppressed is even a special reward for "carrying out the dangerous and thankless duty" of being the "thin blue line" between "civilization on the one side and anarchy and lawlessness on the other." Think about it once again: Terror against the oppressed is not just part of the job, it's also a reward. That is one of the deeper meanings of the story at the start: "Go on, shoot him—it's free!"

Actor Travanti's comments—his conscious concern to improve the image of the police after the turmoil of the '60s, to wipe out the lessons learned through that period of upheaval about the role and nature of the police (along with other things)—bring to mind another story. Someone who had been part of the broad movement of the '60s, and who now has a "civilian" job which, however, brings her into regular contact with the police, told a friend not too long ago: "You know, I used to take part in demonstrations, I was in fights with the police and I called them 'pigs' like a lot of other people; but now that I work around them a lot, it's only now that I actually realize how disgusting they really are!" Well, art, especially art of high quality, can exert a very powerful influence—it can be a very powerful weapon serving one class or another, depending on its content—but it cannot exert as powerful an influence as life itself, overall. Despite Travanti, and his producers and directors, pigs are pigs, and they prove it every day for all to see—except those blinded by class bias and prejudice.

But, maybe some liberals (of the "left" or "right") will object that these stories I've recounted are after all only stories, and even if we allow that they themselves are true stories, still they are only a few cases—the famous "isolated incidents" perhaps. Well, anyone who still really thinks that, or says it, has got to answer one basic question about the following Richard Pryor routine:

> Cops put a hurtin' on your ass, man, you know. They really degrade you. White folks don't believe that shit, don't believe cops degrade;— "Ah, come on, those beatings, those people were resisting arrest, I'm tired of this harassment of police officers." Cause the police live in your neighborhood, see, and you be knowin' 'em as Officer Timpson. "Hello Officer Timpson, going bowling tonight? Yes, uh, nice Pinto you have, ha, ha, ha." Niggers[1] don't know 'em like that. See, white folks get a ticket, they pull over, "Hey, Officer, yes, glad to be of help, here you go." A nigger got to be talkin' 'bout I AM REACH-ING INTO MY POCK-ET FOR MY LICENSE—'cause I don't wanna be no mother-fuckin' accident!
>
> Police degrade you. I don't know, you know, it's often you wonder why a nigger don't go completely mad. No, you do. You get your shit together, you work all week, right, then you get dressed—maybe say a cat make $125 a week, get $80 if he lucky, right, and he go out, get clean, be drivin' with his old lady, goin' out to a club, and the police pull over, "Get outta the car, there was a robbery—nigger look just like you. Alright, put your hands up, take your pants down, spread your cheeks!" Now, what nigger feel like havin' fun after that? "No, let's just go home, baby." You go home and beat your kids and shit—you gonna take that shit out on somebody. (from *That Nigger's*[2] *Crazy*, 1974)

The question is this: Why, at the crucial points of this routine, does Pryor's audience erupt in tense, knowing laughter, coupled with pro-longed applause? Can it be for any other reason than the fact that Pryor has indeed captured and concentrated—with humor, higher than life, as art should be, but the stone truth, all too true, at the same time—a situation that is *typical* for the masses of Black people in the U.S.? Something which, if it has not happened directly to them (and the odds are pretty good that it has), is subject to happen to them tomorrow, or the next day, and has already happened to a relative or friend. To anyone who wants to defend the police, to say nothing of prettifying them, showing them as just ordinary human beings, etc., etc., ad nauseam; and even anyone who wants to raise pious doubts and petty amendments about calling them what they are, without reservation or apology; you can't get around this question: you have to confront it straight up. And don't tell me Pryor's audiences aren't a fair representation: The response will always be the same from any audience that includes a significant number of the masses of Black people, or other oppressed masses (as, in fact, is the case with the audience for Pryor's live performances).

A relevant fact here, drawn directly from "real life." I read in a recent *RW* (No. 188, January 14, 1983), the report about the announcement by the Los Angeles District Attorney that—once again—no charges would be brought against the two pigs who beat and choked a 28-year-old Black man, Larry Morris, to death without any justification, even according to the authorities. The *RW* article went on to expose that "This is just the latest in more than 200 'investigations' of police murders [that is, murders of people by police] since the forming of the D.A.'s 'Operation Rollout.' This program has so far endorsed the police's right to kill every time." And after everything else, we're still bound to hear from some quarters how this is just Los Angeles, where the police are known to be particularly brutal etc., etc. This really shouldn't have to be answered, but it does, so let me answer it by turning again to a Richard Pryor routine, this one from the same performance, in Washington, D.C., in 1978, as the one cited at the start of this article:

"Police in L.A., man, they got a chokehold they use on motherfuckers. Do they do it here, do they choke you to death? (Voices from the audience, *many* voices from the audience: '*Yeah!*') That's some weird shit. 'Cause I didn't know it was a death penalty to have a parking ticket."

But for the masses of Black people in this "great land of freedom and justice for all" it can be—and it has been for hundreds, at least, every year. Of course, this kind of freedom and justice is not reserved for Black people alone in the U.S., though they are special "beneficiaries" of it. It also lashes out and ensnares millions of the masses of other oppressed nationalities, immigrants (so-called "legal" as well as so-called "illegal"), and in general those who are without wealth and therefore without power, including many white people, for whom Officer Timpson is hardly a friend, either.

In short, the armed force of the bourgeois state exists for the purpose of suppressing, by force and arms, the proletariat and all those who would step out of line and challenge this "great way of life" founded on robbery and murder, not only within the U.S. itself but throughout the world. And that, simply, is why pigs are pigs, and will always be pigs—until systems that need such pigs are abolished from the earth. A hard truth—but a liberating truth.

NOTES

Bob Avakian, from *Revolutionary Worker* 928, 10 October 1997.

1. This material is reproduced here as it was performed by Richard Pryor at the time, including the use of the word "nigger"; this is for the sake of accuracy and not out of any disrespect for his feeling, after a trip to Africa, that he should no longer use the word "nigger" because it is dehumanizing.

2. See note 1.

18 Now's the Time

THE RICHARD PRYOR PHENOMENON AND

THE TRIUMPH OF BLACK CULTURE (1998)

SIVA VAIDHYANATHAN

> Times were so hard back then, they didn't even have a name for them. They just called them "Hard Times."
> —Mudbone, a Richard Pryor character

From a nation torn by racial strife—one that elected Richard Nixon twice, showed strong support for George Wallace, and insisted that in order to succeed, African Americans had to dress, talk, and act as unthreatening as possible—emerged Richard Pryor. With a swaggering attitude that challenged the American racial status quo only slightly less than did his chosen vocabulary, Richard Pryor became more than the most influential black stand-up comic in a generation: he was arguably the most successful comedian in America during the 1970s. This was the "Richard Pryor phenomenon," and it deserves a full exploration and explanation. How did a young black man who started out a timid clone of the acceptable Bill Cosby reinvent himself and burst through the color line to emerge as the most bankable act in Hollywood?

Pryor rose from a bit actor and unreliable nightclub act to become the most dominant comic force of the 1970s. He wrote the best bits for Mel Brooks's *Blazing Saddles,* won an Emmy award for writing for the Lily Tomlin comedy special in 1973, and hosted *Saturday Night Live* in its first season. He starred in a series of cinematic hits in which even his small parts stole the show—*Car Wash* (1976), *Silver Streak* (1976), *The Bingo Long Traveling All Stars and Motor Kings* (1976), *The Muppet Movie* (1979), and *Lady Sings The Blues* (1972), among them. He appeared on the cover of *Newsweek* magazine in 1982. Two Pryor stand-up albums from the mid-1970s, *That Nigger's Crazy* (1974) and *. . . Is It Something I Said?* (1975), went gold and won Grammy awards.[1]

There are three possible explanations for the Richard Pryor phenomenon. The first asserts that Pryor was the last and loudest of a series of black comics who had been trying to get over the racial wall in American entertainment, and so he represents the culmination of years of effort and a well-defined tradition. The second explanation has been put forth by Pryor's friend Ishmael Reed. According to Reed, the wall never really came down. Pryor simply leapt it on the strength of his comic genius. Once stranded on the other side of the wall, as Reed sees it, Pryor sunk to creative lows under the influence of Hollywood and its various social and creative pressures.[2]

The best explanation, however, is that the cultural wall was never that formidable to begin with. According to this model, which I call "the triumph of African American culture," American culture has benefited from an undeniable fascination with its African American elements, and these expressions have in the past thirty years emerged as dominant voices in the cultural dialogue. America was never as culturally segregated as it was legally segregated. As a result, the wholesale desegregation of the past fifty years has created a nearly open competitive market for cultural expression. In many areas—such as comedy, popular music, and sports—black culture has established the greatest market share. In others, such as literature and film, African American expression is just beginning to show its might. Richard Pryor was among the most recognizable African Americans to take advantage of the triumph of black culture in the last half of the twentieth century. We must count him with Lena Home, Jackie Robinson, Chuck Berry, Julius Erving, and most recently, Toni Morrison as champions of the triumph. None of their battles were easy, but their victories made possible future triumphs by later artists. Clearly, to understand the rise of Richard Pryor, one must entertain all three explanations.[3]

Two recent books trace Pryor's success with detail and context: *If I Stop I'll Die*, by John and Dennis Williams; and Mel Watkins's *On the Real Side*, an invaluable history of African American humor. Watkins's work is the most encyclopedic resource for examining where Richard Pryor stands in the historical context of African American expression. It is, as most initial histories are, a "great man" epic. *On the Real Side* traces modern African American humor from its African roots through the chain of creative talents who have chipped away at the barriers that segregated African American from mainstream American humor. Watkins describes a cultural wall that sealed African American humor from its mainstream counterpart. Some artists, like Lenny Bruce, were able to borrow from the other side of the wall. But for the most part, it was not until the irresistible crossover appeal of Dick Gregory, Flip Wilson, and Bill Cosby emerged in the 1960s that black comics were taken seriously by the entertainment industry. As Watkins sees it, Richard Pryor launched himself from his immediate predecessors' shoulders and busted down the cultural wall. Once Pryor and his contemporaries crumbled the wall, they could offer the rest of America the purest form possible of African American comic styles and substance.

Pryor's personal rise is an amazing story, but his stylistic triumph is even more impressive. Pryor did not succeed by sugarcoating his act or his personality. He was one of the first major black comedians who did not have to develop two acts—one for white audiences and one for blacks. Pryor showed the same African American experiential ground-ings regardless of his audience. He spoofed misguided liberals as well as dangerous rednecks, even though his audience was often filled with white liberals. Pryor riddled all authority figures with the full arsenal of his comic tools: parody, tricksterism, hyperbole, double-edged vernacu-lar, and rapid-fire revelations of hypocrisy. Pryor generally employed two methods in his stand-up routines: the autobiographical anecdote and the character sketch. Within both methods Pryor's strength was his voice characterization. He could skewer whining whites with a dead-on imita-tion or transform himself into a wise wino. Some voices came from his childhood in Peoria, Illinois. Some came from Hollywood parties.

Pryor's subject matter was even more threatening to whites than his styles were. In his act and in interviews, Pryor described having sex with prostitutes while growing up in Peoria, where his grandmother ran a brothel. He often used anecdotes about his sexual conquests, both interra-cial and extramarital. He boasted of his drug use in ways that equally ad-dicted comics, such as John Belushi, dared not for fear of marring their marketability. Pryor was in a sense freer to paint a negative and dangerous picture of himself because his growing audience loved his unpredictabil-ity and daring. In addition, Pryor subversively used racist assumptions about the proclivity of sexual promiscuity and drug use in his act. Yes, he was bad, but no one else was any better. Pryor's stylistic and substantive experiments touched nerves in an increasingly nervous nation. Some might surmise that a growing desire for racial justice and equality con-tributed to Pryor's rise. This hypothesis may apply more to the success of Gregory, Cosby, and Wilson. But Pryor was often well beyond the toler-ance level of nervous liberals. For these reasons, Watkins rightfully labels the Pryor phenomenon "nothing short of revolutionary."[4]

How did this revolution arise? What sparked it, or at least made it possible? How did Richard Pryor go from a struggling young comic with no sense of personal stage presence to a figure about whom white and black comics of three generations sing his praises? How could this bold and often frightening black man achieve so much commercially and artistically in a nation that still shows its racially sensitive underbelly every other first Tuesday in November? Ishmael Reed—the noted novelist, scholar, and professor of writing at the University of California at Berkeley—says Pryor sparked his own revolution. "Richard's a genius," says Reed; "just outrageous." For Reed, the Richard Pryor phenomenon was the classic story of a hungry genius who struggled, succeeded, and sold out. The fact that Pryor had that wall of stylistic segregation to either destroy or hurdle is a sign, for Reed, of how much more of a genius Pryor had to be than his white contemporaries, for instance, George Carlin or David Brenner.[5]

Reed first saw Pryor perform in a coffee shop in Greenwich Village around 1965 or 1966. Reed's wife was performing in an art troupe that included Yoko Ono, and Pryor opened for them. Pryor immensely impressed Reed because in that setting Pryor, facing a crowd yearning for experimentation, was free to say or do anything. "The talent was there," Reed said of the early Pryor. "The style was different," meaning it was yet to be defined and refined. Reed was among those who helped Pryor define himself in 1969 and 1970. Reed and Pryor grew intellectually close in those years while Pryor was woodshedding in Berkeley. The term "woodshedding" is of special significance here because of its roots in a black culture to which Pryor was closely connected; jazz musicians use the word to describe the gestational process of mastering an instrument and its stylistic canon. For instance, after playing in several mediocre bands around Kansas City in the early 1930s, Charlie Parker took a stack of Lester Young recordings to the Ozarks and mastered all of the older man's licks. When he returned, Parker had found his own voice as well as the technical mastery required to play along with Young.[6] Among their circle of friends were novelists and playwrights such as Claude Brown, Cecil Brown, Al Young, and David Henderson. "[Pryor] was a scholar of comedy" before he got to Berkeley, Reed said. "We just gave him extra materials. We had some long discussions. He was a very experimental comedian, even early on. But even then, he said he wanted to 'get over,'" to be rich and successful in the mainstream world. This was the time of Black Power and the black arts movement. Reed asserts that the movement's attempts to valorize and isolate the blackness of African American expression did not really affect Pryor in those days:

Black arts was confined to Harlem. It frightened people, so it got all the attention. But I don't think black arts had that much significance out here to Richard. He was into Eldridge Cleaver, Richard Wright, Mort Saul, and Lenny Bruce and the people who loosened up things in the 1950s. In Berkeley, we had free speech—taking language performance to an art.

Before 1969, Pryor—especially on television—was doing what Pryor called "that Cosby shit." His material, mostly innocuous stories with some racial tinge, was generally reheated, "safe" material. When Pryor returned to Los Angeles from Berkeley in 1970, he was angry, he was sexual, he was scary, and he was almost instantly successful. Yet to Reed, he was still pure Pryor—immensely talented but flawed by ambition: "Richard should have stayed in Berkeley. Free speech was invented in Berkeley. I don't think Hollywood served him too well. The circle he was running around with here was very positive to him. Hollywood just ruined him. What was that thing he did with Jackie Gleason? *The Toy?* What was that shit? Two geniuses . . ."

If we accept Reed's hypothesis as complete and definitive, then the Pryor phenomenon is explainable because Pryor was a flawed genius willing to mug for the cameras. But we are left with the question of how Pryor was allowed to get away with so much angry and scary material for so long. Six years before Pryor embarrassed himself in *The Toy* (1982), he ad-libbed his lines for a scene in which he convinced Gene Wilder to sport blackface in *Silver Streak,* a scene Williams and Williams describe as a very subversive improvisation. In addition, Pryor's greatest artistic and commercial triumphs were his solo concert films, which were undeniably sexual and daring.[7]

To explain these elements of the Pryor phenomenon, we must look to something much bigger and grander that occurred in the United States during the twenty years or so before Pryor went woodshedding in Berkeley: the culture was deeply and irrevocably Africanized. At the dawn of the twentieth century, W. E. B. Du Bois began an intellectual war against the prevailing racial situation. He set the color line as a battleground on which America might well live up to its promise. Significantly, Du Bois—Napoleon's lessons notwithstanding—declared a two-front war, one political and cultural. The political conflagration rages on, with some significant victories behind it, but the cultural war is nearly over. African American culture has always been—as described by Ralph Ellison—a major "tributary" of American culture. Several influential scholars have agreed with Ellison and have produced books that support the claim for the interdependence of black and white expression. These works of literary history and criticisms show fairly conclusively that from the birth of American letters, both white and black authors have been listening to both white and black voices. The two literary traditions have been engaged in a dialogue of differences and have borrowed style and substance from each other.[8] As Toni Morrison wrote in *Playing in the Dark,* "There seems to be a more or less tacit agreement among literary scholars that, because American literature has been clearly the preserve of white male views, genius, and power, those views, genius, and power are without relationship to and removed from the overwhelming pressure of black people in the United States. . . . the contemplation of this black presence is central to any understanding of our national literature and should not be permitted to hover at the margins of the literary imagination."[9]

In 1903, W. E. B. Du Bois asked, "Would America have been America without her Negro people?"[10] Ralph Ellison answered Du Bois in a 1970 *Time* magazine essay, "What America Would Be like without Blacks": "If we can resist for a moment the temptation to view everything having to do with Negro Americans in terms of racially imposed status, we become aware of the fact that for all the harsh reality of the social and economic injustices visited upon them, these injustices have failed to keep Negroes clear of the cultural mainstream; Negro Americans are in fact one of its major tributaries."[11]

Ellison's description did not go deep enough for 1970. By that time, as Richard Pryor was emerging, that tributary had swollen over its banks, supplying much of what American culture thirsted for: rebelliousness, courage, creativity, and soul. Deep blues had once again shaken the whitewashed world of American rock and roll. Motown had pushed urban rhythm and blues up the white pop charts. A black Muslim was the heavyweight champion of the world. A black pitcher, Bob Gibson, had paralyzed the Detroit Tigers in the 1968 World Series with his intense, angry stare and unhittable fastball. Earl "the Pearl" Monroe and Walt "Clyde" Frazier were about to dazzle the National Basketball Association with their improvisational skills on the hardwood. Neither Richard Pryor nor any of these other figures burst down any cultural walls or dams. The strength of and demand for black cultural expression simply overflowed the levies that white America had futilely built after Reconstruction.

Two authors—both journalists—have described this triumph of

black cultural expression. One is Nelson George, whose *Elevating the Game: Black Men and Basketball* tells the story of how black athletes took over the game in less than fifty years.[12] The other is W. T. Lhamon, who declares in his 1990 book *Deliberate Speed: The Origins of a Cultural Style in the American 1950s* that American youth grew to equate black expressions with youthful, forward-looking style. Black and white youths in the 1950s identified with each other through the works of Vladimir Nabokov, Thelonius Monk, Chuck Berry, Jackson Pollock, Jack Kerouac, and Martin Luther King, Jr.[13]

If, by 1970, black expressions had crowded out non-black forms and had become the dominant voice in some sectors of American culture, how did Richard Pryor fit in? Why was comedy one of these sectors? What did white audiences want from African American humor generally and Richard Pryor specifically? It is important to remember that—as in literature and music—a constant dialogue between black and white storytelling traditions has existed for nearly as long as there have been black and white storytellers on this continent. Although no one has yet traced the interdependence of black and white humor through American history, there are clearly similarities in function, if not structure, between these black and white comic traditions.

One convenient location from which to begin tracing the interdependence of these two traditions of humor is Hannibal, Missouri. Mark Twain—as Shelley Fisher Fishkin shows in *Was Huck Black?*—was enchanted by African American comic storytelling styles. Twain showed a deep respect for African American humor, seeing it as much more than just quaint folk expression. Much like Pryor would do for white voices, Twain spent years trying to master the spoken inflections of African American dialects so he could employ them during his lucrative speaking engagements, which were the nineteenth-century version of the stand-up circuit. Twain, like Elvis, made a good living out of selling black expressions to a white audience who would never think of paying for the real thing. In his book *Mark Twain and the Art of the Tall Tale*, Henry Wonham shows how Twain tapped into the deep American oral tradition of yarn spinning. In his description of the function of the tall tale among a "community of knowers," Wonham provides a clue as to how Pryor's appeal translated itself to white audiences as well as black. Wonham explains that the American pragmatic tradition, as defined by Charles Sanders Peirce and William James, recognized that the truth of a statement depended on its ability to generate consensus among a community. In other words, in America truth is a matter of agreement. Conversely, the community of knowers marks anyone who accepts as "true" a notion they do not accept as outside the community and thus the object of ridicule. Wonham describes the function of tall humor in the United States: "For the group that shares the yarn spinner's privileged point of view, the inflated story of cruelty and suffering—by making those things laughable—may signal a dual victory over both condescending outsiders and the very conditions of life that inspire the tale." In other words, tall tales involve the teller feigning sincerity, stretching credulity, and tricking the outsiders for the amusement of the insiders.[14]

This feigning, or lying, is certainly made easier by the use of a mask, a cold poker face, an innocent-looking simpleton, or a jester in minstrel makeup. Only those who know the authentic identity of the performer would feel included in the joke. As Ralph Ellison wrote, in words that invoke some of the same themes that Wonham explores,

> For the ex-colonials, the declaration of an American identity meant the assumption of a mask, and it imposed not only the discipline of national self-consciousness, it gave Americans an ironic awareness of the joke that always lies between appearance and reality, between the discontinuity of social tradition and that sense of the past which clings to the mind. And perhaps even an awareness of the joke that society is man's creation, not God's. Americans began their revolt from the English fatherland when they dumped the tea into the Boston Harbor, masked as Indians, and the mobility of the society created in this limitless space has encouraged the use of the mask for good and evil ever since. . . . Masking is a play upon possibility and ours is a society in which possibilities are many. When American life is most American it is apt to be most theatrical.[15]

Richard Pryor was a master of the tall tale. He could pose, don a mask, and exaggerate with the best of them. These were skills he observed in elders as a child in Peoria and then rediscovered in Berkeley. For example, Pryor's character Mudbone, the wise street wino, relates a tall tale common in African American humor:

> Ah, that nigger could tell lies. That's how we became friends, see. He tell a lie, I tell a lie, see, and we compliment each other's lies. He make me laugh all day long, bless his soul. He told me this lie one time, told me 'bout the niggers with the big dicks, see. Y'all ever heard it? The niggers had the biggest dicks in the world, and they were trying to find a place where they could have their contest, see. And they wasn't no

freaks, didn't want anybody lookin' . . . They was walking around lookin' for a secret place. So they walked across the Golden Gate Bridge and the nigger seen that water and it make him want to piss, see. Boy say, "Man, I got to take a leak." He pulled out his thing and was pissing. The other nigger pulled his out, took a piss. One nigger say, "Goddamn! This water cold." The other nigger say, "Yeah, and it's deep, too."[16]

Certainly, no outsider would fall for this tall tale. It does not, unlike some of Pryor's jokes, unite a community of knowers and exclude outsiders. But it remains an effective humorous device because it tests the teller of the tale to strike a convincing pose successfully. The delivery is more important than the tale itself. For white audiences in the 1970s, this glimpse into African American humor through Richard Pryor made them feel they were being accepted uneasily into the community of knowers. From the time of Mailer's "White Negroes," the Hipsters, and the beats, white audiences have been trying to buy a seat in the community of knowers and have been borrowing vocabulary as badges of membership. If white audience members got more than half the jokes at a Pryor concert, they could feel included. They could then try to learn what Pryor meant by those jokes they did not get. Pryor mastered this playful inclusion and exclusion of his audience throughout the early 1970s and continued it into the early 1980s, when he stopped making concert films and records. White America desired an avenue into black oral tradition, and Pryor offered it on a large scale at their local theaters. In this way, Pryor masterfully exploited the triumph of black cultural expression.

NOTES

Siva Vaidhyanathan, "Now's the Time: The Richard Pryor Phenomenon and the Triumph of Black Culture," in *New Directions in American Humor*, ed. David E. E. Sloane (Tuscaloosa: University of Alabama Press, 1998), 40–48.

1. For the chronology of Richard Pryor's career, see John A. and Dennis A. Williams, *If I Stop I'll Die: The Comedy and Tragedy of Richard Pryor* (New York: Thunder's Mouth Press, 1991). For a view of Pryor in historical context, see Mel Watkins, *On the Real Side: Laughing, Lying and Signifying; The Underground Tradition of African-American Humor That Transformed American Culture, from Slavery to Richard Pryor* (New York: Simon and Schuster, 1994).

2. Siva Vaidhyanathan, personal interview with Ishmael Reed, 6 December 1994.

3. This notion will be the subject of future work of mine on these and other cultural figures.

4. Watkins, 562.

5. Vaidhyanathan, interview with Reed. For a detailed account of Pryor's hiatus in Berkeley, see Williams and Williams, and Watkins.

6. Significantly, Pryor was supposed to star in a film adaptation of Ross Russell's 1973 biography of Parker, *Bird Lives!* It was never made.

7. Williams and Williams, 84–86.

8. For an exploration of the intermingling of African and African American influences in American culture, see Eric Sundquist, *To Wake the Nations: Race in the Making of American Literature* (Cambridge: Harvard University Press, 1993). See also Shelley Fisher Fishkin, *Was Huck Black?: Mark Twain and African American Voices* (New York: Oxford University Press, 1993); Werner Sollors, *Beyond Ethnicity: Consent and Descent in American Culture* (New York: Oxford University Press, 1986); Paul Gilroy, *The Black Atlantic: Modernity and Double Consciousness* (Cambridge: Harvard University Press, 1993); Michael North, *The Dialect of Modernism: Race, Language, and Twentieth Century Literature* (New York: Oxford University Press, 1994); and Henry B. Wonham, ed., *Criticism on the Color Line: Race and Revisionism in American Literary Studies* (New Brunswick: Rutgers University Press, 1995).

9. Toni Morrison, *Playing in the Dark: Whiteness and the Literary Imagination* (Cambridge: Harvard University Press, 1992), 5.

10. W. E. B. Du Bois, *The Souls of Black Folk* (New York: Penguin Classics, 1989), 215.

11. Ralph Ellison, "What America Would Be like without Blacks," *Going to the Territory* (New York: Random House, 1987), 108.

12. See Nelson George, *Elevating the Game: Black Men and Basketball* (New York: Harper Collins, 1992).

13. W. T. Lhamon, Jr., *Deliberate Speed: The Origins of a Cultural Style in the American 1950s* (Washington, D.C.: Smithsonian Institution Press, 1990), xiii.

14. Henry B. Wonham, *Mark Twain and the Art of the Tall Tale* (New York: Oxford University Press, 1993), 18.

15. Ralph Ellison, "Change the Joke and Slip the Yoke," *Shadow and Act* (New York: Signet, 1964), 68.

16. Pryor, as quoted in Watkins, 550–551.

19 A Pryor Love

THE LIFE AND TIMES OF AMERICA'S COMIC PROPHET OF RACE
(1999)

HILTON ALS

Skin Flick

Winter, 1973. Late afternoon: the entr'acte between dusk and darkness, when the people who conduct their business in the street—numbers runners in gray chesterfields, out-of-work barmaids playing the dozens, adolescents cultivating their cigarette Jones and lust, small-time hustlers selling "authentic" gold wristwatches that are platinum bright—look for a place to roost and to drink in the day's sin. Young black guy, looks like the comedian Richard Pryor, walks into one of his hangouts, Opal's Silver Spoon Cafe. A greasy dive with an R. & B. juke-box, it could be in Detroit or in New York, could be anywhere. Opal's has a proprietor—Opal, a young and wise black woman, who looks like the comedian Lily Tomlin—and a little bell over the door that goes *tink-a-link,* announcing all the handouts and gimmes who come to sit at Opal's counter and talk about how needy their respective asses are.

Black guy sits at the counter, and Opal offers him some potato soup—"something nourishing," she says. Black guy has moist, on-the-verge-of-lying-or-crying eyes and a raggedy Afro. He wears a green fatigue jacket, the kind of jacket brothers brought home from 'Nam, which guys like this guy continue to wear long after they've returned home, too shell-shocked or stoned to care much about their haberdashery. Juke—that's the black guy's name—is Opal's baby, flopping about in all them narcotics he's trying to get off of by taking that methadone, which Juke and Opal pronounce "metha*don*"—the way two old-timey Southerners would, the way Juke and Opal's elders might have, if they knew what that shit was, or was for.

Juke and Opal express their feelings for each other, their shared view of the world, in a lyrical language, a colored people's language, which tries to atomize their anger and their depression. Sometimes their anger is wry: Opal is tired of hearing about Juke's efforts to get a job, and tells him so. "Hand me that jive about job training," she says. "You trained, all right. You highly skilled at not working." But that's not entirely true. Juke has submitted himself to the rigors of "rehabilitation." "I was down there for about three weeks, at that place, working," Juke says. "Had on a suit, tie. Shaving. Acting crazy. Looked just like a fool in the circus." Pause. "And I'm fed up with it." Pause. "Now I know how to do a job that don't know how to be done no more." Opal's face fills with sadness. Looking at her face can fill your mind with sadness. She says, "For real?" It's a rhetorical question that black people have always asked each other or themselves when they're handed more hopelessness: Is this for real?

Night is beginning to spread all over Juke and Opal's street; it is the color of a thousand secrets combined. The bell rings, and a delivery man comes in, carting pies. Juke decides that everyone should chill out—he'll play the jukebox, they'll all get down. Al Green singing "Let's Stay To-gether" makes the pie man and Juke do a little finger-snapping, a little jive. Opal hesitates, says, "Naw," but then dances anyway, and her shyness is just part of the fabric of the day, as uneventful as the delivery man leaving to finish up his rounds, or Opal and Juke standing alone in this little restaurant, a society unto themselves.

The doorbell's tiny peal. Two white people—a man and a woman, social workers—enter Opal's. Youngish, trenchcoated. And the minute the white people enter, something terrible happens, from an aesthetic point of view. They alienate everything. They fracture our suspended disbelief. They interrupt our identification with the protagonists of the TV show we've been watching, which becomes TV only when those social workers start hassling our Juke, our Opal, equal halves of the same resilient black body. When we see those white people, we start thinking about things like credits, and remember that this is a television play, after all, written by the brilliant Jane Wagner, and played with astonishing alacrity and compassion by Richard Pryor and Lily Tomlin on *Lily,* Tomlin's second variety special, which aired on CBS in 1973, and which remains, a little over a quarter of a century later, the most profound meditation on race and class that I have ever seen on a major network.

"We're doing some community research and we'd like to ask you a few questions," the white woman social worker declares as soon as she enters Opal's. Juke and Opal are more than familiar with this line of inquiry, which presumes that people like them are always available for questioning—servants of the liberal cause. "I wonder if you can tell me, have you ever been addicted to drugs?" the woman asks Juke.

Pryor-as-Juke responds instantly. "Yeah, I been addicted," he says. "I'm addicted right now—don't write it down, man, be cool, it's not for the public. I mean, what I go through is private." He is incapable of making "Fuck you" his first response—or even his first thought. Being black has taught him how to allow white people their innocence. For black people, being around white people is sometimes like taking care of babies you don't like, babies who throw up on you again and again, but whom you cannot punish, because they're babies. Eventually, you direct that anger at yourself—it has nowhere else to go.

Juke tries to turn the questioning around a little, through humor, which is part of his pathos. "*I* have some questions," he tells the community researchers, then tries to approximate their straight, white tone: "Who's Pig-meat Markham's Mama?" he asks. "Wilt Chamberlain the tallest colored chap you ever saw?"

When the white people have left and Juke is about to leave, wrapped in his thin jacket, he turns to Opal and says, "You sweet. You a sweet woman. . . . I'll think aboutcha." His eyes are wide with love and need, and maybe fear or madness. "Be glad when it's spring," he says to Opal. Pause. "Flower!"

Lily was never shown again on network television, which is not surprising, given that part of its radicalism is based on the fact that it features a white female star who tries to embody a black woman while communicating with a black man about substantive emotional matters, and who never wears anything as theatrically simple as blackface to do it; Tomlin plays Opal in whiteface, as it were. Nevertheless, "Juke and Opal," which lasts all of nine minutes and twenty-five seconds, and which aired in the same season in which "Hawaii Five-O," "The Waltons," and "Ironside" were among television's top-rated shows, remains historically significant for reasons other than the skin game.

As Juke, Richard Pryor gave one of his relatively few great performances in a project that he had not written or directed. He made use of the poignancy that marks all of his great comedic and dramatic performances, and of the vulnerability—the pathos cradling his sharp wit—that had seduced people into loving him in the first place. Tomlin kept Pryor on the show over objections from certain of the network's executives, and it may have been her belief in him as a performer, combined with the high standards she set for herself and others, that spurred on the competitive-minded Pryor. His language in this scene feels improvised, confessional, and so internalized that it's practically nonverbal: not unlike the best of Pryor's own writing—the stories he tells when he talks shit into a microphone, doing stand-up. And as he sits at Opal's counter we can see him falling in love with Tomlin's passion for her work, recognizing it as the passion he feels when he peoples the stage with characters who might love him as much as Tomlin-as-Opal seems to now.

Although Richard Pryor was more or less forced to retire in 1994, eight years after he discovered that he had multiple sclerosis ("It's the stuff God hits your ass with when he doesn't want to kill ya—just slow ya down," he told *Entertainment Weekly* in 1993), his work as a comedian, a writer, an actor, and a director amounts to a significant chapter not only in late-twentieth-century American comedy but in American entertainment in general. Pryor is best known now for his work in the lackadaisical Gene Wilder buddy movies or for abominations like *The Toy*. But far more important was the prescient commentary on the issues of race and sex in America that he presented through stand-up and sketches like "Juke and Opal"—the heartfelt and acute social observation, the comedy that littered the stage with the trash of the quotidian as it was sifted through his harsh and poetic imagination, and that changed the very definition of the word "entertainment," particularly for a black entertainer.

The subject of blackness has taken a strange and unsatisfying journey through American thought: first, because blackness has almost always had to explain itself to a largely white audience in order to be heard, and, second, because it has generally been assumed to have only one story to tell—a story of oppression that plays on liberal guilt. The writers behind the collective modern ur-text of blackness—James Baldwin, Richard Wright, and Ralph Ellison—all performed some variation on the theme. Angry but distanced, their rage blanketed by charm, they lived and wrote to be liked. Ultimately, whether they wanted to or not, they in some way embodied the readers who appreciated them most—white liberals.

Richard Pryor was the first black American spoken-word artist to avoid this. Although he reprised the history of black American comedy—picking what he wanted from the work of great storytellers like Bert Williams, Redd Foxx, Moms Mabley, Nipsey Russell, La Wanda Page, and Flip Wilson—he also pushed everything one step further. Instead of adapting to the white perspective, he forced white audiences to follow him into his own experience. Pryor didn't manipulate his audiences' white guilt or their black moral outrage. If he played the race card, it was only to show how funny he looked when he tried to shuffle the deck. And as he made blackness an acknowledged part of the American atmosphere he also brought the issue of interracial love into the country's discourse. In a culture whose successful male Negro authors wrote about interracial sex with a combination of reverence and disgust, Pryor's gleeful, "fuck it" attitude had an effect on the general population which Wright's "Native Son" or Baldwin's "Another Country" had not had. His best work showed us that black men like him and the white women they loved were united in their disenfranchisement; in his life and onstage, he performed the great, largely unspoken story of America.

"I LOVE Lily," Pryor said in a *Rolling Stone* interview with David Felton, in 1974, after "Juke and Opal" had aired and he and Tomlin had moved on to other things. "I have a thing about her, a little crush . . . I get in awe of her. I'd seen her on 'Laugh-In' and shit, and something about her is very sensual, isn't it?"

Sensuality implies a certain physical abandonment, an acknowledgment of the emotional mess that oozes out between the seams that hold our public selves together—and an understanding of the metaphors that illustrate that disjunction. (One of Tomlin's early audition techniques was to tap-dance with taps taped to the soles of her bare feet.) It is difficult to find that human untidiness—what Pryor called "the madness" of everyday life—in the formulaic work now being done by the performers who ostensibly work in the same vein as Pryor and Tomlin. Compare the rawness of the four episodes of a television show that Pryor co-wrote and starred in for NBC in 1977 with any contemporary HBO show by Tracey Ullman (who needs blackface to play a black woman): the first Pryor special opens with a close-up of his face as he announces that he has not had to compromise himself to appear on a network-sponsored show. The camera then pulls back to reveal Pryor seemingly nude but with his genitalia missing.

Pryor's art defies the very definition of the word "order." He based his style on digressions and riffs—the monologue as jam session. He reinvented stand-up, which until he developed his signature style, in 1971, had consisted largely of borscht-belt-style male comedians telling tales in the Jewish vernacular, regardless of their own religion or background. Pryor managed to make blacks interesting to audiences that were used to responding to a liberal Jewish sensibility—and, unlike some of his colored colleagues, he did so without "becoming" Jewish himself. (Dick Gregory, for example, was a political comedian in the tradition of Mort Sahl; Bill Cosby was a droll Jack Benny.) At the height of his career, Pryor never spoke purely in the complaint mode. He was often baffled by life's complexities, but he rarely told my-wife-made-me-sleep-on-the-sofa jokes or did "bits" whose sole purpose was to "kill" an audience with a boffo punch line. Instead, he talked about characters—black street people, mostly. Because the life rhythm of a black junkie, say, implies a certain drift, Pryor's stories did not have badda-bing conclusions. Instead, they were encapsulated in a physical attitude: each character was represented in Pryor's walk, in his gestures—which always contained a kind of vicarious wonder at the lives he was enacting. Take, for instance, his sketch of a wino in Peoria, Illinois—Pryor's hometown and the land of his imagination—as he encounters Dracula. In the voice of a Southern black man, down on his luck:

> Hey man, say, nigger—you with the cape. . . . What's your name, boy? Dracula? What kind of name is that for a nigger? Where you from, fool? Transylvania? I know where it is, nigger! You ain't the smartest motherfucker in the world, even though you is the ugliest. Oh yeah, you a ugly motherfucker. Why you don't get your teeth fixed, nigger? That shit hanging all out your mouth. Why you don't get you an orthodontist? . . . This is 1975, boy. Get your shit together. What's wrong with your natural? Got that dirt all in the back of your neck. You's a filthy little motherfucker, too. You got to be home 'fore the sun come up? You ain't lyin', motherfucker. See your ass during the day, you liable to get arrested. You want to suck what? You some kind of freak, boy? . . . You ain't suckin' nothing here, junior.

Pryor's two best comedy albums, both of which were recorded during the mid to late seventies—"Bicentennial Nigger" and "That Nigger's Crazy"—are not available on CD, but his two concert films, *Richard Pryor: Live! in Concert* and *Richard Pryor Live on the Sunset Strip*, which were released in 1979 and 1982, respectively, are out on video. The concert films are excellent examples of what the *Village Voice* critic Carrie Rickey once described as Pryor's ability to "scare us into laughing at his demons—our demons—exorcising them through mass hyperventilation." "Pryor doesn't tell jokes," she wrote, "he tells all, in the correct belief that without punch lines, humor has *more* punch. And pungency." Taken together, the concert films show the full panorama of Pryor's moods: brilliant, boring, insecure, demanding, misogynist, racist, playful, and utterly empathetic.

Before Richard Pryor, there were only three aspects of black male-ness to be found on TV or in the movies: the suave, pimp-style blandness of Billy Dee Williams; the big-dicked, quiet machismo of the football hero Jim Brown; and the cable-knit homilies of Bill Cosby. Pryor was the first image we'd ever had of black male fear. Not the kind of Stepin Fetchit noggin-bumpin'-into-walls fear that turned Buckwheat white when he saw a ghost in the "Our Gang" comedies popular in the twen-ties, thirties, and forties—a character that Eddie Murphy resuscitated in a presumably ironic way in the eighties on "Saturday Night Live." Pryor was filled with dread and panic—an existential fear, based on real things, like racism and lost love. (In a skit on "In Living Color," the actor Damon Wayans played Pryor sitting in his kitchen and looking terrified, while a voiceover said, "Richard Pryor—afraid of absolutely everything.")

"Hi. I'm Richard Pryor." Pause. "Hope I'm funny." That was how he introduced himself to audiences for years, but he never sounded entirely convinced that he cared about being funny. Instead, Pryor embodied the voice of injured humanity. A satirist of his own experience, he revealed what could be considered family secrets—secrets about his past, and about blacks in general, and about his relationship to the black and white worlds he did and did not belong to. In the black community, correct-ness, political or otherwise, remains part of the mortar that holds lives together. Pryor's comedy was high-wire act: how to stay funny to a black audience while satirizing the moral strictures that make black American life like no other.

The standard approach, in magazine articles about Pryor, has been to comment on his anger—in an imitation-colloquial language meant to approximate Pryor's voice. "Richard Pryor said it first: *That Nigger's Crazy*" begins a 1978 article in *People* magazine. And Pryor had fun with the uneasiness that the word "nigger" provoked in others. (Unlike Lenny Bruce, he didn't believe that if you said a word over and over again it would lose its meaning.) Take his great "Supernigger" routine: "Look up in the sky, it's a crow, it's a bat. No, it's Supernigger! Yes, friends, Super-nigger, with X-ray vision that enables him to see through everything except Whitey."

In 1980, in the second of three interviews that Barbara Walters conducted with Richard Pryor, this exchange took place:

WALTERS: When you're onstage . . . see, it's hard for me to say. I was going
　　to say, you talk about niggers. I can't . . . you can say it. I can't say it.
PRYOR: You just said it.
WALTERS: Yeah, but I feel so . . .

PRYOR: You said it very good.
WALTERS: . . . uncomfortable.
PRYOR: Well, good. You said it pretty good.
WALTERS: O.K.
PRYOR: That's not the first time you said it. (*Laughter.*)

Pryor's anger, though, is actually not as interesting as his self-loathing. Given how much he did to make black pride part of American popular culture, it is arresting to see how at times his blackness seemed to feel like an ill-fitting suit. One gets the sense that he called himself a "nigger" as a kind of preemptive strike, because he never knew when the term would be thrown at him by whites, by other blacks, or by the women he loved. Because he didn't match any of the prevailing stereotypes of "cool" black maleness, he carved out an identity for himself that was not only "nigger" but "sub-nigger." In "Live on the Sunset Strip" he wears a maraschino-red suit with silk lapels, a black shirt, and a bow tie. He says, "Billy Dee Williams could hang out in this suit and look cool." He struts. "And me?" His posture changes from cocky to pitiful.

Pryor believed that there was something called unconditional love, which he alone had not experienced. But to whom could he, a "sub-nigger," turn for that kind of love? The working-class blacks who made him feel guilty for leaving them behind? His relatives, who acted as if it were their right to hit him up for cash because he'd used their stories to make it? The white people who felt safe with him because he was neurotic—a quality they equated with intelligence? The women who married him for money or status? The children he rarely saw? He was alienated from nearly everyone and everything except his need. This drama was what made Pryor's edge so sharp. He acted out against his fantasy by testing it with rude, brilliant commentary. A perfect role for Pryor might have been Dostoyevsky's antihero, Alexei, in *The Gambler,* whose bemused nihilism affects every relationship he attempts. (Pryor once told Walters that he saw people "as the nucleus of a great idea that hasn't come to be yet.") That anti-heroic anger prevents him from just telling a joke. He tells it through clenched teeth. He tells it to stave off bad times. He tells it to look for love.

His Life, as a Bit

Black guy named Richard Pryor, famous, maybe a little high, appears on the eleventh Barbara Walters special, broadcast on May 29,

1979, and says this about his childhood, a sad house of cards he has glued together with wit:

PRYOR: It was hell, because I had nobody to talk to. I was a child, right, and I grew up seeing my mother . . . and my aunties going to rooms with men, you understand. . . .

WALTERS: Your grandmother ran a house of prostitution or a whore-house.

PRYOR: Three houses. Three.

WALTERS: Three houses of prostitution. She was the chief madam.

PRYOR: . . . There were no others.

WALTERS: O.K. . . . Who believed in you? Who cared about you?

PRYOR: Richard Franklin Lennox Thomas Pryor the Third.

The isolation that Richard Pryor feels is elaborated on from time to time, like a bit he can't stop reworking. The sad bit, he could call it, if he did bits anymore, his skinny frame twisting around the words to a story that goes something like this: Born in Peoria, on December 1, 1940. "They called Peoria the model city. That meant it had the niggers under control." Grew up in one of the whorehouses on North Washington Street, which was the house of his paternal grandmother, Marie Carter Pryor Bryant. "She reminded me of a large sunflower—big, strong, bright, appealing," Pryor wrote in his 1995 memoir, *Pryor Convictions*. But "she was also a mean, tough, controlling bitch." Pryor called his father's mother "Mama," despite the fact that he had a mother, Gertrude. When Richard's father, Buck Carter, met Gertrude, she was already in-volved in Peoria's nefarious underworld, and she soon began working in Marie's whorehouse. Everything in Richard Pryor's world, as he grew up, centered on Marie, and he never quite recovered from that influence. "I come from criminal people," he told one radio interviewer. At the age of six, he was sexually abused by a young man in the neighborhood (who, after Richard Pryor became Richard Pryor, came to his trailer on a film set and asked for his autograph). And Pryor never got over the division he saw in his mother: the way she could separate her emotional self from her battered body and yet was emotionally damaged anyway.

"At least, Gertrude didn't flush me down the toilet, as some did," Pryor wrote in his memoir. "The only person scarier than God was my mother. . . . One time Buck hit Gertrude, and she turned blue with anger and said 'Okay, motherfucker, don't hit me no more. . . . Don't stand in front of me with fucking undershorts on and hit me, motherfucker.' Quick as lightning, she reached out with her finger claws and swiped at my father's dick. Ripped his nutsack off. I was just a kid when I saw this." Pryor records the drama as a born storyteller would—in the details. And the detail that filters through his memory most clearly is the rhythm of Gertrude's speech, its combination of profanity and rhetoric. Not unlike a routine by Richard Pryor.

Pryor soon discovered humor—the only form of manipulation he had in his community of con artists, hookers, and pimps. "I wasn't much taller than my Daddy's shin when I found that I could make my family laugh," Pryor wrote.

> I sat on a railing of bricks and found that when I fell off on purpose everyone laughed, including my grandmother, who made it her job to scare the shit out of people. . . . After a few more minutes of falling, a little dog wandered by and poo-pooed in our yard. I got up, ran to my grandmother, and slipped in the dog poop. It made Mama and the rest laugh again. Shit, I was really onto something then. So I did it a second time. "Look at that boy! He's crazy!" That was my first joke. All in shit.

When Pryor was ten years old, his mother left his father and went to stay with relatives in Springfield, Illinois, but Pryor stayed with his grandmother. In a biography by John and Dennis Williams, Pryor's teacher Marguerite Yingst Parker remembered him as "perpetually exhausted, sometimes lonely, always likable. . . . He was a poor black kid in what was then a predominantly white school, who didn't mingle with his classmates on the playground." Pryor often got through the tedium of school by entertaining his classmates. Eventually, Parker struck a deal with him: if he got to school on time, she would give him a few minutes each week to do a routine in front of the class. Not long afterward, Pryor met Juliette Whittaker, an instructor at the Carver Community Center. "He was about eleven, but looked younger because he was such a skinny little boy. And very bright," she recalled in the Williams book. "We were rehearsing 'Rumpelstiltskin' and he was watching. He asked if he could be in the play. I told him we only had one part left, and he said, 'I don't care. I'll take anything. I just want to be in the play.' . . . He took the script home and, unbeknownst to anybody, he memorized the entire thing."

When Pryor was in the eighth grade, a teacher who was fed up with his classroom routines asked him to leave school. He slowly became absorbed into the mundane working-class life that Peoria had to offer, taking a job at a packing plant, running errands. When he was seventeen, he discovered that the black woman he was seeing had also been sleeping with his father. Then, in an attempt to escape, Pryor enlisted in the Army, in 1958. He was stationed in Germany, where he was involved in a racial incident: a young white soldier laughed too hard about the painful black parts in the Douglas Sirk film "Imitation of Life," and Pryor and a number of other black inductees beat and stabbed him. Pryor went to jail, and when he was discharged, in 1960, he returned to his grandmother's twilight world of street life and women for hire.

Pryor had some idea of what he wanted to be: a comedian like the ones he had seen on TV, particularly the black comedians Dick Gregory and Redd Foxx. He began performing at small venues in Peoria, telling topical jokes in the cadence of the time: "You know how to give Mao Tse-tung artificial respiration? No. Good!" The humor then "was kind of rooted in the fifties," the comedian and actor Steve Martin told me. "Very straight jokes, you know. The dominant theme on television and in the public's eye was something Catskills. Jokes. Punch lines." And it was within that form that Pryor began to make a name for himself in the local clubs.

But Pryor was ambitious, and his ambition carried him away from Peoria. In 1961, he left behind his first wife and their child, "because I could," and began working the night-club circuit in places like East St. Louis, Buffalo, and Youngstown, Ohio. In 1963, he made his way to New York. "I opened *Newsweek* and read about Bill Cosby," Pryor told David Felton. "That fucked me up. I said, 'God damn it, this nigger's doin' what *I'm* fixin' to do. I want to be the only nigger, ain't no room for two niggers.'" In New York, Pryor began appearing regularly at Cafe Wha?. By 1966, he had begun to make it nationally. He appeared on a show hosted by Rudy Vallee called *On Broadway Tonight*. Then on Ed Sullivan, Merv Griffin, and Johnny Carson—appearing each time with marcelled hair and wearing a black suit and tie that made him look like an undertaker. But his jokes were like placards that read "Joke": "When I was young I used to think my people didn't like me. Because they used to send me to the store for bread and then they'd move." Or "I heard a knock on the door. I said to my wife, 'There's a knock on the door.' My wife said, 'That's pecul-yar, we ain't got no door.'"

He was feted as the new Bill Cosby by such show-business luminaries as Bobby Darin and Sid Caesar, and other comedians and writers counselled him to keep it that way: "Don't mention the fact that you're a nigger. Don't go into such bad taste," Pryor remembers being told by a white writer called Murray Roman. "They were gonna try to help me be nothin' as best they could," he said in the *Rolling Stone* interview. "The life I was leading, it wasn't me. I was a robot. Beep. Good evening, ladies and gentlemen, welcome to the Sands Hotel. Maids are funny. Beep. . . . I didn't feel good. I didn't feel I could tell anybody to kiss my ass, 'cause I didn't have no ass, you dig?"

A drug habit kicked in. Then, in 1967, while Pryor was doing a show in Las Vegas, he broke down. "I looked out at the audience," Pryor wrote. "The first person I saw was Dean Martin, seated at one of the front tables. He was staring right back at me. I checked out the rest of the audience. They were staring at me as intently as Dean, waiting for that first laugh. . . . I asked myself, Who're they looking at, Rich? . . . And in that flash of introspection when I was unable to find an answer, I crashed. . . . I finally spoke to the sold-out crowd: 'What the fuck am I doing here?' Then I turned and walked off the stage."

He was through with what he'd been doing: "I was a Negro for twenty-three years. I gave that shit up. No room for advancement."

In the following years—1968 through 1971—Pryor worked on material that became more or less what we know today as the Richard Pryor experience. A close friend, the comedian and writer Paul Mooney, took him to the looser, more politicized environs of Berkeley, and Pryor holed up there and wrote.

The black folklorist and novelist Zora Neale Hurston once wrote that, although she had "landed in the crib of negroism" at birth, it hadn't occurred to her until she left her home town that her identity merited a legitimate form of intellectual inquiry. It was only after Pryor had left Peoria and wrested a certain level of success from the world that he was able to see his own negroism, and what made it unique. As Mel Watkins writes, in his book *On the Real Side: Laughing, Lying, and Signifying,* after Pryor moved to Berkeley and met the writers Cecil Brown and Ishmael Reed he discovered that "accredited intellectuals" could share "his affection and enthusiasm for the humor and lifestyles of common black folks." Pryor also discovered Malcolm X's speeches and Marvin Gaye's album *What's Going On.* Both taught him how to treat himself as just another character in a story being told. He distanced himself from the more confessional Lenny Bruce—whose work had already influenced him to adopt a hipper approach to language—and "Richard Pryor" became no more important than the winos or junkies he talked about.

Pryor began to reconstruct himself first through the use of sound—imagining the sound of Frankenstein taking LSD, for example, or a baby "being birthed." His routines from this time regularly involved gurgles, air blown through pursed lips, beeps. He also began playing with individual words. He would stand in front of an audience and say "God damn" in every way he could think to say it. Or he'd say, "I feel," in a variety of ways that indicated the many different ways he could feel. And as he began to understand how he felt he began to see himself, to create his body before his audience. He talked about the way his breath and his farts smelled, what he wanted from love, where he had been, and what America thought he was.

In those years, Pryor began to create characters that were based on his own experience; he explored the territory and language of his family and his childhood—that fertile and unyielding ground that most artists visit again and again. The producer George Schlatter, who watched Pryor's transformation at a number of clubs in the late sixties and the early seventies, told me, "Richard grew up in a whorehouse. The language he used, he was entitled to it. Now the kids coming up, they use the word 'fuck' and that becomes the joke. Richard used the word 'fuck' on the way to the joke. It was part of his vocabulary. It was part of his life experience." As Pryor began to recall his relatives' voices, he became able to see them from the outside, not without a certain degree of fondness. "My aunt Maxine could suck a neck-bone, it was a work of art," he'd say. Or:

> My father was one of them eleven-o'clock niggers. [Voice becoming more high-pitched] "Say, say, where you going, Richard? Say, huh? Well, nigger, you ain't ask nobody if you could go no place. What the fuck, you a man now, nigger? Get a job. I don't give a fuck where you go, be home by eleven. You understand eleven, don't you, nigger? *You can tell time, can't you?* . . . Eleven o'clock, bring your ass here. I don't mean down the street singing with them niggers, either. I ain't getting you ass out of jail no more, motherfucker. That's right. [Pause] And bring me back a paper."

Pryor's routines became richer in depth, in imagination—rather like the characters Edgar Lee Masters created for his brilliant, problematic *Spoon River Anthology*. But the most popular and best-known of Pryor's characters—Mudbone, an old black man from Tupelo, Mississippi, whom Pryor created in 1975—also shows how a Pryor character can be *too* well drawn, too much of a crossover tool. Mudbone spoke with a strong Southern dialect and his tales were directly descended from the slave narratives that told (as the critic Darryl Pinckney described them) "of spirits riding people at night, of elixirs dearly bought from conjure men, chicken bones rubbed on those from whom love was wanted." From "Mudbone Goes to Hollywood":

> Old Negro Man's Voice: There was an old man name was Mudbone. . . .
> And he used to sit right here in front of the barbecue shop and he'd dip

snuff . . . and he'd spit. . . . He'd been in a great love affair. That right. He had a woman—he loved her very much—he had to hurt her though 'cause she fucked around on him. He said he knew she was fucking around 'cause I'd leave home and go to work and come back home, toilet seat be up. . . . So I set a little old trap for her there. Went to work early, you know, always did get up early, 'cause I like to hear the birds and shit. . . . So this particular morning, went on to work. Set my trap for this girl. She was pretty, too. Loved her. Sweet as she could be. Breast milk like Carnation milk. So I nailed the toilet seat down and doubled back and I caught that nigger trying to lift it up. So, say, Well, nigger, send your soul to heaven, 'cause your ass is mine up in here.

Mudbone was the character that Pryor's audiences requested again and again. But, as Pauline Kael noted in her review of *Live on the Sunset Strip*, Pryor became tired of him: "Voices, ostensibly from the audience, can be heard. One of them calls, 'Do the Mudbone routine,' and, rather wearily, saying that it will be for the last time, Pryor sits on a stool and does the ancient storyteller [who] was considered one of his great creations. And the movie goes thud . . . Pryor looks defeated."

And he should: Mudbone was the trick he turned and got tired of turning—a safe woolly-headed Negro, a comic version of Katherine Anne Porter's old Uncle Jimbilly. Compare Mudbone, for example, to the innovative and threatening "Bicentennial Nigger" character: "Some nigger two hundred years old in blackface. With stars and stripes on his forehead, lips just a-shining." "Battle Hymn" theme music, and Pryor's voice becomes Stepin Fetchit-like. "But he happy. He happy, 'cause he been here two hundred years. . . . Over here in America. 'I'm so glad y'all took me out of Dahomey.'" Shuckin' and jivin' laugh. "'I used to could live to be a hundred and fifty, now I dies of the high blood pressure by the time I'm fifty-two.'"

By 1973, Richard Pryor had become a force in the entertainment industry. He now appeared regularly in such diverse venues as Redd Foxx's comedy club in Central L.A., where the clientele was mostly black, and the Improv, on Sunset Strip, which was frequented by white show-business hipsters. And he behaved as badly as he wanted to wherever he wanted to—whether with women, with alcohol, or with drugs. "I got plenty of money but I'm still a nigger," he told a radio interviewer. He had become Richard Pryor, the self-described "black greasy motherfucker," whose new style of entertainment was just one of many innovations of the decade —in music (Sly and the Family Stone and the Average White Band), in acting (Lily Tomlin and Ronee Blakley), and in directing (Martin Scorsese and Hal Ashby). Cultural rebellion and political activism defined hip in Hollywood then—an era that is all too difficult to recall now.

"The idea of a black guy going out and saying he fucked a white woman was outrageous . . . but funny," Schlatter told me. "White women dug Richard because he was a naughty little boy, and they wanted some of that. He was talking about real things. Nobody was talking below the waist. Richard went right for the lap, man."

Pryor had directed a film called "Bon Appetit" a few years before—the footage is now lost. "The picture opened with a black maid having her pussy eaten at the breakfast table by the wealthy white man who owned the house where she worked," he recalled in *Pryor Convictions*. "Then a gang of Black Panther types burst into the house and took him prisoner. As he was led away, the maid fixed her dress and called, '*Bon appétit*, baby!'"

Each time someone asked why "that nigger was crazy," Pryor upped the ante by posing a more profound question. On a trip to a gun shop with David Felton in the early seventies, for example, Pryor asked the salesman, "How come all the targets are black?" The salesman smiled, embarrassed. "Uh, I don't know, Richard," he said, shaking his head. "I just—" "No, I mean I always wondered about that, you know?" Pryor said.

Pryor's edginess caught the attention of Mel Brooks, who was already an established Hollywood figure, and in 1972 Brooks hired him to work on a script called "Black Bart," the story of a smooth, Gucci-wearing black sheriff in the eighteen-seventies American West. This was to be Pryor's real crossover gig, not only as a writer but as an actor, but the leading role eventually went to Cleavon Little. Whatever the reason for not casting Pryor (some people who were involved with the movie told me that no one could deal with his drinking and his drug use), there are several scenes in the film (renamed *Blazing Saddles*) that couldn't have been written by anyone else. One scene didn't make it in. It shows a German saloon singer, Lili von Dyke, in her darkened dressing room with Bart, whom she is trying to seduce.

LILI: Here, let me sit next to you. Tell me, *schatzi*, is it true vat zey say about the way you people are gifted? . . . Oh, oh, it's twue, it's twue, it's twue, it's twue.
BART: Excuse me, you're sucking my arm.

Pryor's best performances (in films he didn't write himself) date from these years. There is his poignant and striking Oscar-nominated appearance in Sidney J. Furie's 1972 film, *Lady Sings the Blues*. As the Piano Man to Diana Ross's Billie Holiday, Pryor gives a performance that is as emotional and as surprising as his work in "Juke and Opal." And then there is his brilliant comic turn as Sharp-Eye Washington, the disreputable private detective in Sidney Poitier's 1974 film, "Uptown Saturday Night"—a character that makes use of Pryor's ability to convey paranoia with his body: throughout the movie, he looks like a giant exclamation point. And as Zeke Brown, in "Blue Collar," Paul Schrader's 1978 film about an automobile plant in Detroit, Pryor gives his greatest sustained— if fraught—film performance. In an interview with the writer Kevin Jackson, Schrader recalls his directorial debut:

> There were . . . problems. Part of it was to do with Richard's style of acting. Being primarily versed in stand-up comedy he had a creative life of between three and four takes. The first one would be good, the second would be real good, the third would be terrific, and the fourth would probably start to fall off. . . . The other thing Richard would do when he felt his performance going flat was to improvise and change the dialogue just like he would have done in front of a live audience, and he would never tell me or anyone what he was going to do.

Generally, though, Pryor had a laissez-faire attitude toward acting. One always feels, when looking at the work that he did in bad movies ranging from *You've Got to Walk It like You Talk It or You'll Lose That Beat,* in 1971, to *Superman III,* released twelve years and twenty-seven films later, that Pryor had a kind of contempt for these mediocre projects —and for his part in them. Perhaps no character was as interesting to Richard Pryor as Richard Pryor. He certainly didn't work hard to make us believe that he was anyone other than himself as he walked through shameful duds like *Adios Amigo.* On the other hand, his fans paid all the love and all the money in the world to see him be himself: they fed his vanity, and his vanity kept him from being a great actor.

In September 1977, Lily Tomlin asked Pryor to be part of a benefit at the Hollywood Bowl to oppose Proposition Six, a Californian anti-gay initiative. Onstage, Pryor started doing a routine about the first time he'd sucked dick. The primarily gay members of the audience hooted at first— but they didn't respond well to Pryor's frequent use of the word "faggot." Pryor's rhythm was thrown off. "Shit . . . this is really weird," he exploded. "This is an evening about human rights. And I am a human being . . . I just wanted to test you to your motherfucking *soul.* I'm doing this shit for *nuthin'.* . . . When the niggers was burning down Watts, you motherfuckers was doin' what you wanted to do on Hollywood Boulevard . . . didn't give a shit about it." And as he walked offstage: "You Hollywood faggots can kiss my happy, *rich* black ass."

Pryor liked to tell the truth, but he couldn't always face it himself. Although he spent years searching for an idealized form of love, his relationships were explosive and short-lived. From 1969 to 1978, he had three serious relationships or marriages—two with white women, one with a black woman—and two children. There were also affairs with film stars such as Pam Grier and Margot Kidder, and one with a drag queen. He was repeatedly in trouble for beating up women and hotel clerks. His sometimes maudlin self-involvement when a woman left him rarely involved any kind of development or growth. It merely encouraged the self-pity that informed much of his emotional life.

By the late seventies, Pryor was freebasing so heavily that he left his bedroom only to go to work and even then only if he could smoke some more on the set. He was even more paranoid than he'd always been and showed very little interest in the world. The endless cycle of dependence —from the drinking to the coke to the other drugs he needed to come down from the coke—began to destroy his health. Then, in 1980, he tried to break the cycle by killing himself. He wrote his own account of the episode, in *Pryor Convictions*:

> After free-basing without interruption for several days in a row, I wasn't able to discern one day from the next . . . "I know what I have to do," I mumbled. "I've brought shame to my family . . . I've destroyed my career. I know what I have to do. . . . I reached for the cognac bottle on the table in front of me and poured it all over me. Real natural, methodical. As the liquid soiled my body and clothing, I wasn't scared. . . . I was in a place called There . . . I picked up my Bic lighter. . . . WHOOSH! I was engulfed in flame. . . . Sprinting down the driveway, I went out the gates and ran down the street. . . . Two cops tried to help me. My hands and face were already swollen. My clothes burnt in tatters. And my smoldering chest smelled like a burned piece of meat. . . . "Is there?" I asked. "Is there what?" someone asked. "Oh Lord, there is no help for a poor widow's son, is there?"

Pryor was in critical condition at the Sherman Oaks Community Hospital for seven weeks. When Jennifer Lee—a white woman, whom he married a year later—went to visit him, he described himself as a "forty-year-old burned-up nigger." And, in a sense, Pryor never recovered from his suicide attempt. *Live on the Sunset Strip*, which came out three years later, is less a pulled-together performance than the performance of a man trying to pull himself together. He could no longer tell the truth. He couldn't even take the truth. And, besides, people didn't want the truth (a forty-year-old burned-up nigger). They wanted Richard Pryor—"sick," but not ill.

White Honky Bitch

Jennifer Lee was born and grew up in Ithaca, New York, one of three daughters of a wealthy lawyer. In her twenties, she moved to L.A. to become an actress, had affairs with Warren Beatty and Roman Polanski, and appeared in several B movies. She met Pryor in 1977, when she was hired to help redecorate his house. "We sat on an oversized brass bed in Richard's house," she wrote in an article for *Spin* magazine. "He was blue—heartsick over a woman who was 'running game' on him. He was putting a major dent in a big bottle of vodka. You could feel the tears and smell the gardenias, even with hip, white-walled nasal passages." Since that day, she told me, laughing, as we sat in the garden at the Chateau Marmont, in L.A., last winter, she has always been "the head bitch."

As Jennifer talked with me that afternoon, dressed in black leather pants and a black blazer, her white skin made even whiter by her maroon lipstick, I thought of the photographs I had seen of her with Pryor, some of which were reproduced in her 1991 memoir, *Tarnished Angel.* These images were replaced by others: the white actress Shirley Knight berating Al Freeman, Jr., in the film version of Amiri Baraka's powerful play, "Dutchman," and Diane Arbus's haunting photograph of a pregnant white woman and her black husband sitting on a bench in Washington Square in the sixties. Then I thought of Pryor's routines on interracial sex. From "Black Man, White Woman":

> Don't ever marry a white woman in California. A lot of you sisters probably saying "Don't marry a white woman anyway, nigger." [Pause] Shit. . . . Sisters look at you like you killed yo' Mama when you out with a white woman. You can't laugh that shit off, either. [High-pitched, fake-jovial voice] "Ha ha she's not with me."

From a routine entitled "Black and White Women":

> There really is a difference between white women and black women. I've dated both. Yes, I have. . . . Black women, you be suckin' on their pussy and they be like, "Wait, nigger, shit. A little more to the left, motherfucker. You gonna suck the motherfucker, get down. You can fuck white women and if they don't come they say, "It's all right, I'll just lay here and use a vibrator."

Pryor was not only an integrationist but an integrationist of white women and black men, one of the most taboo adult relationships. The judgments that surround any interracial couple: *White girls who are into black dudes are sluts. White dudes aren't enough for them; only a big-dicked black guy can satisfy them. Black dudes who are into white girls don't like their kind. And, well, you know how they treat their women: they abuse them; any white girl who goes out with one is a masochist.* The air in America is thick with these misconceptions, and in the seventies it was thicker still. Plays and films like *A Taste of Honey, A Patch of Blue, Deep Are the Roots, All God's Chillun' Got Wings,* and *The Great White Hope* gave a view of the black man as both destroyer and nursemaid to a galaxy of white women who were sure to bring him down. But no real relationships exist in these works. The black male protagonists are more illustration than character. (Though they make excellent theatrical agitprop: what a surplus of symbols dangles from their mythic oversized penises!) In his work, Pryor was one of the first black artists to unknot the narrative of that desire and to expose it. In life he had to live through it as painfully as anyone else.

When Jennifer Lee first slept with Pryor, she told me, she touched his hair and he recoiled: its texture was all the difference in the world between them. That difference is part of the attraction for both members of interracial couples. "Ain't no such thing as an ugly white woman," says a character in Eldridge Cleaver's 1968 polemic, *Soul on Ice.* In some ways Pryor found it easier to be involved with white women than with black women: he could blame their misunderstandings on race, and he could take advantage of the guilt they felt for what he suffered as a black man.

Yet, while Pryor may have felt both attracted by and ashamed of his difference from Lee, he also pursued her through all his drug blindness and self-absorption because he saw something of himself in her. "What no one gets," Lee told me, "is that one of the ways Richard became popular was through women falling in love with him—they saw themselves in him, in his not fitting in, the solitude of it all, and his willingness to be vulnerable as women are. And disenfranchised, of course, as women are." That black men and white women were drawn to each other through their oppression by white men was a concept I had first seen expressed in the feminist Shulamith Firestone's book "The Dialectic of Sex." There is a bond in oppression, certainly, but also a rift because of it—a contempt for the other who marks you as different—which explains why interracial romance is so often informed by violence. Cleaver claimed that he raped white women because that was the only kind of empowerment he could find in his brutal world. At times, Pryor directed a similar rage at Jennifer Lee, and she, at times, returned it.

Life in the eighties: Pryor gets up. Does drugs. Drives over to the Comedy Store to work out a routine. Has an argument with Jennifer after a party. Maybe they fly to Hawaii. Come back in a week or so. Some days, Pryor is relaxed in his vulnerability. Other days, he tries to throw her out of the car. Richard's Uncle Dickie says about Jennifer, who is from an Irish family, "Irish are niggers turned inside out." Richard says about Jennifer, "The tragedy was that Jennifer could keep up with me." And she did. They married in 1981. They divorced in 1982.

With Lee, Pryor took the same trajectory that he had followed with many women before her. He began with a nearly maudlin reverence for her beauty and ended with paranoia and violence. In *Tarnished Angel*, Lee describes Pryor photographing her as she was being sexually attacked by a drug dealer he hung out with—a lowlife in the tradition of the people he had grown up with. Pryor could be brutally dissociative and sadistic, especially with people he cared about: he did not separate their degradation from his own. He was also pleased when Lee was jealous of the other women he invariably became involved with. And when she left him, she claims, he stalked her.

Pryor got married again in 1986, to Flynn Be-Laine, two years after she'd given birth to his son Steven. Lee moved back to New York, where she wrote a challenging review of Pryor's film *Jo Jo Dancer: Your Life Is Calling*, for *People*:

> Well, Richard, you blew it. I went to see "Jo Jo Dancer." . . . I went looking for the truth, the real skinny. Well, guess what? It wasn't there . . . How sad. After all, it was you who was obsessed by the truth, be it onstage or in your private life . . . You had no sacred cows. That's why I fell in love with you, why I hung in through the wonder and madness . . . Listen to your white honky bitch, Richard: Ya gotta walk it like you talk it or you'll lose that beat.

But later the same year, when Lee interviewed Pryor for *Spin*, they had reached a kind of detente:

LEE: What about the rage, the demons?
PRYOR: They don't rage much anymore.
LEE: Like a tired old monster?
PRYOR: Very tired. He hath consumed me.
LEE: Has this lack of rage quieted your need to do standup?
PRYOR: Something has. I'm glad it happened after I made money.

Pryor had gone sober in 1983 and he soon recognized that, along with alcohol, he needed to relinquish some of the ruthless internal navigations that had given his comedy its power. He performed live less and less. There were flashes of the old brilliance: on Johnny Carson, for example, when he responded to false rumors that he had AIDS. And when his public raised its fickle refrain—"He's sick, he's washed up"—he often rallied, but in the last eight years of his performing life he became a more conventional presence.

Pryor divorced Flynn in 1991, and in 1994 he placed a call to Jennifer. He was suffering from degenerative multiple sclerosis, he told her, and wouldn't be able to work much longer. "He said, 'My life's a mess. Will you help me out?' " she recalls. "I thought long and hard about it . . . I wasn't sure it would last, because Richard loves to manipulate people and see them dance. But, see, he can't do that anymore, because he finally bottomed. That's the only reason Richard is allowing his life to be in any kind of order right now."

Lee came back to Pryor in July of that year. "When I got there, he was in this ridiculous rental for, like, six thousand dollars a month," she told me. "Five bedrooms, seven bathrooms. Honey, it was classic. You couldn't write it better." Lee helped him to find a smaller house in Encino, and she has cared for him since then. He has two caregivers and is bathed and dressed in a collaborative effort that has shades of Fellini. He spends his days in a custom-made wheelchair, while others read to him or give him physical or speech therapy. Every Friday, he goes to the movies. According to Lee, he can speak well when he wants to, but he doesn't often want to. "Sometimes he'll say, 'Leave me the fuck alone, Jenny,' " she tells me, laughing. "Just the other day, Richard was sitting, staring out the window, and his caregiver said, 'Mr. Richard, what are you thinking about?' He said, 'I'm thinking about how much money I pay all you motherfuckers.' " He doesn't see his children much, or his other ex-wives, or the people he knew when he still said things like "I dig show business. I do . . . I wake up every morning and I kiss it. Show business, you fine bitch."

Blue Movie

"Was that corny?" Lily Tomlin said to me one afternoon last winter when I told her I'd heard that certain CBS executives hadn't wanted her to kiss Pryor good night at the close of *Lily,* back in 1973. After all, Pryor was then a disreputable black comic with an infamous foul mouth, and Lily Tomlin had just come from *Laugh-In,* where she had attracted nationwide attention. Tomlin kissed him anyway, and it was, I think, the first time I had ever seen a white woman kiss a black man—I was twelve—and it was almost certainly the first time I had ever seen Richard Pryor. Tomlin and I were sitting with Jane Wagner, her partner and writer for thirty years, in a Cuban restaurant—one of their favorite places in Los Angeles. Tomlin and Wagner were the only white people there.

"We just loved Richard," Tomlin told me. "He was the only one who could move you to tears. No one was funnier, dearer, darker, heavier, stronger, more radical. He was everything. And his humanity was just glorious."

"What a miracle 'Juke and Opal' got on," Wagner said. "The network treated us as if we were total political radicals. I guess we were. And they hated Richard. They were so threatened by him."

CBS had insisted that Tomlin and Wagner move "Juke and Opal" to the end of the show, so that people wouldn't switch channels in the middle, bringing down the ratings. "It threw the whole shape of the show off," Tomlin recalled in a 1974 interview. "It made 'Juke and Opal' seem like some sort of Big Message, which is not what I intended . . . I wasn't out to make any, uh, heavy statements, any real judgments."

"Everybody kept saying it wasn't funny, but we wanted to do little poems. I mean, when you think of doing a drug addict in prime time!" Wagner told me. And what they did *is* a poem of sorts. It was one of the all too few opportunities that Tomlin had to showcase, on national television, the kind of performance she and Pryor pioneered.

"Lily and Richard were a revolution, because they based what they did on real life, its possibilities," Lorne Michaels, the producer of *Saturday Night Live,* told me. "You couldn't do that kind of work now on network television, because no one would understand it. . . . Lily and Richard were the exemplars of a kind of craft. They told us there was a revolution coming in the field of entertainment, and we kept looking to the left, and it didn't come."

It is odd to think that Richard Pryor's period of pronounced popularity and power lasted for only a decade, *really*—from 1970 to 1980. But comedy is rock and roll, and Pryor had his share of hits. The enormous territory he carved out for himself remains more or less his own. Not that it hasn't been scavenged by other comedians: Eddie Murphy takes on Pryor's belligerent side, Martin Lawrence his fearful side, Chris Rock his hysteria, Eddie Griffin his ghoulish goofiness. But none of these comedians approaches Pryor's fundamental strangeness, vulnerability, or political intensity. Still, their work demonstrates the power of his influence: none of them would exist at all were it not for Richard Pryor. The actor Richard Belzer described him to me as "the ultimate artistic beacon." "It was like he was the sun and we were planets," Belzer said. "He was the ultimate. He took socially complex situations and made you think about them, and yet you laughed. He's so brilliantly funny, it was revelatory. He's one of those rare people who define a medium."

According to Lee, Pryor has been approached by a number of artists who see something of themselves in him. Damon Wayans and Chris Rock wanted to star in a film version of Pryor's life. The Hughes Brothers expressed interest in making a documentary. In 1998, the Kennedy Center gave Pryor its first Mark Twain Prize, and Chevy Chase, Whoopi Goldberg, Robin Williams, and others gathered to pay tribute to him. Pryor's written acceptance of the award, however, shows a somewhat reluctant acknowledgment of his status as an icon: "It is nice to be regarded on par with a great white man—now that's funny!" he wrote. "Seriously, though, two things people throughout history have had in common are hatred and humor. I am proud that, like Mark Twain, I have been able to use humor to lessen people's hatred!"

In some ways, Pryor probably realizes that his legendary status has weakened the subversive impact of his work. People are quick to make monuments of anything they live long enough to control. It's not difficult to see how historians will view him in the future. An edgy comedian. A Mudbone. But will they take into account the rest of his story: that essentially American life, full of contradictions; the life of a comedian who had an excess of both empathy and disdain for his audience, who exhausted himself in his search for love, who was a confusion of female and male, colored and white, and who acted out this internal drama onstage for our entertainment.

NOTE

Hilton Als, "A Pryor Love: The Life and Times of America's Comic Prophet of Race," *The New Yorker,* 13 September 1999, 68–81.

20 Conclusion

WE OWE A DEBT TO RICHARD PRYOR

AUDREY THOMAS MCCLUSKEY

Sometimes I laugh just to keep from crying.
—blues lyric

Novelist Ralph Ellison once described the blues personality as one who "fingers the jagged edge" of life to transcend personal catastrophe through honesty and tenacity of spirit. Richard Pryor—whose recent death released him from more than a decade of the crippling effects of multiple sclerosis, an illness that rendered his body unable to respond to his tenacious, irreverent spirit—was the embodiment of the blues personality. His genius (an overused and misapplied word, to be sure) as well as much of his personal trouble and many of his well-known foibles can be located in his unwillingness to tolerate any public pretense. He began his scorching social critique, the mainstay of his comedic performance, with a display of brutal honesty and vulnerability. Rather than surrender to the pain of life, Richard Pryor made art out it. The winner of five Grammy awards and a posthumous lifetime achievement award for his comedy albums, he performed not from a desire to churn out one-liners and jokes, but from a need to share lived and deeply felt experience that linked our common humanity. He left his audiences bowled over, laughing so hard that they would be crying, too. In the blues tradition, laughing to keep from crying can be a transcendent response to the fickleness of life.

Though his comedy was often bawdy and raw, he avoided stereotypical "cooning and clowning." He frequently used racial and sexual themes, and laid bare issues that made some black people squirm. Yet whites could not feel safe from the scorching truth-telling that exposed white racism and hypocrisy. In his best stand-up, a lesson, a protest, even a moral message was imparted. Pryor spared no one, especially himself. He was a man of bad habits, laced with good intentions, who admired the qualities of those who would not give in to injustice.

A poignant example of this is shown in his story about football great Jim Brown. Brown, as the league's all-time leading rusher, had to deal with the racism of early 1960s NFL opponents who would stomp on him after an overdue tackle and call him the N-word. "Jim has so much integrity," said Pryor, "He would get up slowly, go back to the huddle and calmly tell the quarterback to 'give me the ball.' " Now, that is not necessarily funny, but with Pryor's insistent voice imitations and manner, his re-telling became not only funny, but a treatise on heroic action.

Pryor's solidarity with the underdog, and disregard for secrets—society's as well as his own—stemmed from his biography. Growing up in a bordello in Peoria, Illinois, under the tutelage of a wise and unsentimental grandmother, and in the shadow of a larger-than-life father, he was exposed to all types of human frailty and need. Pryor invented sympathetic rendering of flawed, deeply human, and affecting characters from winos and drug addicts to the inimitable Mudbone, the southern transplant who fled racism on a "borrowed" tractor, and Miss Rudolph, the dispenser of magic potions and punishment.

Leaving Peoria and the Army, he worked his way east and reinvented himself as the next Bill Cosby. His G-rated routines showed tremendous physical agility and comic delivery and landed him on network television. But it was not long before he exited that stage, giving up on what he felt was a lucrative fraud, to let his inner voice—the voices of the winos, drug addicts, and everyday people struggling to hold onto their dignity—shine through.

Pryor was not the first to satirize race relations, but he was the first to draw a huge crossover audience who paid to hear him poke fun at them. When, for example, he contrasted the behavior of blacks and whites at funerals, showing whites acting reserved and composed and blacks crying and moaning, both groups laughed in recognition of the essential truth in that exaggeration. His success led to a productive movie career that extended beyond comedic roles. For a brief time, Pryor was the biggest black personality in Hollywood, with a multiple-movie deal and several notable performances in films such as *Blue Collar* (1978), *Lady Sings the Blues* (1972), and *Bingo Long and the Traveling All-Stars* (1976), plus several hit comedies with Gene Wilder, including *Silver Streak* (1976) and *Stir Crazy* (1980). He had a good share of duds, too, *The Toy* (1982) and *Brewster's Millions* (1985) among them.

Today's comedians of all races owe him a debt for shaking up the status quo and creating a new standard of performance. Because he was an original, Pryor will continue to be imitated, which just makes us miss him more. If he is in heaven, he, no doubt, has God bowled over in laughter. If he is in that other place, he is matching wits with the devil, and in that pairing, Richard Pryor has got to be the favorite.

NOTE

This chapter by Audrey Thomas McCluskey was originally published in the editorial pages of the Bloomington *Herald Times*, 22 January 2006. It is slightly revised here.

SELECTED CHRONOLOGY: THE LIFE AND TIMES OF RICHARD PRYOR

1940	Born, Dec. 1, Richard Franklin Lennox Thomas Pryor in Peoria, Ill., to Leroy Pryor and Gertrude Thomas. Lived with large extended family that included parents and grandmother Marie Carter Bryant, who ran a brothel
1946	Molested by neighbor named "Hoss"
1951	Cast in play, *Rumpelstiltskin,* by teacher Juliette Whittaker at the Carver Community Center
1954	Dropped out of high school; worked odd jobs
1957	Renee Pryor, first of his seven children from different relationships and seven marriages, was born (Other children are: Richard Jr. [1961], Elizabeth [1967], Rain [1969], Stephen Michael [1984], Kelsey [1987], and Franklin Matthew Mason [1987]. Pryor was married to Patricia Price [1960–61]; Shelley Bonus [1967–69]; Deboragh McGuire [1977–79]; Flynn BeLaine [1986–1987;1990–91]; Jennifer Lee [1981–82; 2001–2005])
1958	Enlisted in U.S. Army
1960	Discharged from Army
1960–63	Performed as a stand-up comic at black clubs in Midwest
1963	Moved to New York City (performed at Apollo Theatre)
1964–66	Television debut: "On Broadway Tonight"; other TV appearances: *The Tonight Show; Ed Sullivan Show; Merv Griffin Show; Kraft Music Hall*
1967–68	First album, *Richard Pryor;* beginning of film career: *The Busy Body; The Green Berets; Wild in the Streets*
1969–71	Moved to Berkeley, Calif.; involved with West Coast black intellectuals, writers, artists, and activists
1971	Played Piano Man in *Lady Sings the Blues* with Diana Ross
1973	Emmy Award for television writing: *The Lily Tomlin Special*
1974–76	Gold records and two Grammy Awards for *That Nigger's Crazy* and . . . *Is It Something I Said?; Bicentennial Nigger* (he considered this his most political album)
1976–77	The well-received *Richard Pryor Television Special* followed the next year by short-lived *Richard Pryor Show;* four episodes
1976–81	During this period he became most prolific and best-known black actor "in history"; appeared in dozens of movies including: *Car Wash* (1976); *Bingo Long and the Traveling Motor Kings* (1976); *Silver Streak* (1976); *Greased Lightening* (1977); *Which Way Is Up?* (1977); *Blue Collar* (1978); *The Wiz* (1978); *Stir Crazy* (1980); *Bustin' Loose* (1981)
1979	Released comedy albums: *Richard Pryor: Live! in Concert; Wanted* First trip to Africa (Kenya, East Africa). Swore off of using the word "nigger" in his routines
1979–80	Founded Indigo Productions with other blacks, including actor and ex-athlete Jim Brown, who became president
1980	Suffered third-degree burns on most of his body in freebasing drug incident

1982	*Richard Pryor Live on the Sunset Strip* (concert film)
1983	*Here and Now* comedy album released
1986	Diagnosed with multiple sclerosis
	Jo Jo Dancer: Your Life Is Calling, starred in film loosely based on his life
1990	Suffered a heart attack
1992	American Comedy Lifetime Achievement Award
1998	Recipient, inaugural Kennedy Center Mark Twain Award Humor Prize
2004	Voted number one on Comedy Central's list of 100 Greatest Stand-up Comics of all time
2005	December 10, died of cardiac arrest in Encino, California

ADDITIONAL SOURCES

Books/Articles

Acham, Christie. *Revolution Televised: Prime Time and the Struggle for Black Power.* Minneapolis: University of Minnesota Press, 2004.

Beavers, Herman. "'The Cool Pose': Intersectionality, Masculinity, and Quiescence in the Comedy and Films of Richard Pryor and Eddie Murphy." In *Race and the Subject of Masculinities,* ed. Harry Stecopoulos and Michael Uebel. Durham, N.C.: Duke University Press, 1997.

Brown, Kate E., and Howard I. Kushner. "Eruptive Voices: Coprolallia, Malediction, and the Poetics of Cursing." *A Journal of Theory and Interpretation* 32, no. 3 (Summer 2001): 537–562.

Butler, Judith. *Excitable Speech: A Politics of the Performative.* New York: Routledge, 1997.

Coleman, Larry G. "Black Comic Performance in the African Diaspora: A Comparison of the Comedy of Richard Pryor and Paul Keens-Douglas." *Journal of Black Studies* 15, no. 1 (September 1984): 67–78.

Gates, Henry L., and Cornel West. "Richard Pryor—1980–1989." In *The African American Century: How Black Americans Have Shaped Our Country.* New York: Touchstone, 2002.

George, Nelson. *Blackface: Reflections on African-Americans and the Movies.* New York: Harper Collins, 1994.

Gray, Herman. *Watching Race: Television and the Struggle for Blackness.* Minneapolis: University of Minnesota Press, 2004.

Hall, Stuart. "Encoding and Decoding in the Television Discourse." Centre for Contemporary Cultural Studies, University of Birmingham (England), 1973. Reprinted in *Culture, Media, Language: Working Papers in Cultural Studies, 1972–79,* ed. Stuart Hall et al. London: Hutchison, 1980. 197–208.

Haskins, James. *Richard Pryor, a Man and His Madness: A Biography.* New York: Beaufort Books, 1984.

Hunt, Darnell M., ed. *Channeling Blackness: Studies on Television and Race in America.* New York: Oxford University Press, 2005.

Johnson, Albert. "Moods Indigo: A Long View." *Film Quarterly* 44, no. 2 (Winter 1990–1991): 13.

Johnson, Anne Jeannette. "Richard Pryor (1940–): Comedian, Actor, Writer." *Contemporary Black Biography* 3 (18 April 2002).

Kael, Pauline. "Richard Pryor Live on the Sunset Strip." In *For Keeps: Thirty Years at the Movies.* New York: E. P. Dutton, 1994.

——. "Time Warp Movies: A Review of Superman III." In *State of the Art.* New York: E. P. Dutton, 1985.

Keels, Crystal. "James Alan McPherson Lecture Highlights Richard Pryor Film Retrospective." *Black Camera* 16, no. 2 (Fall/Winter 2001).

——. "The Richard Pryor Film Retrospective." *Black Camera* 16, no. 2 (Fall/Winter 2001).

Leland, John. *Hip: The History.* New York: Harper Collins, 2004. (Includes several references to Richard Pryor.)

Merrit, Bishetta. "Pryor, Richard: U.S. Comedian/Actor." *Museum of Broadcast Communications Encyclopedia of Television* 2 (1997): 1308.

Nazel, Joseph. *Richard Pryor: The Man behind the Laughter.* Los Angeles: Holloway House, 1981.

Neal, Mark Anthony. *What the Music Said: Black Popular Music and Black Public Culture.* New York: Routledge, 1999.

Parker, Janice. *Great African Americans in Film.* New York: Crabtree, 1997.

Pryor, Richard, with Todd Gold. *Pryor Convictions, and Other Life Sentences.* New York: Pantheon Books, 1995.

Rahman, Jacqueline. *It's a Serious Business: The Linguistic Construction of Middle-Class White Characters by African American Narrative Comedians (Richard Pryor, Adele Givens, Steve Harvey).* ProQuest Information and Learning, 2005.

Robbins, Fred, and David Ragan. *Richard Pryor: This Cat's Got Nine Lives!* New York: Delilah, 1982.

Rovin, Jeff. *Richard Pryor: Black and Blue.* London: Orbis, 1984.

Simon, Roger L., et al. *Family Dream: Bustin' Loose.* Universal City, Calif.: Universal City Studios, 1979.

Vaidhyanathan, Siva. "Now's the Time: The Richard Pryor Phenomenon and the Triumph of Black Culture." In *New Directions in American Humor,* ed. David E. Sloane. Tuscaloosa: University of Alabama Press, 1998.

Watkins, Mel. *On the Real Side: Laughing, Lying, and Signifying—: The Underground Tradition of African-American Humor That Transformed American Culture, from Slavery to Richard Pryor.* New York: Simon and Schuster, 1994.

Williams, John A., and Dennis A. Williams. *If I Stop I'll Die: The Comedy and Tragedy of Richard Pryor.* New York: Thunder's Mouth Press, 1991.

Online Articles

Breckman, Andy. "Nobody Move! It's Richard Pryor!" 12 August 2002. http://www.wfmu.org/LCD/20/pryor.html (accessed 2 May 2004).

Garrone, Max. "*Blazing Saddles:* Mel Brooks remembers working with Richard Pryor, and a time when farting jokes were as offensive as it gets." *Salon,* 8 May 2001. http://www.salon.com/ent/movies/dvd/review/2001/05/08/blazing/ (accessed 18 April 2002).

Gross, Jason. "King of Comedy." *Iron Minds,* 19 October 2000. http://www.ironminds.comlironminds/issues/001019/humor.shtml (accessed 18 April 2002).

Ingram, Billy. "The Richard Pryor Show." *TVparty.* http://www.tvparty.com/pryor.html (accessed 18 April 2002).

McClelland, Justin. "Richard Pryor . . . and It's Deep, Too." *Rock and Roll Reporter,* 1 July 2001. http://www.rocknrollreporter.com/july0l/pryor.htm (accessed 18 April 2002).

Nelson, Jill. "Brilliant Careers: Pryor Knowledge." *Salon,* 24 November 1998. http://www.salon.com/bc/1998/11/24bc.html (accessed 18 April 2002).

Popular Press

Als, Hilton. "A Pryor Love: The Life and Times of America's Comic Prophet of Race." *New Yorker,* 13 September 1999, 68.

Armstrong, Stephen. "Richard Pryor: Live in Concert: An Email Interview." *Sunday Times* (London), 30 May 2004, Culture section:9.

Avakian, Bob. "Richard Pryor Routines or Why Pigs Are Pigs." *Revolutionary Worker* 928 (10 October 1997): 3.

Brashler, William. "Berserk Angel." *Playboy,* December 1979, 243–248, 292–296.

Burr, Ty. "Pryor Engagements." *Entertainment Weekly,* 30 April 1993, 22.

"Comedian Richard Pryor Tells How His Life Is No Laughing Matter in New Book 'Pryor Convictions.' " *Jet,* 5 June 1995, 58.

"Comedian Richard Pryor's Serious Side." *Essence,* March 1986, 78.

Cox, Tom. "Screen Grab: He turned personal tragedy into a brilliant, comic celebration of life." *The Daily Telegraph* (London), 26 June 2004, Arts section:18.

"Damon Wayans to Portray Richard Pryor in Movie." *Jet,* 8 January 1996, 18.

Esckilsen, Erik. "Richard Pryor's Searing Fire." *Entertainment Weekly,* 10 June 1994, 76.

Felton, David. "Jive Times: Richard Pryor, Lily Tomlin and the Theatre of the Routine." *Rolling Stone,* 10 October 1974, 38–39.

Flamm, Matthew. "Tears of a Clown." *Entertainment Weekly,* 26 May 1995, 76.

George, Nelson. "The Rumors of His Death Have Been Greatly Exaggerated." *New York Times,* 17 January 1999, 28.

Handelman, David. "The Last Time We Saw Richard." *Premiere* 5, no. 5 (January 1992): 78.

——. "Richard the First." *TV Guide,* 16 January 1999, 28.

"The Hollywood Portfolio." *Vanity Fair,* April 2001, 349.

"In Case You Haven't Heard . . ." *Alcoholism and Drug Abuse Weekly,* 10 July 1995, 6.

Lawson, Terry. "Shock, Laughs in Pryor TV Series." *Detroit Free Press* Entertainment News, 24 March 2004.

Leavy, W. "Three Generations of Black Comedy." *Ebony,* January 1990, 102.

Martin, Denise. "Comedy Central Has Pryor Committed." *Variety,* 6 November 2003, 3.

Martin, Weston. "Richard Pryor: 'Every Nigger Is a Star.' " *Ebony,* September 1976, 55–60.

McNary, Dave. "Comics No Longer King." *Variety,* 5 January 2004, 14.

McPherson, James Alan. "The New Comic Style of Richard Pryor." *The New York Times Magazine,* 27 April 1975, 20ff.

Mitchell, Elvis. "Take '71 Pryor; Add Funky Chicken." *New York Times,* 5 May 2000, E28.

Molotsky, Irvin. "Laughs Mix with Pathos at Richard Pryor Tribute." *New York Times,* 22 October 1998, E4.

Murphy, Frederick. "Richard Pryor: Teetering on Jest, Living by His Wit," in *Encore American and Worldwide News,* 24 November 1974, 27–29.

"The 'N' Word." *New Yorker,* 29 April 1996, 50.

Plummer, William, and F. X. Feeney. "Nowhere to Hide." *People,* 29 May 1995, 76.

"Pryor Engagement." *New Yorker,* 10 July 1995, 25.

"Pryor Experience." *GQ: Gentlemen's Quarterly,* March 2004, 205.

Pryor, Richard, and Todd Gold. "Pryor Convictions." *Ebony,* September 1995, 92.

"Pryor Wants to Get Back to Performing on Stage." *Jet,* 31 August 1992, 59.

"Pryor Working on Own Book." *The New York Post,* 14 June 2004, 10.

"Richard Pryor Awarded Star on Hollywood Walk of Fame." *Jet,* 7 June 1993, 54.

"Richard Pryor Honored With First Mark Twain Prize for American Humor." *Jet,* 9 November 1998, 16.

"Richard Pryor Is Toasted and Roasted at All-Star Gala in Beverly Hills." *Jet,* 14 October 1991, 24.

"Richard Pryor Makes Comeback as Stand-up Comedian Despite MS Disease." *Jet,* 5 October 1992, 56.

"Richard Pryor Proves He Can Take the Heat During Friars Roast." *Jet,* 14 October 1991, 54.

"Richard Pryor Wins His Master Recordings in Lawsuit Settlement." *Jet,* 25 March 2002, 21.

"Richard Pryor's Hometown Names Street for Him." *Jet,* 5 November 2001, 6.

Robinson, Louie, "Richard Pryor Talks. . . ." *Ebony,* January 1978, 116–122.

Rosenberg, M., and L. Armstrong. "Glad to Be Alive." *People,* 2 December 1991, 103.

Schickel, Richard. "Vroomy Movie: A Review of *Greased Lightening.*" *Time,* 15 August 1977, 61.

Sheffield, Rob. "Richard Pryor: The Real Slim Shady." *Rolling Stone,* 15 March 2001, 28.

Shumacher, David. "Richard Pryor's Biggest Fight." *Ebony,* September 1993, 100.

Shumacher, David, and Jeffery Newbury. "Richard Pryor in His Own Words." *Entertainment Weekly,* 30 April 1993, 16.

Watkins, Mel. "How He Kept 'Em in Stitches." *New York Times,* 27 November 1994, H34.

Spoken Word

African American Profiles in History. Vol. 1. Narrated by Joe Carter. Richmond, Va.: Dynamic Education Tapes, 1990.

Black History in Music Sampler. Los Angeles: Rhino Entertainment, 1998.

But Seriously . . . the American Comedy Box (1915–1994). Los Angeles: Rhino, 1995.

Carrey, Jim, David Letterman, Richard Pryor, et al. *The Comedy Store Twentieth Birthday.* Westlake Village, Calif.: Uproar Entertainment, 1996.

Comedy Classics. Manitoba: K-tel International, 1981.

Comedy Classics. Plymouth, Minn.: K-tel International (USA), 1987.

Foxx, Redd, Richard Pryor, L. Page, et al. *The Kings and Queens of Comedy.* Encino, Calif.: Encore International, 1990.

Gross, Terry, and Richard Pryor. *Richard Pryor, Comedian.* Washington, D.C.: National Public Radio, 1995.

Jackson, Jesse, Kim Weston, Jimmy Jones, Richard Pryor, et al. *Wattstax: The Living Word.* Memphis, Tenn.: Stax, 1973.

Joe Henry. New York: Mammoth Records, 2001.

Larry King: Laughs. New York: Simon and Schuster Audio, 1993.

Twenty-Five Years of Recorded Comedy. Los Angeles: Warner Bros. Records, 1977.

Discography

Pryor, Richard. *After Hours.* Los Angeles: Laff Records, 1980.

——. *Are You Serious???* New York: Loose Cannon/Laff Records: Manufactured and marketed by Island Records, 1990.

——. *Bicentennial Nigger.* Burbank, Calif.: Warner Bros. Records, 1976.

——. *Black Ben the Blacksmith.* New York: Island Records, 1994.

——. *Craps (After Hours).* New York: Loose Cannon, 1994 (1971).

——. *Greatest Hits.* Warner Brothers, 1990.

——. *Here and Now.* Burbank, Calif.: Warner Bros. Records, 1983.

——. *Insane.* Los Angeles: Laff, 1976.

——. *. . . Is It Something I Said?* Burbank, Calif.: Reprise, 1994.

——. *L.A. Jail.* New York: Tiger Lily Records, 1976.

——. *Live.* Rahway, N.J.: Phoenix Entertainment and Talent, 1982.

——. *Live Recording.* Atlanta: DB Records, 1983.

——. *Pryor Convictions, and Other Life Sentences.* New York: Random House AudioBooks, 1995.

——. *Rev. Du Rite.* Los Angeles: Laff Records, 1976.

——. *Richard Pryor Meets Richard and Willie and the S.L.A.* Los Angeles: Laff, 1976.

——. *Richard Pryor's Greatest Hits.* Burbank, Calif.: Warner Bros. Records, 1977.

——. *Supernigger.* New York: Loose Cannon, 1990.

——. *That Nigger's Crazy.* Warner Brothers, 1990.

——. *The Very Best of Richard Pryor.* Los Angeles: Laff Records, 1982.

——. *Wanted/Richard Pryor Live in Concert.* Burbank, Calif.: Warner Bros. Records, 1978.

——. *Who Me? I'm Not Him.* New York: Island Records, 1994.

——. *The Wizard of Comedy.* New York, N.Y.: Found Money, 1995.

Pryor, Richard, and Redd Foxx. *Down and Dirty.* Los Angeles: Laff Records, 1975.

Pryor, Richard, L. W. Page, Redd Foxx, George Carlin, et al. *Legends of Comedy.* Westlake Village, Calif.: Uproar Entertainment, 1996.

Pryor, Richard, Reggie Collins, and Steve Pokorny. *". . . And It's Deep Too": The Complete Warner Brothers Recordings (1968–1972).* Los Angeles: Warner Bros. Records; Rhino Entertainment Company, 2000.

——. *The Anthology (1968–1992).* Los Angeles: Warner Brothers, 2001.

Pryor, Richard, Slappy White, Rusty Warren, George Carlin, et al. *Hooked on Comedy.* Los Angeles: Laff Records, 1982.

Tomlin, Lily, Bill Cosby, Richard Pryor, et al. *Comedy Classics Collector's Edition of Your Favorite Comedy Routines.* Hopkins, Minn.: ERA Records; distributed by Dominion Music Corp., 1983.

White People. Washington, D.C.: National Public Radio, 1982.

Television and Video

Baker, W., C. Armstrong, et al. *Unforgettable.* Los Angeles: KHJ-TV, Inc.; KCAL-TV, 1989.

The Best of Saturday Night Live 1975. Alexandria, Va.: Distributed by Time Life Video, 1991.

Chase, Chevy, John Belushi, Richard Pryor, et. al. *The Best of Chevy Chase.* Burbank, Calif.: Warner Home Video, 1990.

Cocaine Drain. National Basketball Players Association; Oregon Cable Television Association, 1988.

DePasse, D., B. Mischer, Richard Pryor, et al. *Motown Twenty-Five: Yesterday, Today, Forever.* New York: NBC; Motown Pictures, 1983.

DePasse, D., B. Mischler, S. Coston, et al. *Motown Returns to the Apollo: Celebrating Fifty Years of Great Entertainment.* New York: NBC; Motown Pictures; Inner City Broadcasting Corp., 1985.

Foxx, Redd, D. Wilson, B. Yorkin. *Sanford and Son. Where's the Money? Collector's Edition.* Terre Haute, Ind.: Columbia House; distributed by Columbia House Video Library, 1997.

The Funniest Comedians: The Early Years. New York: Goodtimes Home Video, 1988.

Great T.V. Comedians, the Early Years: Richard Pryor; Jack Benny. New York: Goodtimes, 1986.

Here and Now. Columbia Tristar, 1998.

Krass, E. M., Richard Pryor, L. Klainberg, et al. *Mo' funny: Black Comedy in America.* Los Angeles: HBO Documentaries, 1993.

Richard Pryor—I Ain't Dead Yet, #*%$#@!! (Uncensored). Paramount Home Video, 2004.

Richard Pryor Live and Smokin' (1971). Mpi Home Video, 2001.

Richard Pryor: Live! in Concert (1979). Mpi Home Video, 1998.

Richard Pryor Live on the Sunset Strip (1982). Columbia/Tristar Studios, 2003.

The Richard Pryor Show, Vols. 1 & 2 plus Bonus Disc. Image Entertainment, 2004.

Saturday Night Live [with] Richard Pryor. New York: Warner Home Video, 1982.

Schlatter, G., B. Margolis, B. Kohan, et al. *Sammy Davis, Jr.'s 60th Anniversary Celebration.* New York: ABC Television; George Schlatter Productions, 1990.

Tomlin, Lily, Richard Pryor, Alan Alda. *The Lily Tomlin Special, Volume One.* Karl Home Video, 1973.

Very Best of the Ed Sullivan Show, Volume Two. Hosted by Burt Reynolds. Burbank, Calif.: Distributed by Buena Vista Home Video, 1992.

Walters, Barbara. *Barbara Walters Interviews Richard Pryor.* New York: ABC News, 1981.

Photo Archive

Black Film Center/Archive. Indiana University. Motion picture stills, various productions.

Schultz, Michael. *Which Way Is Up?* Collection of motion picture stills.

Websites

Ingram, Billy. "The Richard Pryor Show." http://www.tvparty.com/pryor.html (18 April 2002).

Pryor, Richard. http://www.richardpryor.com/ (21 January 2005).

Merrit, Bishetta D. http://www.museum.tv/archives/etv/P/htmlP/pryorrichar/pryo rrichar.htm (21 January 2005).

Motion Picture Filmography

Available at: http//www.imdb.com

Richard Pryor Filmography from the Black Film Center/Archive (Indiana University)

Dynamite Chicken (1969)
Black Brigade [a.k.a. *Carter's Army*] (1970)
Lady Sings the Blues (1972)—parts 1 and 2
The Mack (1973)
Wattstax (1973)
Uptown Saturday Night (1974)—16mm
Bingo Long Traveling All-Stars and Motor Kings (1976)—16mm
Car Wash (1976)
Silver Streak (1976)
Greased Lightening (1977)—16mm
The Wiz (1978)
Blue Collar (1978)
Richard Pryor: Live in Concert (1979)
In God We Tru$t (1980)
Bustin' Loose (1981)
Richard Pryor Live and Smokin' (1981)
Some Kind of Hero (1981)
Richard Pryor Live on the Sunset Strip (1982)
Richard Pryor: Here and Now (1983)
Pryor's Place, vols. 1–4 (1984 to 1985)
Brewster's Millions (1985)
Critical Condition (1986)

Jo Jo Dancer: Your Life Is Calling (1986)
Moving (1988)
Harlem Nights (1989)
See No Evil, Hear No Evil (1989)
A Laugh, A Tear (1990)
Another You (1991)

Other Richard Pryor Films

Green Berets (1968) [bit part]
Wild in the Streets (1968)
The Phynx (1970)
You've Got to Walk It like You Talk It or You'll Lose That Beat (1971)
Some Call It Loving (1972)
Hit! (1973)
Adios Amigo (1975)
Which Way Is Up? (1977)
California Suite (1978)
The Muppet Movie (1979)
Stir Crazy (1980)
Wholly Moses (1980)
The Toy (1982)
Superman III (1983)
Mad Dog Time [a.k.a. *Trigger Happy*] (1996)
Lost Highway (1997)
Sam Kinison: Why Did We Laugh? (1998)

Selected List of Richard Pryor Television Appearances

On Broadway Tonight (1964)
The Wild, Wild West—"The Night of the Eccentrics" (1965)
The Kraft Summer Music Hall (1966)
The Partridge Family—"Soul Club" (1970)
Flip Wilson Show (1970)
The Lily Tomlin Special, vol.1 (1973)
Martin—"The Break Up," part 1 (1992)
Chicago Hope—"Stand" (1994)
Malcolm and Eddie—"Do the KC Hustle" (1996)
The Norm Show—"Norm vs. the Boxer" (1999)
Biography—Richard Pryor: Biography (1987, 2000)

PERMISSIONS AND CREDITS

Als, Hilton
>   *The New Yorker Magazine, NYC*
Avakian, Bob
>   *The Revolutionary Worker*
Felton, David
>   *Rolling Stone*
George, Nelson
>   *Blackface: Reflections on African Americans and the Movies,* by permission of the author
Kael, Pauline
>   *State of Art,* E. P. Dutton, Curtis Brown, Ltd, New York
>   *For Keeps: Thirty Years at the Movies,* E. P. Dutton, Penguin Group (USA)
McPherson, James Alan
>   James Alan McPherson, by permission of the author
Nazel, Joseph
>   *Richard Pryor: The Man Behind the Laughter,* Holloway Publishing House, Los Angeles
Sheffield, Rob
>   *Rolling Stone*
Vaidhyanathan, Siva
>   University of Alabama Press
John A. Williams and Dennis Williams
>   *If I Stop I'll Die: The Comedy and Tragedy of Richard Pryor,* Thunder's Mouth Press, 1991

Photographs

See No Evil, Hear No Evil
>   Copyright 1989 TriStar Pictures, Inc.
>   All Rights Reserved
>   Courtesy of Columbia Pictures
Stir Crazy
>   Copyright 1980 Columbia Pictures Industries, Inc.
>   All Rights Reserved
>   Courtesy of Columbia Pictures
Wholly Moses
>   Copyright 1980 Columbia Pictures Industries, Inc.
>   All Rights Reserved
>   Courtesy of Columbia Pictures

CONTRIBUTORS

HILTON ALS is a writer for the *New Yorker*. He is also a fiction writer and author of the memoir *The Women*.

BOB AVAKIAN is a Marxist-Leninist-Maoist author of several books that espouse his political views. He is a contributing editor of *Revolution* (formerly the *Revolutionary Worker*). He went into self-imposed exile after being charged with assault at a protest rally during the visit of Premier Deng Xiaoping of China. His current whereabouts are not widely known.

KATE E. BROWN is an independent scholar who specializes in Victorian Studies. Her work has appeared in several journals, including *ELH* and *Novel: A Forum on Fiction*.

MARGO NATALIE CRAWFORD is an assistant professor of African American literature and culture in the department of English at Indiana University. She is editor (with Lisa Gail Collins) of *New Thoughts on the Black Arts Movement* and author of *Rewriting Blackness*.

DAVID FELTON is a widely published author and frequent contributor to *Rolling Stone* magazine.

NELSON GEORGE is an award-winning journalist, cultural critic, and filmmaker. He is the author of numerous books, including *Post-Soul Nation* and *The Death of Rhythm and Blues*, and contributor to the *Village Voice* and the *Amsterdam News*. He was also a consulting producer on HBO's *The Chris Rock Show* and director of the Emmy-nominated HBO film *Life Support*.

KEITH M. HARRIS currently teaches in the departments of English and Film and Visual Culture at the University of California–Riverside and is author of *Boys, Boyz, Boies: An Ethics of Masculinity in Popular Film, Television and Video* and "'Untitled': D'Angelo and the Visualization of the Black Male Body" in *Wide Angle*.

PAULINE KAEL (1919–2001) wrote essays and movie reviews for the *New Yorker* magazine. She was considered the most influential film critic of her era. Her fourth book, *Deeper into Movies,* was the first nonfiction book about movies to win a National Book Award. Her first book, *I Lost It at the Movies,* established her reputation for a spirited, personal style of writing.

MAXINE A. LEGALL is an associate professor of communication arts at the University of the District of Columbia. A folktale researcher and storyteller, she is a founding member of the National Association of Black Storytellers and the festival director of its Third Annual International Storytelling Festival. Her work has been published in *Jump Up and Say* (edited by Linda Goss and Clay Goss) and in the *Washington Post*.

AUDREY THOMAS McCLUSKEY is a professor of African American and African diaspora studies and former director of the Black Film Center/Archive at Indiana University. Her recent publications include *Imaging Blackness: Race and Racial Representation in Film Poster Art* and *Frame by Frame III: A Filmography of the African Diasporan Image* (both from Indiana University Press, 2007). Her forthcoming book is titled *The Devil You Dance With: Film Culture in the New South Africa.*

MALIK D. McCLUSKEY, an Indiana University administrator and lecturer, earned a Ph.D. in philosophy from the University of North Carolina at Chapel Hill. His research interests are ethics and black cultural aesthetics. His essay on the Cosby–Dyson debate was published in *Black Renaissance/ Renaissance Noir* in 2006.

JAMES ALAN McPHERSON is a prolific author of both fiction and nonfiction works. He is a past recipient of the Pulitzer Prize for his collection of short stories, *Elbow Room,* a Guggenheim fellowship, and in 1981, a MacArthur "genius" fellowship. He is a professor of English and creative writing at the University of Iowa.

JOSEPH NAZEL (1944–2006) authored several books on outstanding black Americans, including Langston Hughes, Ida B. Wells, B. B. King, and Martin Luther King, Jr. His writing achievements also extend to several works of fiction, including mysteries.

MICHAEL SCHULTZ, director of the cult-like favorite *Cooley High,* has extensive directorial credits and awards. He has been equally prodigious in directing for television, film, and stage productions. His more recent feature work includes *Woman Thou Are Loosed* and several films in pre-production. Schultz also directed episodes of the hit television series *Jag, Ally McBeal,* and *Cold Case,* among others.

ROB SHEFFIELD writes music reviews and covers the music and popular culture scenes for *Rolling Stone,* the *Village Voice,* and other publications.

TYRONE R. SIMPSON, an assistant professor of English and American culture at Vassar College, is the recipient of the 2007–2008 Woodrow Wilson Fellowship for minority professional development, and is at work on his manuscript, "Under Psychic Apartheid: Literary Ghettoes and the Making of Race in the Twentieth-Century American Metropolis."

SIVA VAIDHYANATHAN is a cultural historian and media scholar. He is the author of several articles and books, including *Copyrights and Copywrongs: The Rise of Intellectual Property and How It Threatens Creativity,* and he recently co-edited *Rewiring the Nation: The Place of Technology in American Studies.*

JOHN A. WILLIAMS is a celebrated novelist with over a dozen published works of fiction, including the politically potent hit *The Man Who Cried I Am.* He is also a journalist and the author of several nonfiction works. His son, DENNIS A. WILLIAMS, is a journalist and freelance writer who formerly worked as a staff reporter for *Newsweek* and has written features for *Essence* and *Ebony.*

INDEX

Italicized page numbers indicate illustrations.

Audrey Thomas McCluskey is a professor of African American and African diaspora studies and former director of the Black Film Center/Archive at Indiana University. Her recent publications include *Imaging Blackness: Race and Racial Representation in Film Poster Art* and *Frame by Frame III: A Filmography of the African Diasporan Image* (both from Indiana University Press, 2007).